For Reference

Not to be taken from this room

All Things Chaucer

All Things Chaucer

An Encyclopedia of Chaucer's World

VOLUME 1

A–J

Shannon L. Rogers

GREENWOOD PRESS
Westport, Connecticut • London

Library of Congress Cataloging-in-Publication Data

Rogers, Shannon L.
   All things Chaucer : an encyclopedia of Chaucer's world / Shannon L. Rogers.
      p. cm.
   Includes bibliographical references and index.
   ISBN 0–313–33253–3 (v. 1 : alk. paper)—ISBN 0–313–33254–1 (v. 2 : alk. paper)—
ISBN 0–313–33252–5 (set : alk. paper)
   1. Chaucer, Geoffrey, d. 1400—Encyclopedias.   2. Poets, English—Middle English,
1100–1500—Biography—Encyclopedias.   3. Civilization, Medieval, in literature—
Encyclopedias.   I. Title.
   PR1903.R55 2007
   821′.1—dc22   2006027206

British Library Cataloguing in Publication Data is available.

Library of Congress Catalog Card Number: 2006027206

ISBN: 0–313–33252–5 (set)
      0–313–33253–3 (vol. 1)
      0–313–33254–1 (vol. 2)

First published in 2007

Greenwood Press, 88 Post Road West, Westport, CT 06881
An imprint of Greenwood Publishing Group, Inc.
www.greenwood.com

Printed in the United States of America

The paper used in this book complies with the
Permanent Paper Standard issued by the National
Information Standards Organization (Z39.48–1984).

10 9 8 7 6 5 4 3 2 1

The publisher has done its best to make sure the instructions and/or recipes in this book
are correct. However, users should apply judgment and experience when preparing recipes,
especially parents and teachers working with young people. The publisher accepts no
responsibility for the outcome of any recipe included in these volumes.

For Ben,
still my muse

Contents

Preface   ix

Acknowledgments   xi

Alphabetical List of Entries   xiii

Guide to Related Topics   xvii

Introduction   xxiii

Chronology of Important Events in Chaucer's Time   xxxv

All Things Chaucer   1

Appendices   469

   Genealogy of Edward III   471

   Map of Route to Canterbury   475

Bibliography   479

Index   491

Preface

While much of the appeal of *The Canterbury Tales* lies in its universal assessment of human nature and character, there remain many elements within this and other of Chaucer's works that can make his world seem to be an alien landscape. Issues of time and place, unfamiliar language or word usage, and differences in moral, religious, and other social and cultural attitudes can all baffle the modern reader. These volumes are intended to demystify Chaucer's world: to explain the background to his works, to place him contextually, and to add historical resonance to any reading of his poetry.

These two volumes will survey the texts of Chaucer's writing, provide historical background and information on items mentioned in all of his works, and serve as a portal to medieval culture, identifying for readers the individual items that make up the physical culture of Chaucer's time. These items include weapons, clothing, housing, food, money, and tools and will be discussed in detail, going beyond mere definitions to explain form and function of everyday and obscure items. The book will hopefully broaden any reader's understanding of Chaucer and contribute to her ability to interpret and analyze his writings. In addition to physical things, this book also explores the customs, rituals, and belief systems that comprise medieval culture. Although this work is intended for a wide readership, I have utilized primary source materials and analyzed the impact of rituals, superstitions, politics, and other aspects of daily life in a way to be useful to multiple levels of expertise, including professional scholars.

As such, the book is intended to be a companion to Chaucer. It is meant, above all, to be a resource to which one can refer while reading Chaucer. The individual entries are arranged alphabetically, in encyclopedic form.

There is some overlap between the content of related articles, which is intentional. If one were, for instance, to refer to the entry on the Knight, one would also find similar material covered in the entries on Weapons and Chivalry. Likewise, the suggestions for "Further Reading" that are included at the end of each entry sometimes refer to similar or identical sources. However, each individual entry is a focused assessment of the subject in question and includes its relevance to Chaucer's works. Most are introduced by a related quotation from Chaucer, in both Middle English and modern translation. Throughout the text are specific references to Chaucer's works as they relate to the entry in question, either in quotation form or simply by line references.

In addition to individual suggestions for further reading, there is also a full bibliography referencing all of the works used in this compilation. This might be of most interest to readers who are interested in more broadly conceived subjects, along with the "Guide to Related Topics." For those readers who seek specific subjects—to learn a more narrow topic in depth or to consult a specific question raised by a close reading of a Chaucerian text—the individual entries themselves, introduced by the "Alphabetical List of Entries," will provide information on a specific subject. At the close of each entry, in order to serve the needs of all readers, are "See Also" directives to seek information in related topics.

In order to set Chaucer's life and work into its proper historical context, I have tried to provide ample biographical details about him in the introduction. The interaction between his professional career and his poetic are discussed at length, accompanied by details about his family. I have also included a broad discussion of the intellectual trends of his time and where he fits into them. For those who would like a simple reference guide to what was going on during Chaucer's life, there is a chronology, listing both important historical events and personal Chaucerian moments.

In addition to the many illustrations that accompany the text, the entries are followed by two appendices that help place Chaucer both historically and geographically. The first is a genealogical chart of the lineage of Edward III, showing Chaucer's close marital relationship to the royal family. The second is a map of the route of the Canterbury pilgrims, which illustrates for the modern reader the amount of distance covered by the group of 29, who made the trip on horseback and on foot.

Finally, all references are to Larry Benson's magisterial *The Riverside Chaucer,* and thus all Middle English passages are from this work as well. Any errors in transcription are my own, as are the translations. They are certainly not the sort of masterful and poetic translations I read in the course of this work, but they are functional and should be of service to anyone unfamiliar with Middle English. I do, however, encourage even the most novice reader to give the Middle English originals a try. Read them out loud, pronouncing every letter. It is surprising how the language flows and begins to make sense.

Acknowledgments

The task of categorizing Chaucer's world is an especially daunting one, and I could not have done it without the help of a number of people. In the broader sense, I am in debt to all of those who have come before me to write the scholarship on Chaucer and fourteenth-century England that made this work possible. I would also like to thank the staff of a number of libraries, including the interlibrary loan folks at the Kingston Public Library and the staffs of Juniata College and Penn State Wilkes-Barre. Their prompt response to my numerous requests for increasingly arcane books is admirable and most appreciated.

I would also like to thank Professor Benjamin Hudson of the History Department at the Pennsylvania State University. I would never have been introduced to Greenwood without him, nor would I have probably ever finished my doctorate without his fine mentoring and constant enthusiastic support. Thanks to my patient and long-suffering Greenwood editor, George Butler, for all of his guidance and understanding. I'll bet he thought we'd never get to this stage. I would like to thank my mother for always being excited about this project, even if she still doesn't quite know who Chaucer is.

And finally, any acknowledgements page would be empty without thanking Benjamin Moores. You've been a part of this through every stage. Thank you for the distractions, which helped me keep my sanity, even if I lost a little in focus. Thank you for always being proud of me, even if you pretend you aren't. And thank you for being who you are, because you always inspire me to be more than I am. Rwy'n dy garu di.

Alphabetical List of Entries

Abigail
Abraham
Absalom
Achates
Achilles
Actaeon
Adam
Adonis
Aeneas
Agriculture
Alchemy
Alcyone
Aldgate
Alexandria
Algeciras
Allegory and Dream Visions
Allusions, Biblical
Allusions, Classical
Amphion
Animals
Apollo
Architecture
Ariadne
Armor

Astrolabe
Astrology and Astronomy

Bacchus
Baptism
Bath
Birds
Birth
Black Death
Blanche, Duchess of Lancaster
Boar
Boccaccio
Boethius
Bruges
Burgundy
Business and Commerce

Calendar
Caliope
Cambridge
Canterbury
Cassandra
Castles
Catalonia
Cathedrals

Childhood
Chivalry
Cities, Towns, and Villages
Clerk
Courtly Love
Crow
Cuckoo

Daedalus
Daily Life
Daniel
Daphne
Deianira
Demophon
Dog
Dove
Dreams

Eagle
Echo
Education
Edward III
Edward, the Black Prince
Entertainment
Estates
Esther
Eve

Falcon
Fame
Fashion
Feudalism
Food
Fortune
Four Humors
Fox
Franklin
Friar
Froissart
Furniture

Games
Gentilesse
Goose
Great Schism
Grenada

Hare
Helen of Troy
Heraldry
Heresy
Holidays and
    Holy Days
Horse
Humanism
Hundred Years War
Hunting
Hygiene
Hypsipyle

Indulgences

Jerusalem
Jews
Job
John of Gaunt
Joseph
Judas

Knight

Lamech
Law
Leather
Lithuania
Lollardy
London
Lucrece

Macedonia
Manciple
Marriage
Medea
Medicine
Merchant
Miller
Monarchy
Money
Monk
Morocco
Music

Names
Narcissus
Nun

Pardoner
Parson
Peasant Revolt
Philosophy
Physician
Pilgrimage
Priapus
Prioress
Private Houses
Prussia

Reeve
Religion
Richard II
Rooster and Hen
Russia

Science
Scrope-Grosvenor Trial
Sex
Sheep
Shipman
Sittingbourne
Southwark
Squire
St. Augustine
St. Benedict
St. Bernard
St. Cecilia
St. Christopher
St. Cuthbert

St. Denis
St. Dunstan
St. Edward
St. Eligius
St. Frideswide
St. Giles
St. Jerome
St. Julian
St. Neot
St. Ronan
St. Valentine
Stratford-at-Bow
Summoner
Syria

Tapestry
Taverns
Teutonic Knights
Thessaly
Thomas à Becket
Tournaments
Travel
Trojan War

Weapons
Westminster Abbey
Wolf
Wood
Wool

Yeoman
Ypres

Guide to Related Topics

Art and Architecture

Architecture

Castles
Cathedrals

Private Houses

Tapestry

Business and Industry

Business and Commerce

Leather

Merchant
Money

Shipman

Wood
Wool

Daily Life

Baptism
Birth
Black Death
Business and Commerce

Calendar
Castles
Cathedrals

Childhood

Daily Life
Dreams

Education
Entertainment
Estates

Fashion
Feudalism
Food
Furniture

Games

Holidays and
    Holy Days
Hunting
Hygiene

Leather

Marriage
Medicine
Monarchy
Money
Music

Names

Pilgrimage
Private Houses

Sex

Taverns
Travel

Wood
Wool

Literature

Abigail
Abraham
Absalom
Achates
Achilles
Actaeon
Adam
Adonis
Aeneas
Alcyone
Allegory and Dream Visions
Allusions, Biblical
Allusions, Classical
Amphion
Apollo
Ariadne

Bacchus
Boccaccio
Boethius

Caliope
Cassandra

Daedalus
Daniel
Daphne
Deianira
Demophon

Echo
Esther
Eve

Helen of Troy
Hypsipyle

Jews
Job
Joseph

Judas
Lamech
Lucrece

Medea

Narcissus

Priapus

Nature

Animals

Birds
Boar

Crow
Cuckoo

Dog
Dove

Eagle

Falcon
Fox

Goose

Hare
Horse

Rooster and Hen

Sheep

Wolf

People

Abigail
Abraham
Absalom
Achates
Achilles
Actaeon
Adam
Adonis
Aeneas
Alcyone
Amphion

Apollo
Ariadne

Bacchus
Blanche, Duchess of Lancaster
Boccaccio
Boethius

Caliope
Cassandra
Clerk

Daedalus
Daniel
Daphne
Deianira
Demophon

Echo
Edward III
Edward, the Black Prince
Esther
Eve

Fame
Fortune
Franklin
Friar
Froissart

Helen of Troy
Hypsipyle

Jews
Job
John of Gaunt
Joseph
Judas

Knight

Lamech
Lucrece

Manciple
Medea
Merchant
Miller
Monk

Narcissus

Nun

Pardoner
Parson
Physician
Priapus
Prioress

Reeve
Richard II

Shipman
Squire
St. Augustine
St. Benedict
St. Bernard
St. Cecilia
St. Christopher
St. Cuthbert
St. Denis
St. Dunstan
St. Edward
St. Eligius
St. Frideswide
St. Giles
St. Jerome
St. Julian
St. Neot
St. Ronan
St. Valentine
Summoner

Thomas à Becket

Yeoman

Places

Alexandria
Algeciras
Alisaundre

Bath
Bruges
Burgundy

Cambridge
Canterbury
Catalonia

Grenada

Jerusalem

Lithuania
London

Macedonia
Morocco

Prussia

Russia

Sittingbourne
Southwark
Stratford-at-Bow
Syria

Thessaly

Westminster Abbey

Ypres

Religion

Calendar
Canterbury
Clerk

Great Schism

Heresy
Holidays and Holy Days

Indulgences

Jerusalem
Jews

Lollardy

Monk
Music

Nun

Pardoner
Parson
Pilgrimage
Prioress

St. Augustine
St. Benedict

St. Bernard
St. Cecilia
St. Christopher
St. Cuthbert
St. Denis
St. Dunstan
St. Edward
St. Eligius
St. Frideswide
St. Giles
St. Jerome
St. Julian
St. Neot
St. Ronan
St. Valentine
Summoner

Thomas à Becket

Rituals and Myths

Allusions, Biblical
Allusions, Classical

Baptism
Birth

Dreams

Fame
Fortune

Religion

Town and Country

Agriculture
Aldgate

Castles
Cathedrals
Cities, Towns, and Villages

Science

Alchemy
Astrolabe
Astrology and Astronomy

Black Death

Four Humors

Hygiene

Medicine

Physician

Science

War and the Knightly Ethos

Armor

Chivalry
Courtly Love

Gentilesse

Heraldry
Hundred
   Years War

Knight

Squire

Teutonic Knights
Tournaments
Trojan War

Weapons

Introduction

Whan that Aprill with his shourse soote
The droghte of March hath perced to the roote,
And bathed every veyne in swich licour
Of which vertu engendred is the flour;
Whan Zephirus eek with his sweete breeth
Inspired hath in every holt and heeth
The tendre croppes, and the yonge sonne
Hath in the Ram his half cours yronne,
And smale foweles maken melodye,
That slepen al the nyght with open ye
(So Priketh hem Nature in hir corages),
Thanne longen folk to goon on pilgrimages,
And palmeres for to seken straunge strondes,
To ferne halwes, kowthe in sundry londes;
And specially from every shires ende
Of Engelond to Caunterbury they wende,
The hooly blisful martir for to seke,
That hem hath holpen whan that they were seeke.

When April with its sweet showers
Has pierced to the root the drought of March,
And bathed every plant in such moisture
That every flower is engendered with life;
When the west wind with his sweet breath
Has inspired in every wood and heath
The tender shoots to spring, and the young sun
Has traveled halfway through the sign of Aries,
And little birds make sweet melodies,
Which sleep all night with open eyes
(As Nature prompts them to do, and encourages),

Then folks long to go on pilgrimages,
And pilgrims seek strange lands,
To foreign halls, renowned in many distant lands;
And especially from every shire's end
In England they all find their way to Canterbury,
To seek the holy blissful martyr,
Who will give them help when they are sick.

(*Canterbury Tales*, General Prologue, I A, 1–18)

Thus run the opening lines of one of the most famous and influential pieces of English literature, Geoffrey Chaucer's *Canterbury Tales*. Begun most likely in the year of the poet's wife's death, the *Canterbury Tales* represent a lifetime of experience and learning, as well as a keen eye for understanding and describing human behavior. The structure of the *Tales* was most probably modeled upon Boccaccio's *Decameron,* which also uses the device of group entertainment through the telling of tales. For Boccaccio the framing scenario was the passing of time by a group of young nobles who have fled the Black Death. For Chaucer, the tales are told by a socioeconomically mixed group who are on a pilgrimage to visit the shrine of Thomas à Becket in Canterbury Cathedral. They meet at the Tabard Inn in Southwark, not far from where Chaucer spent most of his married life, and proceed from there, providing readers with a compelling glimpse into the personalities and social structure of fourteenth-century England as they make their way from London to Canterbury.

Geoffrey Chaucer was born sometime between 1340 and 1344. The precise date of his birth is uncertain; however, we know a great deal more about his life than we do about other literary figures, including Shakespeare. This is thanks, in part, to his years of service within the households of royalty and within the government. England's most famous poet was, at the end of the day, a civil servant, and as such his history is reasonably well documented. Because he lived through interesting times, Chaucer's placement within the inner circle of England's government would make him historically important even if he had never written a single line of poetry.

Given the highly stratified class system of the Middle Ages, at first consideration it would seem unlikely that Geoffrey Chaucer would ever have risen to serve a king or befriend the king's brother. Chaucer's father, John, was a vintner or wine merchant originally from Ipswich who had settled in London on Thames Street, a wealthy mercantile area. This area would have brought Geoffrey into contact with Italian merchants, which would account for his later command of the language that made him useful in royal diplomatic missions. Chaucer's mother, Agnes de Copton, was a wealthy middle-class heiress. Agnes had previously been married to the Baron of the Exchequer and Keeper of the King's Purse. Her marriage to John Chaucer was her second, and it was perhaps her connections from the first marriage that enabled young Geoffrey to move easily in aristocratic circles.

However his placement there was achieved, it is certain that Geoffrey became a page in the household of Elizabeth, Countess of Ulster, in 1357. Elizabeth was married to Edward III's brother Lionel, Duke of Clarence. This was quite a step upward socially for the son of middle-class mercantilists. It was in this position that he most likely met both his later patron, John of Gaunt, another of Edward's brothers, and his future wife, Phillippa de Roet, who was also in the countess's household. Philippa was the daughter of Sir Paon de Roet, a Flemish knight in the retinue of Philippa of Hainault, Edward III's queen.

Although his parents were able to afford to educate him prior to this time, it is uncertain to what degree, if at all, they did so. It is, however, far more probable that he received a reasonably thorough course of training while in the countess's household (see Education). This education would encompass some modification of the liberal arts program of the trivium (grammar, dialectic, and rhetoric) and the quadrivium (arithmetic, music, astronomy, and geometry). Given his adult command of so many areas of learning—including French, classical literature, and astronomy—it is clear that he learned several languages, including Latin, and received some education in arithmetic, theology, music, and philosophy.

It is also a possibility that Chaucer attended the law schools of the Inns of Court sometime in the early 1360s, because there exists a mention in the record books of the Inner Temple of a "Geffrye Chaucer" who was "fined two shillings for beatinge a Franciscan Fryer in fletestreate" (*fined two shillings for beating a Franciscan friar in Fleet Street*). In order to be fined by the society, he would have had to have been a student there. It unclear whether this was the same Geoffrey Chaucer as the poet; however, his thorough knowledge of legal matters and his characterization of the Man of Law seem to indicate some familiarity with the profession (see Law).

All speculation on his completed education aside, the next official mention of Chaucer is as a soldier in the king's forces under the Duke of Clarence. This would have involved Chaucer in the action of the major martial conflict of his time, the Hundred Years War (see Hundred Years War). While besieging Rheims in 1359, Chaucer was captured by the French and held for ransom. This ransom—£16—was eventually paid by the Keeper of the King's Wardrobe. That perhaps Chaucer was not considered to be a vital part of the army is revealed by the fact that this figure is slightly less than the ransom paid for Sir Robert de Clynton's horse. This experience among soldiers, however, may have provided Chaucer with his rather cynical attitude toward the knighthood that is reflected so many times throughout the *Canterbury Tales,* not only in his portrayal of the Knight and the Squire, but in details from several tales, including the "Tale of Sir Thopas" (see Chivalry, Knight, and Squire).

Not long after he was ransomed, Chaucer was employed by Prince Lionel in October 1360 to carry letters from Calais to England. After that mission, the next six years of Chaucer's life are a complete mystery to us today. It is possible that he accompanied Lionel to Ireland when the Duke became Viceroy there. Or, more probably, Chaucer moved into some form of service with the king. Whatever the case may be, we next find him in the record books in February 1366, when he was granted safe transport by Charles II of Navarre. The precise nature of his business and why he required such safe passage, however, remains unknown.

That same year was accompanied by personal changes on both ends of the emotional spectrum. Sadly, Chaucer's father died (the year of his mother's death remains unknown). On a happier note, however, Chaucer married Philippa, who had by now become an attendant to Philippa of Hainault, Edward III's queen. The queen awarded Philippa Chaucer an annual annuity of 10 marks or roughly £7. The first recorded mention of Chaucer himself within the royal household is from June 1367, when he was awarded an annual salary of 20 marks (£13). The nature of his service is uncertain—he is described in the records as both a squire and a valet.

It is clear that Chaucer's career at the heart of the royal court was on the rise. He rapidly advanced within the ranks of being one of forty or so men in the king's service whose duties ranged from anything including serving meals to traveling on official business. Chaucer traveled to Spain in 1368 with the Black Prince, and may have carried messages to Prince Lionel who was in Milan. Later that same year, Chaucer officially became an Esquire to the King's Household. When John of Gaunt's first wife, Blanche, died in September, Gaunt awarded Chaucer a lifetime annuity of £10, perhaps as a reward for writing the *Book of Duchess* (see Blanche, Duchess of Lancaster and John of Gaunt). Although the figures behind the characters of the Black Knight and Duchess White have been debated, it is generally accepted that the grief-stricken Knight is John of Gaunt who has lost his Blanche (meaning "white") to an untimely demise. His dangerous heartbreak is chronicled in the *Book of the Duchess* along with an admonition to try to get beyond it for his own physical and mental safety. Chaucer's exploration of grief and its physical toll on the human body is remarkably modern here and has been born out by medical evidence. His closeness to the personages involved, in a capacity apparently beyond that of trusted and paid servant, is alluded to in the deeply personal understanding of the Knight's grief as well as by the assumption that Gaunt asked Chaucer to write something in Blanche's honor.

It is clear that Chaucer had already been widely recognized as a poet of considerable talent. While the dating of some of the shorter poems is uncertain, his first probable work would have been his translation of the *Roman de la Rose*. The first definite original poetic work would then be the *Book of the Duchess*. However, the fact that Gaunt asked Chaucer to write this work in honor of Blanche is a strong indication that he was already known as a poet, and that reputation would have to have been based upon some real poetic evidence. Earlier poems may have been lost or were merely presented orally at court. Unfortunately, the lack of any prior poetic output is another frustrating hole in the historical record.

Chaucer's career continued to advance throughout the 1360s and 1370s, with perhaps his most important assignment occurring in 1372 when he was sent to Italy to negotiate the use of English ports by Genoese merchants. While there, he discussed with the Duke of Genoa which ports might be used by these merchants as permanent headquarters, a crucial financial arrangement for both Genoa and England. From there, he traveled to Florence to negotiate some government loans. While staying in Florence, it is quite probable that Chaucer not only obtained a copy of Dante's *Divina Commedia* (*Divine Comedy*) but met Petrarch and Boccaccio. Any one of these three events would have made a deep impact on the English poet. The possibility that he was exposed to the three most important Italian poets of his time is an event of potentially monumental import to his development as a wordsmith.

Upon his return to England in May 1374, Chaucer was given the dubious reward of the position of Controller of the Customs of Wools, Skins, and Hides for the port of London. Because wool was England's chief export, this position carried a great deal of importance and demonstrated the high degree of confidence on the part of the crown in Chaucer's abilities. However, it was a position that was also fraught with an equal amount of burdensome responsibility. The taxes collected on wool and leather funded the costs of war and the running of the government and thus were a chief source of the king's annual revenue. The position carried a salary of £10 per annum, which was added to his annuity of £13. Chaucer was also given the use of a house over Aldgate rent free, an award that was made to him by the mayor and aldermen of the city. His only costs for the use of the house would be for upkeep and repairs. Chaucer was also required to allow its use in times of war if it was needed defensively.

Geoffrey and Philippa must have been quite comfortably well off at this time, with their combined incomes and lack of living expenses. He had also been awarded a gift from Edward III of a gallon of wine each day for life—probably in reward for writing a poem for the king. This he collected until 1378, when he had it commuted to an annuity of 20 marks. Keeping up with court life and fashion was no doubt of some expense. However, the Chaucers had a modestly sized family of two or three children—two sons, Thomas and Lewis, and a possible daughter, Elizabeth—which meant that their household upkeep was minimized while the combined income of him and his wife totaled somewhere near £99. It is therefore rather sad that he felt a financial pinch in his final years, as is evidenced by the poem "The Complaint of Chaucer to His Purse." His expenditures on an impressive library of more than sixty books make it clear that Chaucer spent what he earned.

In 1376 and 1377 he traveled again to the Continent on royal business. It is known that he was in France, potentially to conduct truce negotiations. Later, he appears to have traveled there again to conduct betrothal negotiations for the young Richard II and a French princess—negotiations that eventually fell through, as Richard would ultimately marry Anne of Bohemia in 1382. In 1378, Chaucer again traveled to the Continent on business connected with the war with France, this time going to Lombardy. The following year, it is probable that he began working on the *House of Fame*.

The 1380s brought a variety of events for the Chaucers. In 1380, Geoffrey would face serious charges of *raptu,* a legal term that could indicate either rape or abduction. The details of the case are completely unknown, except that the woman in question, Cecily Chaumpaigne, eventually released Chaucer from all charges. However, during the course of the proceedings, he must have faced many moments of anxiety about the outcome and the potential effects on his family and career.

1381 brought the Peasant Revolt, or Wat Tyler's Rebellion (see Peasant Revolt and Richard II), a defining moment in English history in which the peasants of Kent and Essex rose in rebellion in response to the substantial poll tax levied by Richard II. It is again unknown how much of the revolt Chaucer witnessed personally (see Aldgate). However, his connection with court life would have given him an enviable position to learn inside details of the event. Many of the peasants who were eventually killed came from the area of the city where Chaucer grew up and still owned a house. Four days after the revolt, Chaucer sold his father's house to a merchant by the name of Henry Herbury. His reasoning for doing so is unclear and forever hidden by the intervening time. It would be farfetched, however, to speculate that the area's connection with the revolt made his house unpleasant to him. More likely, it had become a burden to maintain or he had better uses for the money it was worth. It is around this time that Chaucer wrote the *Parliament of Fowls,* in honor of Richard II's engagement to Anne of Bohemia.

In 1382, Chaucer's official duties expanded when he was awarded the controllership of Petty Customs, which included collecting import and export duties on wine and other miscellaneous merchandise. Even with these additional duties, Chaucer continued to travel on official business. He was appointed a deputy to cover his responsibilities when he was traveling, demonstrating that his service was highly valued in both positions to the degree that the king was willing to incur extra expense to allow Chaucer to continue to act in all capacities.

As the 1380s progressed, however, Chaucer appears to have increasingly withdrawn from London life. He employed a permanent deputy in 1385 to handle his controller duties. In October of that same year, he was elected as Justice of the Peace in Kent, a very important position because the French were threatening to invade there. In 1386, he would be elected to the House of Commons as a Knight of the Shire in Kent and gave up his lease on the Aldgate house in order to relocate outside the city. During this same period, Chaucer's poetic output was immense, demonstrating a reduction in time necessary to be devoted to his official capacities. He wrote *Troilus and Criseyde* in 1385 and began his translation of Boethius. In 1386, he also probably wrote the *Legend of Good Women* and started the ambitiously conceived *Canterbury Tales,* which would occupy the next decade of his life. It would remain unfinished upon his death.

In June 1387, Philippa Chaucer disappears from the official records, an indication that she had died. It is unknown how she died or how Chaucer took the news. Despite the many sarcastic jibes he makes about the institution of marriage in his works, most evidence indicates that his marriage was a happy one, so it is fairly safe to assume that her loss was a blow to him emotionally. We do know that later that same year he traveled to Calais on undisclosed business. This would be his last official journey, which can be interpreted as either a loss of court support (although not necessarily royal support) or a certain withdrawal from public affairs after his wife's death in order to pursue other interests. The prior interpretation is supported by the fact that three of the men he worked with at the Customs House were executed in 1388. This was at the insistence of the Merciless Parliament, which was dominated by enemies of the king who later would be executed by Richard II when he had regained the reigns of power that had rested shakily in his hands for many years (see Richard II).

That Chaucer retained the king's support is clear from his appointment in 1389 as Clerk of the King's Works. In this capacity, he oversaw the building and repair of 10 royal residences in and around London—including the Tower, Sheen Manor, and Westminster Palace—as well as care and maintenance of all of the hunting lodges in the royal forests (see Wood). Chaucer's salary was two shillings per day, which was three times his salary at the Custom's House. However, when he left this position in 1391, he was owed the entire amount of his three-year tenure there. Clearly, the king was having trouble in managing all aspects of his government at this time, a state of affairs that no doubt contributed greatly to his downfall and eventual overthrow and murder.

The king made good on some of the money owed when he awarded Chaucer a gift of £10 in 1393 and granted him an annual annuity of £20. During the preceding two years, Chaucer had worked for him as Deputy Forester in the Royal Forest of North Petherton in Somerset. It is unknown what his salary was there and whether he was ever paid his overdue wages from being Clerk of the King's Works. He seems to have continued in this position until 1399, living at Park House, when he decided to return to London and leased a house in the gardens of Westminster Abbey. The last recorded payment to him is for June 5, 1400. He died October 25 of that year and was buried in the abbey. This placement of his grave was most likely because he was a tenant there and not for any reasons of honor or position. It is therefore ironic that his tomb would become the focus for the later Poet's Corner.

Introduction

Through all of his career's movement and his personal developments, Chaucer the civil servant was accompanied by Chaucer the poet. Certainly his work and life experiences must have colored his writing, but nowhere is it blatantly obvious. Or, rather, it is very rarely obvious. As mentioned, he wrote a complaint about the emptiness of his purse and he seems to have used his experiences as a soldier as a background to his portrayals of knights. His mercantile roots more than likely are reflected in his characterizations of the Merchant and the Wife of Bath, among others. The Peasant Revolt is mentioned briefly in the "Nun's Priest's Tale":

Certes, he Jakke Straw and his meynee
Ne made nevere shoutes half so shrille
Whan that they wolden any Flemyng kille,
As thilke day was maad upon the fox.

For certain, Jack Straw and his men
Never made a noise quite so shrill
When they were killing Flemings
As was made this day upon the fox.

(*Canterbury Tales*, "The Nun's Priest's Tale,"
VIII, 3394–97)

The Book of the Duchess and the *Parliament of Fowls* were written in response to specific court events: the death of Blanche of Lancaster and the engagement of Richard II, respectively. However, there are few specific references or allusions to contemporary events in Chaucer's works as a whole.

His strengths in providing historical significance instead lie in his characterization of the people and attitudes of his times. Chaucer's works reveal a great deal about the changing shape of society, both in class perceptions and socioeconomic realities. They reveal a good deal about the decline of the feudal system. And, most famously perhaps, they reveal even more about the changing role of the Church.

While all times can be characterized as times of change, fourteenth-century Europe—and England in particular—are especially good examples of this statement. This century was poised at the cusp of change from medieval attitudes to something that can be described as closer to modern. Although any generalizations about a particular time are fraught with potential for misspeaking, it is clear that the fourteenth century can honestly be characterized as a period of great transition. Many belief systems and social structures that had been in place for centuries were beginning to show signs of wear and decline and new ones were rising to take their place. A very homogeneous society with hierarchies rather statically defined would emerge at the end of the century much more fragmented and fluid. Change was ultimately gradual, but it was punctuated by a number of cataclysmic moments that hastened these inevitable changes.

The first of these moments would be the coming of the Black Death in 1348 (see Black Death). While the causes and origins of the disease remain hotly debated, it is clear that the effects of the disease were to change the shape of European society drastically. After the plague had swept northward from Italy through Scandinavia, roughly one-quarter to one-third of the population was gone. The economy, because of the lost population, was in dire straits along with the Church and the feudal structure. Villages were depleted, agricultural production was in shambles, and those who were left to pick up the pieces of the society were facing what must have seemed insurmountable odds.

However, as the cliché goes, when one door closes, another opens, and the survivors of the Black Death soon discovered myriad opportunities for change. These were changes that no doubt would have occurred in due time as European society was moving in that direction anyway. However, the catastrophic losses caused by the Black Death accentuated and hastened these changes. Peasants suddenly found themselves in a position of power that they had never known before. There was much work to be done and few to do it. No longer would it be enough to simply provide a cottage and a strip of land in return for full-time labor. Now, peasants began to demand, and receive, real wages as well as rights. They would be willing to die to protect these advances, as is proven by Wat Tyler's Rebellion in 1381 as well as several other revolts across Europe.

Nobles, in order to protect their assumed position in society, retaliated first by seeking wage caps and later by switching the focus of their land from agriculture to the rearing of livestock—in particular, sheep. This development is crucial to the ascension of England as a major economic power in the coming decades and lasting for the next 600 years. With the domination of the woolen trade, England came to dominate in nearly every other aspect of the economy and politics.

The fact that the nobility was physically susceptible to the disease eroded the faith that they were somehow inherently superior to those who were not of aristocratic birth and, therefore, qualified to rule unquestioned. The changing face of warfare compounded this effect as well. Common foot soldiers and pikemen were the driving force behind a number of English victories in the Hundred Years War. The place of the knight as sole protector of society was slowly slipping away, and both of these factors combined to wear away the golden façade of aristocratic privilege that had existed for so many centuries.

The belief in the ability of the Church to protect its faithful also wavered in the face of high mortality rates among its clergy and the unwillingness of many priests to administer last rites for fear of contamination. The resulting questioning of the Church's role and suitability to be responsible for the salvation of all the world's souls is reflected in the hostility toward the clergy and other religious figures that is apparent in Chaucer's works (see Friar, Monk, Nun, Parson, Prioress, and Religion). It would also lead directly into the Reformation, as various heretical groups gained traction among the faithful.

From this point forward, individuality rather than community and homogeneity began to assert itself as a value. Individuals sought their own salvation through means that did not involve priestly intercession, in methods such as the pilgrimage that forms the framework of the *Canterbury Tales*. Peasants sought to better their financial position through cash wages and the selling of surplus goods at markets. Cash could be accumulated in order to buy land, or it could be used to travel to a city where one could pursue a nonagricultural trade or take up a mercantile pursuit. The options for those of common birth, in other words, were becoming much more complex.

For the nobility, the interdependence of the agricultural life-style was replaced by the lower maintenance and less communal one of raising sheep. For the knightly class, their position as the primary fighting force and protectors of society was being undermined by new developments in weaponry—in particular, the use of gunpowder—that rendered them obsolete as well as a new reliance on common foot soldiers to wield pikes (see Armor, Estates, Knight, and Weapons). For many centuries the nobles had dominated through their insistence upon their inborn superiority. Too many arguments were rising to refute that idea, weakening their control of the social structure.

The effects of this change are apparent in Chaucer's works. Current in his society were attitudes that reflected a certain degree of uncertainty about the future and an air of the excitement of possibilities, and Chaucer's work reflects these ideas. One of the more pervasive ideas of his time was the image of Dame Fortune and her wheel. The wheel turns indiscriminately, taking people to the heights of achievement and back down into despair and failure, often with no more reasonable explanation than the whims of the goddess (see Fortune). Chaucer uses the image of Fortune and her wheel throughout all of his works, even devoting a short poem to her.

There was also a notion current in Chaucer's day that life itself is like a pilgrimage, with a goal in mind that should essentially bring, if not salvation, some sort of positive outcome. The adventures along the way are what guide us to our end goal and shape the way that we arrive there. Chaucer must have intended his tales to end with the arrival at the tomb of St. Thomas or, as Harry Bailly plans, with the return to the Tabard Inn. The fact that he never achieved either of these potential goals can be viewed as a sort of existential commentary on the uncertainty of our individual journeys through life. However, along the way, he allows us to experience the rich panorama of teeming London life that he was exposed to every day.

This very richness is what has made Chaucer such a beloved and enduring part of our literary culture. He teaches us plenty about his own time through his characters, especially in the *Canterbury Tales,* but he also provides a window into the very essence of human nature. His relevance is timeless for the very reason that the issues and situations he explores are still with us today. He is as much a product of his own time as outside of it, in much the way that Shakespeare would be. Both writers had a keen grasp of human motivations and emotions, the inner worlds that inspire and drive us all. For that reason, his place is assured both as the focal point of the Poet's Corner in Westminster Abbey and as the father of English poetry.

Chronology of Important Events in Chaucer's Time

1327   Edward II is overthrown by his queen Isabella and her lover, Roger de Mortimer. Edward III takes the throne but is controlled by his mother.

1330   Edward III seizes power in his own name, banishing Isabella and executing Mortimer.

1339   Edward III invades France, claiming the French crown as his own and starting the Hundred Years War.

1340   England naval victory at Sluys.

1343   Probable birth year of Chaucer.

1346   Battle of Crécy, resulting in a French defeat by the English. The English also defeat the Scots at the Battle of Neville's Cross.

1347   Truce between England and France. Black Death begins in Italy.

1348   Black Death arrives in England.

1353   Publication of Boccaccio's *Decameron*.

1356   Battle of Poitiers.

1357   Chaucer enters the household of Elizabeth, Countess of Ulster, wife of Lionel, Duke of Clarence and son of Edward III.

1359   Chaucer goes to France with Edward III's army and is captured at the siege of Rheims.

1360   The Treaty of Bretigny ends first phase of Hundred Years War. Chaucer is ransomed for £16.

1361   The publication of Langland's *Piers Plowman*.

1366   Chaucer marries Philippa de Roet, a lady-in-waiting to Queen Philippa of Hainault.

1367   Edward the Black Prince leads expedition to Spain to aid Pedro the Cruel, deposed King of Castile.

1369   Hostilities resume in the Hundred Years War.

1374   Chaucer moves to house above Aldgate and is appointed Controller of Customs.

1376   Death of the Black Prince.

1377   Death of Edward III. Crown passes to his grandson, Richard II.

1378   Pope Gregory XI elected. Start of Great Schism.

1379   Chaucer writes the *House of Fame*.

1380   John Wycliffe is dismissed from the Oxford faculty for teaching religious reform. The Lollards would form heretical pre-Lutheran sect around his teachings.

1381   Wat Tyler's Rebellion.

1382   Richard II marries Anne of Bohemia. Wycliffe translates Bible into English. Chaucer is appointed Controller of Petty Customs on Wines.

1383   Death of John Wycliffe.

1385   Probable date of composition of *Troilus and Criseyde*.

1386   John of Gaunt leads unsuccessful expedition to Spain to claim crown of Castile in the name of his second wife. Chaucer writes first sections of the *Canterbury Tales*. Also moves to Greenwich and is appointed Justice of the Peace and Knight of the Shire.

1387   Probable year of death of Philippa Chaucer.

1399   Death of John of Gaunt. Richard II is deposed by Henry of Bolingbroke (John of Gaunt's son), who takes the crown as Henry IV.

1400   Death of Richard II and of Geoffrey Chaucer.

1478   William Caxton publishes first printed edition of the *Canterbury Tales*.

A

Abigail

Abigail (Old Testament) was the wife of a sheep farmer named Nabal. When Nabal refused to provide hospitality to a group of men sent by King David, David retaliated in anger. He sent an armed force of men, hoping to teach Nabal a very painful, even deadly, lesson. Abigail realized her husband's great danger before he did and managed to save him by preparing lavish gifts for David.

King David was so pleased with Abigail's devotion that, when Nabal eventually died, David took her as his own wife.

She is mentioned twice in *The Canterbury Tales* as the archetype of the "good wife":

Lo Abigayl, by good conseil how she
Saved hir housbonde Nabal whan that he
Sholde han be slayn;

See Abigail and how by her good advice
She saved her husband Nabal when it seemed
Certain that he would be killed.

(*Canterbury Tales,*
"The Merchant's Tale," IV, (E), 1369–71)

Abygail delivered Nabal hir housbonde fro David the kyng, that wolde have slayn hym, and apaysed the ire of the kyng by her wit and by hir good conseillyng.

Abigail saved her husband Nabal from King David, who would have killed him, and appeased the anger of the king with her wit and charm and her good advice to her husband.

(*Canterbury Tales,*
"The Tale of Melibee," VIII, 1099)

FURTHER READING

Brown, Peter, ed. *A Companion to Chaucer.* Malden, MA: Blackwell, 2002.

Frye, Northrop. *Biblical and Classical Myths: The Mythological Framework of Western Culture.* Buffalo, NY: University of Toronto Press, 2004.

Manser, Martin H. *The Facts On File Dictionary of Classical and Biblical Allusions.* New York: Facts On File, 2003.

Abraham

Abraham (Old Testament) is regarded as the patriarch of the Israelites, making him a key figure in the three leading religions of the world—Christianity, Islam, and Judaism—all of which are referred to as "Abrahamic religions." Similar accounts of his life are given in the Bible and the Qur'an, where he is described as blessed by God. His two sons, Isaac and Ishmael, would go on to found the two Semitic peoples, the Jews and the Arabs, respectively. For the Christians, Abraham's willingness to sacrifice Isaac at God's command provides a precursor to God's later sacrifice of his own son, Jesus.

Abraham's first wife Sarah bore him Isaac when she was in old age, while her handmaiden, Hagar, bore Ishmael. It was through the birth of Isaac, promised by God, that the right of circumcision was initiated. After the death of Sarah at the age of 127 years, Abraham married Cetura and fathered six more children.

The Wife of Bath mentions Abraham in the prologue to her tale as one of the many examples of those men who are respected by posterity yet married many times (*Canterbury Tales,* "The Wife of Bath's Tale," III (D), 44–55).

FURTHER READING

Brown, Peter, ed. *A Companion to Chaucer.* Malden, MA: Blackwell, 2002.

Frye, Northrop. *Biblical and Classical Myths: The Mythological Framework of Western Culture.* Buffalo, NY: University of Toronto Press, 2004.

Manser, Martin H. *The Facts On File Dictionary of Classical and Biblical Allusions.* New York: Facts On File, 2003.

Absalom

The handsome and rebellious son of King David, Absalom (Old Testament), died tragically after rising up against his father. Although David gave specific instructions to spare his son's life, Joab deliberately went against them and killed Absalom in a cowardly way. When Absalom was running from Joab's men, who were in hot pursuit, his neck became caught in the forked branches of a tree. As he hung there defenseless, Joab approached and slew him.

His is the ironic name of Alison's unwanted suitor in "The Miller's Tale." He is also referenced in "The Parson's Tale" and in *The Legend of Good Women:* "Hyd, Absolon, thy gilte tresses clere" (*Look, Absalom, with your beautiful golden hair*) (*Legend of Good Women*, 249).

FURTHER READING

Brown, Peter, ed. *A Companion to Chaucer.* Malden, MA: Blackwell, 2002.
Frye, Northrop. *Biblical and Classical Myths: The Mythological Framework of Western Culture.* Buffalo, NY: University of Toronto Press, 2004.
Manser, Martin H. *The Facts On File Dictionary of Classical and Biblical Allusions.* New York: Facts On File, 2003.

Achates

A character from the *Aeneid,* Achates was the friend and armor-bearer of Aeneas, with whom he flees upon the fall of Troy. He is mentioned in *The House of Fame* aiding Aeneas in his wooing of Dido (*House of Fame*, 225–52) as well as in *The Legend of Good Women*'s "Legend of Dido":

He hadde a knight, was called Achates,
And hym of all his felawshipe he ches
To gon with hyn, the cuntre for t'espie.
He tok with hym no more companye,
But forth they gon, and lafte his shipes ryde,
His fere and he, withouten any gyde.

He had a knight who was called Achates
And of all the friends around him he chose Achates
To go with him to see the country.
He took with him no other company,
And off they went, leaving his ships behind,
His friend and him, without any other guide.

(*Legend of Good Women*, 964–69)

FURTHER READING

Brown, Peter, ed. *A Companion to Chaucer.* Malden, MA: Blackwell, 2002.
Frye, Northrop. *Biblical and Classical Myths: The Mythological Framework of Western Culture.* Buffalo, NY: University of Toronto Press, 2004.

Hansen, William F. *Classical Mythology: A Guide to the Mythical World of the Greeks and Romans.* New York: Oxford University Press, 2005.

Manser, Martin H. *The Facts On File Dictionary of Classical and Biblical Allusions.* New York: Facts On File, 2003.

Morford, Mark P. O. *Classical Mythology.* 7th ed. New York: Oxford University Press, 2003.

Nolan, Barbara. *Chaucer and the Tradition of the Roman Antique.* New York: Cambridge University Press, 1992.

Powell, Barry B. *Classical Myth.* Translated by Herbert M. Howe. 4th ed. Upper Saddle River, NJ: Pearson/Prentice Hall, 2004.

Price, Simon, and Emily Kearns, eds. *The Oxford Dictionary of Classical Myth and Religion.* New York: Oxford University Press, 2003.

Achilles

The tragic hero of the Trojan War, Achilles appears in "The Man of Law's Tale" as an example of a death that is fated:

In sterres, many a wynter therbiforn,
Was writen the deeth of Ector, Achilles,
Of Pompei, Julius, er they were born;
The strif of Thebes; and of Ercules,
Of Sampson, Turnus, and of Socrates
The deeth; but mennes wittes ben so dulle
That no wight kan wel rede it atte fulle.

In the stars, many a winter long before,
Was written the death of Hector, of Achilles,
Of Pompey, of Julius Caesar, before they were even born.
The war of Thebes; and the death of Hercules,
Of Sampson, of Turnus, and Socrates too.
But men's wits are so dull
That they cannot even read the truth before them

(*Canterbury Tales,*
"The Man of Law's Tale," II (B1), 197–203)

In both "The Nun's Priest's Tale" and *The Book of the Duchess,* Achilles appears as the killer of Hector, and interestingly, in *The House of Fame,* he is mentioned as one of a series of faithless men. Since *Troilus and Criseyde* centers around the Trojan War, it might be assumed that Achilles plays a pivotal role. However, despite the fact that he slays Troilus, his appearance in the tale is brief. He first kills Hector, "Unwar of this, Achilles thorugh the maille / And thorugh the body gan hym for to ryve; / And thus this worthi knyght was brought of lyve" (*Unaware of this, Achilles ran him through his mail / and through his body / and in this way this worthy knight lost his life*) and then kills Troilus, "Despitously hym slough the fierse Achille" (*The fierce Achilles slew him without pity*) (*Troilus and Criseyde*, V, 1559–61, 1806).

FURTHER READING

Brown, Peter, ed. *A Companion to Chaucer*. Malden, MA: Blackwell, 2002.

Frye, Northrop. *Biblical and Classical Myths: The Mythological Framework of Western Culture*. Buffalo, NY: University of Toronto Press, 2004.

Hansen, William F. *Classical Mythology: A Guide to the Mythical World of the Greeks and Romans*. New York: Oxford University Press, 2005.

Manser, Martin H. *The Facts On File Dictionary of Classical and Biblical Allusions*. New York: Facts On File, 2003.

Morford, Mark P. O. *Classical Mythology*. 7th ed. New York: Oxford University Press, 2003.

Nolan, Barbara. *Chaucer and the Tradition of the Roman Antique*. New York: Cambridge University Press, 1992.

Powell, Barry B. *Classical Myth*. Translated by Herbert M. Howe. 4th ed. Upper Saddle River, NJ: Pearson/Prentice Hall, 2004.

Price, Simon, and Emily Kearns, eds. *The Oxford Dictionary of Classical Myth and Religion*. New York: Oxford University Press, 2003.

Actaeon

Actaeon was the unfortunate hunter who accidentally saw a nude Artemis/Diana preparing to bathe with her nymphs. Overcome with lust, he attempted to ravish the goddess and, as punishment, she turned him into a stag. Actaeon's hounds, already on the hunt, turned upon their owner and tore him to pieces.

Actaeon's story appears in "The Knight's Tale," painted upon the walls of Diana's temple as Emily prays to the goddess to allow her to preserve her virginity:

Goddesse of maydens, that myn herte hast knowe
Ful many a yeer, and woost what I desire,
As keepe me fro thy vengeaunce and thyn ire,
That Attheon aboughte cruelly.
Chaste goddesse, wel wostow that I
Desire to ben a mayden al my lyf,
Ne nevere wol I be no love ne wyf.

Oh goddess of maidens, who my heart has known well
For many years, and who knows what I most desire,
Keep me from your vengeance and anger
That Actaeon bought so cruelly.
Chaste goddess, well you know my

Desire to remain a maiden my entire life,
And that I never wish to be a lover or a wife.

(*Canterbury Tales,*
"The Knight's Tale," I (A), 2300–6)

FURTHER READING

Brown, Peter, ed. *A Companion to Chaucer*. Malden, MA: Blackwell, 2002.

Frye, Northrop. *Biblical and Classical Myths: The Mythological Framework of Western Culture*. Buffalo, NY: University of Toronto Press, 2004.

Hansen, William F. *Classical Mythology: A Guide to the Mythical World of the Greeks and Romans*. New York: Oxford University Press, 2005.

Manser, Martin H. *The Facts On File Dictionary of Classical and Biblical Allusions*. New York: Facts On File, 2003.

Morford, Mark P. O. *Classical Mythology*. 7th ed. New York: Oxford University Press, 2003.

Nolan, Barbara. *Chaucer and the Tradition of the Roman Antique*. New York: Cambridge University Press, 1992.

Powell, Barry B. *Classical Myth*. Translated by Herbert M. Howe. 4th ed. Upper Saddle River, NJ: Pearson/Prentice Hall, 2004.

Price, Simon, and Emily Kearns, eds. *The Oxford Dictionary of Classical Myth and Religion*. New York: Oxford University Press, 2003.

Adam

Adam (Old Testament) was the first man, created by God in his own image to live in the earthly paradise of Eden. Lonely in his solitude, Adam asked God to make him a wife. In response, God made Eve from one of Adam's ribs.

It would be her temptation by Satan (in the form of a snake) into eating from the forbidden Tree of Knowledge—the moment known as Original Sin—that would precipitate humanity's expulsion from Eden. The subsequent consequences are illness, pain, and the existence of death as an earthly eventuality.

Adam is the Monk's second example in his tale and he is mentioned in "The Parson's Tale":

Looke that in th'estaat of innocence, whan Adam and Eve naked weren in Paradys, and nothyng ne hadden shame of hir nakednesse, / how that the serpent, that was moost wily of alle othere beestes that God hadde maked, seyde to the womman, "'Why comaunded God to yow ye sholde nat eten of every tree in Paradys?' / The womman answerde: 'Of the fruyt,' quod she, 'of the trees in Paradys we feden us, but soothly, of the fruyt of the tree that is in the myddel of Paradys, God forbad us for to ete, ne nat touchen it, lest per aventure we sholde dyen." / … There may ye seen that deedly synne hath, first, suggestion of the feend, as sheweth heere by the naddre; and afterward, the delit of the flessh, as sheweth heere by Eve; and

Various stories from Psalm 84: driving Adam and Eve out of the Terrestrial Paradise, Adam and Eve working, Annunciation, and Saint Joseph sitting behind the Virgin. © Bibliothèque nationale de France.

after that, the consentynge of resoun, as sheweth heere by Adam. / For trust wel, through so were that the feend tempted Eve—that is to seyn, the flessh—and the flessh hadde delit in the beautee of the fruyt defended, yet certes, til that resoun—that is to seyn, Adam—consented to the etynge of the fruyt, yet stood he in th'estaat of innocence. / Of thilke Adam tooke we thilke synne original, for of hym flesshly descended be we alle, and engendred of vile and corrupt mateere.

See that in the state of innocence, when Adam and Eve were naked in Paradise, and neither had shame of that nakedness / How the snake Satan, which is the most wily of all of the creatures God has created, said to Eve the woman, "Why did God not allow you to eat from every tree that grows in Paradise?" / She replied, "We eat all of the fruit of the trees of Paradise except for one that grows in the middle. God told us that we should never eat it, nor even touch it, or we would die." / There you can see that deadly sin, first suggested by the devil, which is the joys of the flesh, or lust—shown by Eve—and later the consenting to her urging—shown by Adam. / For trust my word, though it is true that the devil tempted Eve to the sins of the flesh, and her flesh had joy in the delicious-ness of the fruit, yet it is true that until he gave in to her and agreed to eat the fruit too, Adam continued to exist in a state of innocence. / And from Adam's own sin we all take on the original sin, because we are all descended from him, and are all made of vile and corrupted matter.

(*Canterbury Tales*,
"The Parson's Tale," X (I), 324–35)

FURTHER READING

Brown, Peter, ed. *A Companion to Chaucer*. Malden, MA: Blackwell, 2002.

Frye, Northrop. *Biblical and Classical Myths: The Mythological Framework of Western Culture*. Buffalo, NY: University of Toronto Press, 2004.

Manser, Martin H. *The Facts On File Dictionary of Classical and Biblical Allusions*. New York: Facts On File, 2003.

Adonis

The handsome Adonis had the complicated fate to be loved both by Venus and Persephone. In order to satisfy both goddesses, Jupiter decreed that he should spend one third of every year with each of them. The third portion of the year could be spent wherever Adonis chose. He invariably chose to spend the final third with Venus.

Adonis would be killed tragically, gored by a boar on hunting trip. Some legends attribute his untimely and youthful demise to the jealousy of Venus's lover Ares. His death is the basis of the creation of the rose, one of which grew from each drop of blood that fell from his dying body. He appears in both "The Knight's Tale," as Palamon prays to Venus, and in *Troilus and Criseyde*, as Troilus explains to Pandarus the pains of love:

For thilke love thow haddest to Adoon,
Have pitee of my bittre teeris smerte,
And taak myn humble preyere at thyn herte.

For the love that you bore for Adonis,
Take pity on my bitter tears that hurt,
And take my most humble prayers into your heart.

(*Canterbury Tales*,
"The Knight's Tale," I (A), 2224–26)

And if ich hadde, O Venus ful of myrthe,
Aspectes badde of Mars or of Saturne,
Or thow combust or let were in my birthe,
Thy fader prey al thilke harm disturne
Of grace, and that I glad ayein may turne,
For love of hym thow lovedest in the shawe—
I meene Adoun, that with the boor was slawe.

O Venus full of mirth, if I was under the influences
Of Mars or of Saturn at my birth or
If you Venus were made powerless by the strength of the sun,
Then pray to your father for me to stop these
Evil celestial influences, so that I can again be glad
Please do this for the love of him who you loved in the woods,
I mean Adonis, who was slain by the boar.

(*Troilus and Criseyde,* Book III, 715–21)

FURTHER READING

Brown, Peter, ed. *A Companion to Chaucer.* Malden, MA: Blackwell, 2002.

Frye, Northrop. *Biblical and Classical Myths: The Mythological Framework of Western Culture.* Buffalo, NY: University of Toronto Press, 2004.

Hansen, William F. *Classical Mythology: A Guide to the Mythical World of the Greeks and Romans.* New York: Oxford University Press, 2005.

Manser, Martin H. *The Facts On File Dictionary of Classical and Biblical Allusions.* New York: Facts On File, 2003.

Morford, Mark P. O. *Classical Mythology.* 7th ed. New York: Oxford University Press, 2003.

Nolan, Barbara. *Chaucer and the Tradition of the Roman Antique.* New York: Cambridge University Press, 1992.

Powell, Barry B. *Classical Myth.* Translated by Herbert M. Howe. 4th ed. Upper Saddle River, NJ: Pearson/Prentice Hall, 2004.

Price, Simon, and Emily Kearns, eds. *The Oxford Dictionary of Classical Myth and Religion.* New York: Oxford University Press, 2003.

Aeneas

A hero of the Trojan war, Aeneas was the son of Venus and Anchises and the cousin of Hector. After the fall of Troy, he would lead the survivors into wandering exile to find a new place to settle. Virgil in the *Aeneid* chronicled Aeneas's many adventures—romantic and otherwise—in his travels. Chaucer seems to hold a very low opinion of him and only mentions his misogynistic activities.

In *The House of Fame, The Book of the Duchess,* and *The Legend of Good Women,* Chaucer chronicles Aeneas's betrayal of Dido, who committed suicide when he left her. In *Troilus and Criseyde,* Chaucer makes no mention of his military prowess and alludes to him merely as a friend of Poliphete, the man who victimized and harassed Criseyde with legal troubles.

FURTHER READING

Brown, Peter, ed. *A Companion to Chaucer.* Malden, MA: Blackwell, 2002.

Frye, Northrop. *Biblical and Classical Myths: The Mythological Framework of Western Culture.* Buffalo, NY: University of Toronto Press, 2004.

Hansen, William F. *Classical Mythology: A Guide to the Mythical World of the Greeks and Romans.* New York: Oxford University Press, 2005.

Manser, Martin H. *The Facts On File Dictionary of Classical and Biblical Allusions.* New York: Facts On File, 2003.

Morford, Mark P. O. *Classical Mythology.* 7th ed. New York: Oxford University Press, 2003.

Nolan, Barbara. *Chaucer and the Tradition of the Roman Antique.* New York: Cambridge University Press, 1992.

Powell, Barry B. *Classical Myth.* Translated by Herbert M. Howe. 4th ed. Upper Saddle River, NJ: Pearson/Prentice Hall, 2004.

Price, Simon, and Emily Kearns, eds. *The Oxford Dictionary of Classical Myth and Religion.* New York: Oxford University Press, 2003.

Agriculture

With hym ther was a PLOWMAN, was his brother,
That hadde ylad of dong ful many a fother;
A trewe swynkere and a good was he,
Lyvynge in pees and parfit charitee.
God loved he best with al his hoole herte
At alle tymes, thogh him gamed or smerte,
And thanne his neighebor right as hymselve.

With him there was a Plowman who was his brother
And who had carried many a full cart of dung;
He was a good hard worker,
Who lived in peace and perfect charity.
He loved God best with his whole heart
All of the time, whether it was to his gain or his detriment,
And he treated his neighbor as he would himself.

(*Canterbury Tales,*
General Prologue, I (A), 529–35)

As in any time of human history, feeding the populace was an ongoing and critical concern of medieval society. Because it was period of increased urbanization, a situation in which a growing segment of the population had no access to food beyond what was produced and brought in to market, the Middle Ages presented new challenges that had to be overcome to feed a growing population and foster other cultural and societal developments.

For many centuries, societies were strongly agriculturally based. Certainly each successive European empire had its share of cities and along with them the sorts of artisans and craftsmen who flourished in urbanized areas. However, it was Chaucer's era that would finally witness the real growth of urban centers in which the inhabitants were completely dependent on imported foodstuffs from the outlying agricultural centers. Transported food was also of vital importance in keeping armies on their feet in the nearly constant warfare that characterized the period. No matter what one's station in life, one had to eat, and thus the growing of crops and preserving of food was perhaps the most important aspect of medieval life.

By Chaucer's day, agricultural production had become a rather sophisticated system. In England and on the Continent, this system combined elements of Byzantine and Arab techniques with indigenous methods to create methods of farming that were appropriate to each individual climate. Key to the success of any agricultural endeavor were the arability and availability of land and the variety of natural resources nearby. Certainly the area that enjoyed a bounty of these factors was fortunate indeed, but generally farmers and peasants had to make the best of their situations. Therefore, in drier climates, or in fields that were located far away from rivers, irrigation systems developed by the Arabs were built to keep crops watered. Intricate terracing based on Byzantine methods prevented soil erosion in arid or hilly lands. Crop rotation and as wide a variety of vegetables and grains as soil

A farming scene from Jean of Montlucon's fifteenth-century *Book of Hours.* © Bibliothèque nationale de France.

and climate conditions would sustain were ways to prevent depletion of nutrients as well as to provide the populace with a healthy and varied diet.

The three-field system was developed at some point during the Middle Ages in order to fulfill these goals. An elaboration on the tried and true, but not especially productive, two-field system, the three-field system consisted of dividing arable land into thirds. One field per year was left fallow so that it could recoup nutritive losses to the soil and enter the following year's growing season fresher and potentially more productive. One of the remaining two would be planted in the spring with a grain such as wheat, and in the fall with oats or barley. This provided for the village's or manor's grain needs and at the same time utilized a limited amount of soil nutrients. The third field would be planted with other vegetable crops, such as peas, corn, or greens. The following year the fields would rotate, the fallow being planted with wheat, and so forth. In this fashion, each field was replenished by a year of rest as well as by the different nutritional demands and benefits of each successive crop that was planted there.

The manorial system was the glue that held the agricultural world together. Each manor, given to a noble overlord by his feudal lord (often the king), contained the many fields as well as the peasant housing, village, the

Shearing sheep and bringing in the harvest from the fifteenth-century *Les Tres Riches Heures* from the collection of Duc du Berry. Courtesy of the Dover Pictorial Archive.

lord's manor house, and equipment and livestock. Since oxen teams and the heavy plow were both expensive and difficult to turn in small spaces, peasants were forced to cooperate with one another to a remarkable degree. If the lord did not provide the plow team, not only did the peasants have to pool their financial resources to purchase a communal team, they had to work the land cooperatively. Fields were plowed in long narrow strips, and the lands of each individual peasant would fall along the continuum, along with the overlord's lands. Thus, as the shared plow made its way through the long field, it crossed over

The hay harvest from the fifteenth-century *Playfair Book of Hours.* © Victoria & Albert Museum, London / Art Resource, NY.

the lands of many before turning and traversing the same lands in reverse order. This deep sense of interdependence perhaps was one of the factors that helped to unify the peasant population to the degree that they were able to organize themselves in order to revolt so many times and so nearly successfully against the time-honored and Church-endorsed social system.

Chaucer captures a bit of this spirit of cooperation in his description of the hardworking and affable Plowman.

See also Feudalism; Food; Peasant Revolt

FURTHER READING

Attreed, Lorraine Christine. *The King's Towns: Identity and Survival in Late Medieval English Boroughs.* New York: P. Lang, 2001.

Bisson, Lillian M. *Chaucer and the Late Medieval World.* New York: St. Martin's Press, 1998.

Bloch, Marc. *Feudal Society.* Translated by L. A. Manyon. New York: Routledge, 1961; 1989.

Brewer, Derek. *Chaucer and His World.* Cambridge, England: D. S. Brewer, 1978; reprinted 1992.

Britnell, Richard, ed. *Daily Life in the Late Middle Ages.* Stroud, England: Sutton, 1998.

Brown, Peter, ed. *A Companion to Chaucer.* Malden, MA: Blackwell, 2002.

Gies, Frances, and Joseph Gies. *Cathedral, Forge, and Waterwheel.* New York: Harper Collins, 1994.

Masschaele, James. *Peasants, Merchants, and Markets: Inland Trade in Medieval England, 1150–1350.* New York: St. Martin's Press, 1997.

Morgan, Gwyneth. *Life in a Medieval Village.* New York: Cambridge University Press, 1975.

Singman, Jeffrey L., and Will McLean. *Daily Life in Chaucer's England.* Westport, CT: Greenwood Press, 1995.

Thirsk, Joan. *Alternative Agriculture: A History. From the Black Death to the Present Day.* Oxford, England: Oxford University Press, 1997.

Alchemy

What sholde I tellen ech proporcion
Of thynges whiche that we werche upon—
As on fyve or sixe ounces, may wel be,
Of silver, or som oother quantitee—
And bisye me to telle yow the names
Of orpyment, brent bones, iren squames,
That into poudre grounden been ful smal;
And in an erthen pot how put is al,
And salt yput in, and also papeer,
Biforn thise poudres that I speke of heer;
And wel ycovered with a lampe of glas;

...

Ther is also ful many another thyng
That is unto oure craft apertenyng.

...

As boole armonyak, verdegrees, boras,
And sondry vessels maad of erthe and glas,
Oure urynales and oure descensories,
Violes, crosletz, and sublymatories

...

And herbes koude I telle eek many oon,
As egremoyne, valerian, and lunarie,
And othere swiche, if that me liste tarie;
Oure lampes brennyng bothe nyght and day,
To brynge aboute oure purpos, if we may;

...

Unslekked lym, chalk, and gleyre of an ey,
Poudres diverse, asshes, donge, pisse, and cley,
Cered pokkets, sal peter, vitriole,
And diverse fires maad of wode and cole;
Sal tarter, alkaly, and sal preparat,
And combust materes and coagulat;

...

I wol yow telle, as was me taught also,
The foure spirites and the bodies sevene,

...

The firste spirit quyksilver called is,
The seconde orpyment, the thridde, ywis,
Sal armonyak, and the ferthe brymstoon.
The bodyes sevene eek, lo, hem heere anoon:
Sol gold is, and Luna silver we threpe,
Mars iren, Mercurie quyksilver we clepe,
Saturnus leed, and Juppiter is tyn,
And Venus coper, by my fader kyn!

Do I really need to tell you of the proportions
Of the ingredients that we work on—
For instance, we might use five or six ounces
Of silver, or maybe some other quantity—
Or should I busy myself to tell you the names of these things,
Orpiment, or burnt bones, or iron flakes,
And grind them all into a very fine power.
And how, into an earthen pot,
We add some paper, and some salt as well,
Along with the powders I spoke of before,
And cover it all tightly with a sheet of glass.
…
There are also many other matters
That pertain to our craft
…
Such as Armenian bole, verdigris, and borax;
And the various vessels, made of earthenware or glass,
And our urinals and our vessels for distilling,
Our flasks, and vials, and crucibles.
…
And of herbs I could tell you of many a one,
Such as agrimony, and valerian, and moonwort,
And others if I could waste time on listing them.
Our lamps burned night and day
In order to accomplish our purpose.
…
I could tell you of unslaked lime, the chalk, and the white of an egg,
The many different powders, the dung, the piss, and the clay,
The waterproofed bags, the saltpeter, and the vitriol,
And all of the fires made of wood and coal.
And there is the salt of tartar and the alkali, and the common salt,
That combusts and coagulates.
…
And I will tell you, as it was told to me,
Of the four spirits and the bodies seven.
…
The first spirit is called quicksilver,
And the second orpiment, the third,
Sal ammoniac, and the fourth brimstone.
The bodies seven; listen! Here they are
Gold is the sun, and silver is the moon,
Mars iron, and Mercury is quicksilver we say.
Saturn is lead, and Jupiter is tin,
And Venus is copper, by my father's teaching!

(*Canterbury Tales,*
"The Canon's Yeoman's Tale," VIII (G), 754–897)

Title page of a sixteenth-century pamphlet with an illustration showing the tree of knowledge, 1515. Courtesy of the Library of Congress.

Rembrant's sketch of an alchemist, 1632. Courtesy of the Dover Pictorial Archive.

Alchemy, in its most straightforward definition, was the secret and mysterious process by which base metals could be transformed into gold. This, for obvious reasons, made it one of the most popular forbidden activities of the Middle Ages. This one-dimensional perception of alchemy, however, is an oversimplification of the spiritual aspects of the philosophy's deeper goals.

Alchemy in its deepest sense was intended to unlock the mysteries of the universe. The monk Ferrarius defined alchemy as "the science of the Four Elements, which are to be found in all created substances but are not of the vulgar kind. The whole practice of the art is simply the conversion of these Elements into one another." The central tenet of alchemy is that all things are perfectible. Because there is an ideal Absolute that can be attained by altering one's perception, it is possible to reach not only the archetypal absolute, but also the "eternal perfection." Gold, according to alchemists, is simply the most perfect of all metals. Thus, through alchemical processes, lead—a base type of metal—can achieve and become the archetype.

Interest and participation in alchemical experimentation was widespread in spite of the fact that the Church prohibited it. Apparently, as was the case with astrology, the Church did not actively persecute alchemists unless they became problematic. Richard II, for instance, personally owned alchemical texts. However, it remained a technically forbidden, even heretical, activity and so texts were written in obscure riddles and illustrated with fantastical symbolism so that the true alchemical process would be nearly impossible to decipher for all but the initiated.

The texts themselves generally took one of two forms. The first are little more than recipe books, detailing the "ingredients" and steps necessary to make the so-called Philosopher's Stone, which was the primary ingredient in the alchemical process. The second type of texts were of special use to the "puffers"—the name given to those who were so frantic to make gold that they puffed the bellows at the fire with great energy, so much so that they sometimes blew themselves up. These texts purported, in obscure and often indecipherable language, to provide the secret to changing lead to gold.

"The Canon's Yeoman's Tale," in fact, alludes to this habit of puffing. In the tale's prologue, Harry Bailly asks the Yeoman why his face is so discolored. The Yeoman responds by describing his former master's activities, and his urge to quickly make a fortune by turning base metals to gold. The constant blowing of the bellows over the fire has permanently darkened his skin:

I am so used in the fyr to blowe
That it hath changed my colour, I trowe.
I am nat wont in no mirour to prie,
But swynke soore and lerne multiplie.

I am so used to the fire blowing in my face,
That it has permanently changed my color, I'm afraid.
I'm not likely to look in the mirror to find out,
But instead work myself to death in trying to transmute base metals.

(*Canterbury Tales,*
"The Canon's Yeoman's Tale," VIII (G), 666–83)

Alchemy was essentially, in its scientific sense, the precursor to chemistry, and medieval chemists were responsible for the discovery of alcohol in the twelfth century, as well as nitric, hydrochloric, and sulfuric acids in the thirteenth century. Through the work of Paracelsus (1493–1541), alchemy also aided the development of medicine. Its legendary father was Hermes Trismegistus, who created what is known as the Emerald Table. This table contains a number of aphorisms that seek to develop an alchemist's "innerstanding" that will bring him to the Absolute. The theory behind reaching the Absolute was to turn everything into its opposite, thus making all things one.

The *Materia Prima* ("first matter") was the first step for the alchemist and without it none of the processes were possible. The problem for the new alchemist, however, was that the substance was never clearly identified. Whatever it was, it had to be mined, but only under the signs of Aries, Taurus, or Gemini. After mining under these special conditions, it then had to be purified. Along with the first matter, the alchemist had to prepare the *Ignis Innaturalis,* also known as the "secret fire," which appears to be a salt by-product of cream of tartar (and what is apparently described by the

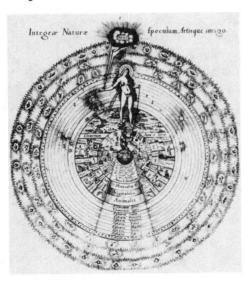

Integra Naturæ *Speculum Artisque imago*

An illustration from a fifteenth-century manuscript by Robert Fludd. Courtesy of the National Library of Medicine.

Canon's Yeoman in the passage above). It is described in alchemical texts as a "dry water that does not wet the hands" and a "fire burning without flames." Once these two products were prepared—no easy task—then the Philosophic Egg could be formed. The *Materia Prima* was pulverized with the *Ignis Innaturalis* in an agate mortar, moistened with dew, and placed in a hermetically sealed vessel inside a special furnace. Various color changes occurred from the chemical reaction that provides the inspiration behind the allegorical nature of alchemical art. Each drawing of a red king or a peacock was meant to convey a direction in the process. When the red substance joins with the white within the egg, the Philosopher's Stone is achieved and can be used to create gold. For the spiritually minded, this would then lead to the discovery of the Elixir of Life and the answer to the mysteries of the universe. For the greedy, it meant that inexpensive piles of lead could be transformed into gold bars of untold worth.

Chaucer's "The Canon's Yeoman's Tale" is the most alchemical of his works and during his time earned him a slightly racy reputation as one who most probably dabbled in the forbidden art. The tale begins with a lengthy discussion of what was involved in the alchemical process, so detailed that Chaucer seems to give away the ancient secrets known only to adepts.

See also Astrology and Astronomy; Four Humors; Medicine; Science

FURTHER READING

Brown, Peter, ed. *A Companion to Chaucer*. Malden, MA: Blackwell, 2002.

De Rola, Stanislas Klossowski. *Alchemy: The Secret Art*. New York: Bounty Books, 1973.

Kibre, Pearl. *Studies in Medieval Science: Alchemy, Astrology, Mathematics, and Medicine*. London: Hambledon Press, 1984.

Alcyone

The daughter of Aeolus and Enarete, Alcyone is the devoted wife who exhorts Juno to send her a dream about her missing husband's fate. Juno answers Alcyone's prayer by sending Morpheus to animate the body of her husband, Ceyx. Ceyx tells her he has been drowned and that she must bury his body. He gives her detailed instructions about where to find him and, upon the discovery of his corpse, Alcyone commits suicide by throwing herself into the sea. The gods pity Alcyone and Ceyx for her devotion and reward them by changing them into sea birds.

When waves wash away their nests on the edge of the water, Jupiter responds in pity by forbidding the winds to blow during the two weeks in winter that comprise their breeding season. These days would come to be known as "halcyon days," a period of calm and tranquility.

In *The Book of the Duchess*, the narrator reads Alcyone's story in Ovid, and then dreams of the Black Knight and his overpowering grief (*Book of the Duchess*, 62–269).

FURTHER READING

Brown, Peter, ed. *A Companion to Chaucer*. Malden, MA: Blackwell, 2002.

Frye, Northrop. *Biblical and Classical Myths: The Mythological Framework of Western Culture*. Buffalo, NY: University of Toronto Press, 2004.

Hansen, William F. *Classical Mythology: A Guide to the Mythical World of the Greeks and Romans*. New York: Oxford University Press, 2005.

Manser, Martin H. *The Facts On File Dictionary of Classical and Biblical Allusions*. New York: Facts On File, 2003.

Morford, Mark P. O. *Classical Mythology*. 7th ed. New York: Oxford University Press, 2003.

Nolan, Barbara. *Chaucer and the Tradition of the Roman Antique*. New York: Cambridge University Press, 1992.

Powell, Barry B. *Classical Myth*. Translated by Herbert M. Howe. 4th ed. Upper Saddle River, NJ: Pearson/Prentice Hall, 2004.

Price, Simon, and Emily Kearns, eds. *The Oxford Dictionary of Classical Myth and Religion*. New York: Oxford University Press, 2003.

Aldgate

Aldgate was one of the original four gates into London, built into the city walls during the Roman occupation in the 300s. City walls were a defensive maneuver designed to protect the urban center and its inhabitants from invasion. Gates were placed strategically for ease of passage for those who were approved to be admitted, but could be closed and secured when an enemy army approached. When the Romans withdrew in 410, the Anglo-Saxons continued to fortify the defensive walls and built more structures on top of them. By Chaucer's day, the original four—Aldgate at the East End, Ludgate at the west, Bridgegate at the south over the Thames River, and Aldersgate at the north—had expanded to seven. Aldgate provided entrance into Whitechapel and London's East End, known today for its distinctive Cockney accent and colorful culture. The gate was rebuilt in the thirteenth century and, during Chaucer's time, consisted of two double gates. A heavy iron portcullis, presenting a formidable challenge to invaders, protected each outer gate from artillery attacks.

Houses were built on the walls above the gate, and it was one of these on the southern end that Chaucer rented from 1374 to 1386. The house was provided to him free of charge as part of his compensation as Controller of Wool Customs and Subsidy for the Port of London. One of the more notable sights he must have witnessed from his home would have been the procession of the angry mob traveling to meet with Richard II at Mile End during the Peasant Revolt of 1381. It was here at Aldgate that Chaucer would compose most of his poetry before leaving his post and retiring to Greenwich. His bird's eye view of daily London life may well have provided Chaucer with details for some of his more colorful characters and scenes in *The Canterbury Tales.*

See also London; Peasant Revolt

FURTHER READING

Archer, Lucy. *Architecture in Britain and Ireland, 600–1500.* London: Harvill Press, 1999.

Brewer, Derek. *Chaucer and His World.* Cambridge, England: D. S. Brewer, 1978; reprinted 1992.

Carlin, Martha. *Medieval Southwark.* Rio Grande, OH: Hambledon Press, 1996.

Hanawalt, Barbara A., ed. *Chaucer's England: Literature in Historical Context.* Minneapolis: University of Minnesota Press, 1992.

———. *Growing Up in Medieval London: The Experience of Childhood in History.* New York: Oxford University Press, 1993.

Alexandria

In 331 B.C., Alexander the Great founded Alexandria as the capital of his empire in Egypt. For many centuries it represented the epitome of culture and learning in the east. Alexandria's library was world renowned and its lighthouse at Pharos was named one of the Seven Wonders of the World. In 969, however, the construction of Cairo contributed to Alexandria's ultimate decline, a descent that was hastened by the conquest of Egypt by the Muslims.

The General Prologue to *The Canterbury Tales* declares that the Knight was in Alexandria "whan it was wonne" [*when it was won*] (*Canterbury Tales,* General Prologue, I A, 51). This would place him in Alexandria in October 1365, when troops led by Peter I of Cyprus captured the city, massacred its inhabitants, and abandoned it within one week. Such bloodthirsty behavior is not in keeping with the claim that the Knight is a model of perfect chivalry. While it was acceptable in the eyes of the Church to wage war upon the infidel, Chaucer seems to be slyly implying that such behavior is hypocritical.

In the end, the chief lasting conquest of Alexandria in the fourteenth century appears to have been accomplished by nature when a series of tidal waves and earthquakes struck the port city. The most devastating of these quakes would destroy the Pharos lighthouse in 1323.

See also Knight

FURTHER READING

Cantor, Norman. *The Civilization of the Middle Ages.* Rev. ed. New York: Harper Collins, 1993.

Jones, Terry. *Chaucer's Knight: The Portrait of a Medieval Mercenary.* Baton Rouge: Louisiana State University Press, 1980.

Kaeuper, Richard W. *Chivalry and Violence in Medieval Europe.* New York: Oxford University Press, 1999.

Labarge, Margaret Wade. *Medieval Travellers.* New York: Norton, 1983.

Le Beau, Bryan F., and Menachem Mor, eds. *Pilgrims and Travelers to the Holy Land.* Omaha, NE: Creighton University Press, 1996.

Tyerman, Christopher. *England and the Crusades, 1095–1588.* Chicago: University of Chicago Press, 1988.

Verdon, Jean. *Travel in the Middle Ages.* Notre Dame, IN: University of Notre Dame Press, 2003.

Algeciras

Algeciras is a port city in southern Spain, located on the Strait of Gibralter and known as the gateway to Morocco. Its name comes from the Arabic for "the peninsula," *al jazeera,* and dates to its domination by Muslim invaders. Alfonso XI, king of Castile and León, took it from the Moors in 1344. It was in this siege the Knight participated, most likely as a mercenary:

In Gernade at the seege eek hadde he be
Of Algezir, and ridden in Belmarye.

He had been at the siege of Algeciras
In Grenada, and had ridden in Morocco.

(*Canterbury Tales,*
General Prologue, I A, 56–57)

This activity on the part of the Knight further underlines Chaucer's sly indication that the Knight is not all that his initial classification as the highest-ranking member of the party would indicate.

Alfonso would die in 1350 while besieging Gibralter. He would be succeeded by his son, Peter the Cruel, who would figure prominently in John of Gaunt's bid for the throne of Castile, a bid bolstered by his marriage to the granddaughter of Alfonso, Constance.

See also John of Gaunt; Knight

FURTHER READING

Cantor, Norman. *The Civilization of the Middle Ages*. Rev. ed. New York: Harper Collins, 1993.

Jones, Terry. *Chaucer's Knight: The Portrait of a Medieval Mercenary*. Baton Rouge: Louisiana State University Press, 1980.

Kaeuper, Richard W. *Chivalry and Violence in Medieval Europe*. New York: Oxford University Press, 1999.

Labarge, Margaret Wade. *Medieval Travellers*. New York: Norton, 1983.

Le Beau, Bryan F., and Menachem Mor, eds. *Pilgrims and Travelers to the Holy Land*. Omaha, NE: Creighton University Press, 1996.

Tyerman, Christopher. *England and the Crusades, 1095–1588*. Chicago: University of Chicago Press, 1988.

Verdon, Jean. *Travel in the Middle Ages*. Notre Dame, IN: University of Notre Dame Press, 2003.

Algezir. See Algeciras

Alisaundre. See Alexandria

Allegory and Dream Visions

Defaute of slep and hevynesse
Hath sleyn my spirit of quyknesse
That I have lost al lustyhede.
Suche fantasies ben in myn hede
So I not what is best to doo.

But men might axe me why soo
I may not slepe and what me is.
But natheles, who aske this
Leseth his asking trewely.
Myselven can not telle why
The sothe; but trewly, as I gesse,
I holde hit be a sicknesse
That I have suffred this eight yeer;
And yet my boote is never the ner,
For there is phisicien but oon
That may me hele; but that is don.

Lack of sleep and sadness
Have robbed my spirit of lightness
And I have lost all of my zest for life.
Terrible ideas have been in my head
And I don't know what to do.
One might ask me why it is
That I can't sleep and what is wrong with me

Yet, whoever asks this
Will not receive an answer.
As I can't tell why I can't sleep,
But I guess that I have been
Stricken by a sickness of the heart
That has afflicted me for eight long years;
And yet there is no remedy near
There is only one doctor who can heal me;
But it is not to be and so must be done without.

(Book of the Duchess, 25–40)

As a literary device, dream visions were one of the most important and distinctive conceits of the medieval period. The dream vision formed a kind of homage to classical and biblical stories, which were often framed in similar ways by the narrator sleeping and telling a fantastic tale of what was seen in the unconscious state. The Old Testament, for example, is full of dreams and visions, from Joseph to Ezekiel. In the New Testament, the Book of Revelation is perhaps the most famous and disturbing example. In classical literature, Virgil includes a vision of the underworld in the *Aeneid*, Plato of the cave in *The Republic*, and—most relevant to Chaucer—Macrobius comments on the dream of Scipio. The use of the dream vision as a literary device also makes use of the medieval belief that dreams can illuminate the dreamer with some type of wisdom. For instance, Chauntecleer tells Pertelote:

as touching daun Catoun,
That hath of wysdom swich a greet renoun,
Though that he bad no dremes for to drede,
By God, men may in olde books rede
Of many a man moore of auctorite
Than evere Caton was, so moot I thee,
That al the revers seyn of this sentence,
And han wel founden by expenence
That dremes been significaciouns
As wel of joye as of tribulaciouns
That folk enduren in this lif present.

As touching upon Cato,
Who has such great renown as a wise man
Although he may have said that bad dreams are nothing to dread,
Nevertheless, men may read in old books
Of many men of more authority
Than ever Cato was on this subject, so your point is moot,
As they all say the opposite
That dreams are significant signs

> *Of happiness to come as well as trouble*
> *That people endure in their daily lives.*

(*Canterbury Tales*,
"The Nun's Priest's Tale," VII, 2970–3170)

<hr>

See also Troilus and Criseyde, Book II, 925–31; *Troilus and Criseyde,* Book V, 364–92, 1233–47, 1275–88; *The Legend of Good Women,* 1295–1300, 2658–62; *The Book of the Duchess,* 119–21.

Dream visions generally followed a predictable series of plot stages. The dreamer would initially be beset by some psychological trouble—a problem in need of resolution or an emotional upheaval. While puzzling over what to do, the dreamer would drift off to sleep. The dream would take the dreamer (usually male) to some incredibly verdant place where he would meet his guide. The guide would show the dreamer a number of allegorical situations, about which the dreamer would attempt to question the guide as to meaning. These attempts are nearly always frustrated, and, just as he is beginning to move toward a resolution on his own, some force internal to the dream jars the dreamer awake.

In times when making political criticisms or pointed social commentary could carry serious negative repercussions, the dream vision or allegory allowed the author an "out." A writer could claim that, if his or her words offended, it was only a dream. The untimely awakening served the dual purpose of allowing both the reader to reach his or her own conclusions about the lessons of the dream and the author to avoid making any potentially incriminating pronouncements.

Chaucer himself made frequent use of the dream vision to frame his narratives. *The Parliament of Fowls, The Book of the Duchess,* and *The House of Fame* are all examples of the dream vision as a literary device to separate the writer by one level from the tale being told. Chaucer's works, as we might assume from such an innovative writer, had idiosyncrasies peculiar to him. All three of his dream visions begin with a book by a classical writer. In *The Book of the Duchess,* the narrator takes up Ovid's *The Metamorphosis* in order to "drive the night away; / For me thoughte it better play / Then playe either at ches or tables" (*drive away the night / because I thought it was better to read / Than to play chess or tables*) (*Book of the Duchess,* 49–51). *The Metamorphosis* also inspires parts of *The House of Fame,* although in this work, Virgil's *Aeneid* is the specific book that directly leads to the dream vision. In fact, the *Aeneid* plays an integral role in the visual structure of the poem itself, as paintings depicting scenes from Virgil's poem appear within the dream. *The Parliament of Fowls,* which focuses upon the romantic choices of a formel eagle, finds the narrator reading Cicero's *Dream of Scipio* prior to falling asleep.

Another of Chaucer's innovations in the form is to leave his own problem unclear, focusing instead upon the tribulations of the characters. This draws attention further away from him as the author/narrator/creator. This is particularly apparent in *The Book of the Duchess*, in which the true focus of the narrative is on the grief of the man in black (presumably John of Gaunt). Yet, the narrator's vague depression at the beginning of the poem mirrors the depression of loss. He speaks of his insomnia and the eight-year "sicknesse" (sadness) that has robbed him of sleep and vigor.

Finally, Chaucer is probably the first writer to use the dream vision explicitly for social and political commentary. *The Book of the Duchess*, by general critical consensus, is believed to deal with the death of the wife of his patron, John of Gaunt. Chaucer was close to both Gaunt and Blanche of Lancaster, and so the poem becomes not only a personal elegy to a lost friend, but a means of ingratiating himself further with a powerful man in the English nobility. *The Parliament of Fowls* addresses, through the means of eagles choosing mates, the courtship by Richard II of his future wife, Anne of Bohemia. Finally, *The House of Fame* describes the poet's visit to the palace of the goddess Fama, a whirling and wobbly house of wicker that allegorically describes the precarious quest to become famous.

And al thys house of which y rede
Was mad of twigges, falwe, rede,
And grene eke, and somme weren white,
Swiche as men to these cages thwite,
Or maken of these panyers,
Or elles hottes or dossers;
That for the swough and for the twygges,
This hous was also ful of gygges,
And also ful eke of chirkynges,
And of many other werkynges

And the entirety of this house which I saw
Was made of twigs and branches, of yellow, red,
And green, and some were white.
Like the kind that men use to whittle for cages
Or to make bread baskets,
Or the sorts of wicker baskets carried on one's back;
And for all the sound of the wind and the twigs themselves
The house was full of squeaking noises
And constant creakings
As well as many other sounds.

(*House of Fame*, 1935–44)

The squeaking of the twigs in the wind mirrors the rumors and whisperings of fame by which men define themselves and their success. In each of these examples, Chaucer maintains a delicate balance between philosophical profundity and humor, seeming to shake his head at how silly yet endearing human nature can be. Even the otherwise dark *The Book of the Duchess* contains small moments of amusing human nature.

See also Dreams; Fame; John of Gaunt; Richard II

FURTHER READING

Bowden, Muriel. *A Reader's Guide to Geoffrey Chaucer.* Syracuse, NY: Syracuse University Press, 2001.

Brown, Peter, ed. *A Companion to Chaucer.* Malden, MA: Blackwell, 2002.

Gray, Douglas, ed. *The Oxford Companion to Chaucer.* New York: Oxford University Press, 2003.

Lerer, Seth, ed. *The Yale Companion to Chaucer.* New Haven, CT: Yale University Press, 2006.

Rigby, S. H. *Chaucer in Context: Society, Allegory, and Gender.* New York: Manchester University Press, 1996.

St. John, Michael. *Chaucer's Dream Visions: Courtliness and Individual Identity.* Burlington, VT: Ashgate, 2000.

Allusions, Biblical

Although Chaucer's works are far more heavily weighted with allusions to classical literature, he was certainly familiar with the Bible, as his audience would be, and so we find a fair number of references to figures from both the Old and New Testaments. Allusions, of course, are a long-utilized literary device that uses the resonance of reference to a culturally familiar person or story in order to increase the meaning and symbolic import of the author's own perspective. The Bible was a common mine for such references, being full of moral stories and towering figures of allegorical and moral significance. Many of the figures in the Bible, even as early as Chaucer's time, had taken on metaphorical stature as archetypes. While many of the figures referenced by Chaucer will have at least a passing familiarity to even the least religious person merely by virtue of their cultural significance, Chaucer also employed a number of minor characters who would have been recognizable to his contemporary audience. Interestingly, statistically speaking, Chaucer alludes far more frequently to characters from the Old Testament than he does to the New Testament.

See also Abigail; Abraham; Absalom; Adam; Daniel; Esther; Eve; Job; Joseph; Judas; Lamech

FURTHER READING

Brown, Peter, ed. *A Companion to Chaucer.* Malden, MA: Blackwell, 2002.

Frye, Northrop. *Biblical and Classical Myths: The Mythological Framework of Western Culture.* Buffalo, NY: University of Toronto Press, 2004.

Manser, Martin H. *The Facts On File Dictionary of Classical and Biblical Allusions.* New York: Facts On File, 2003.

Allusions, Classical

As rich as Chaucer's works are with biblical allusions, it is in his classical references that his command of other literature shines. His knowledge of ancient Greek and Roman legends is impressive, and he is able to nuance a tale through a wealth of past literature that would have been familiar to his audience.

Allusions are a long-utilized literary device that uses the resonance of reference to a culturally familiar person or story in order to increase the meaning and symbolic import of the author's own perspective. Like the Bible, the classics were an important source for such references, being full of stories and personalities that reflected human behavior on a grand and allegorical scale. As with the Bible, many of the figures from classical literature were important for their status as archetypes.

See also Achates; Achilles; Actaeon; Adonis; Aeneas; Alcyone; Amphion; Apollo; Ariadne; Bacchus; Caliope; Cassandra; Daphne; Deianira; Demophon; Echo; Helen of Troy; Hypsipyle; Lucrece; Medea; Narcissus; Priapus

FURTHER READING

Brown, Peter, ed. *A Companion to Chaucer.* Malden, MA: Blackwell, 2002.

Frye, Northrop. *Biblical and Classical Myths: The Mythological Framework of Western Culture.* Buffalo, NY: University of Toronto Press, 2004.

Hansen, William F. *Classical Mythology: A Guide to the Mythical World of the Greeks and Romans.* New York: Oxford University Press, 2005.

Manser, Martin H. *The Facts On File Dictionary of Classical and Biblical Allusions.* New York: Facts On File, 2003.

Morford, Mark P. O. *Classical Mythology.* 7th ed. New York: Oxford University Press, 2003.

Nolan, Barbara. *Chaucer and the Tradition of the Roman Antique.* New York: Cambridge University Press, 1992.

Powell, Barry B. *Classical Myth.* Translated by Herbert M. Howe. 4th ed. Upper Saddle River, NJ: Pearson/Prentice Hall, 2004.

Price, Simon, and Emily Kearns, eds. *The Oxford Dictionary of Classical Myth and Religion.* New York: Oxford University Press, 2003.

Amphion

The son of Jupiter/Zeus and Antiope, Amphion was abandoned with his brother Zethus by his mother when she fled the wrath of her father, Nycteus. The boys were raised by shepherds, unaware of their lineage. On his deathbed, the vengeful Nycteus makes his brother promise to punish Antiope for her loose morals. His brother, Lycus, responds by keeping her as his slave wife, a questionable choice. When Antiope is able to escape, she seeks the protection of her sons, who upon learning the truth, kill Lycus and his wife.

Not only is Amphion known for his loyalty to his mother, but he exhibited amazing musical talent. In one legend attributed to him, he was able to make stones move with the power of his lyre playing. His end, as with so many figures from classical literature, is tragic. He eventually married Niobe, but his children were killed by Apollo and Artemis because Niobe refused to honor them. In his grief and despair, Amphion committed suicide.

He is mentioned in "The Knight's Tale" as both Palamon and Arcite are descended from him (*Canterbury Tales*, "The Knight's Tale," I (A), 1546). Chaucer references his musical abilities in "The Merchant's Tale" when the music at January and May's wedding is compared to Amphion's: "Biforn hem stoode instrumentz of swich soun / That Orpheus, ne of Thebes Amphioun, / Ne maden nevere swich a melodye" (*Before him stood instruments of such beautiful sound / That neither Orpheus nor Amphion of Thebes / Would have been able to make such a melody*) (*Canterbury Tales*, "The Merchant's Tale," IV (E), 1715–17).

The Manciple also briefly references Amphion in his tale, comparing Phebus's singing with that of Amphion: "Certes the kyng of Thebes, Amphioun, / That with his syngyng walled that citee, / Koude nevere syngen half so wel as hee" (*For certain, Amphion, the King of Thebes, / who walled the city with his singing / could never have sung even half as well as he*) (*Canterbury Tales*, "The Manciple's Tale," IX (H), 116–18).

FURTHER READING

Brown, Peter, ed. *A Companion to Chaucer*. Malden, MA: Blackwell, 2002.

Frye, Northrop. *Biblical and Classical Myths: The Mythological Framework of Western Culture*. Buffalo, NY: University of Toronto Press, 2004.

Hansen, William F. *Classical Mythology: A Guide to the Mythical World of the Greeks and Romans*. New York: Oxford University Press, 2005.

Manser, Martin H. *The Facts On File Dictionary of Classical and Biblical Allusions*. New York: Facts On File, 2003.

Morford, Mark P. O. *Classical Mythology*. 7th ed. New York: Oxford University Press, 2003.

Nolan, Barbara. *Chaucer and the Tradition of the Roman Antique*. New York: Cambridge University Press, 1992.

Powell, Barry B. *Classical Myth*. Translated by Herbert M. Howe. 4th ed. Upper Saddle River, NJ: Pearson/Prentice Hall, 2004.

Price, Simon, and Emily Kearns, eds. *The Oxford Dictionary of Classical Myth and Religion*. New York: Oxford University Press, 2003.

Animals

Animal stories and allegories date back to the time of the ancient Greeks. Familiarity with and dependence on animals for survival, both wild and domestic, led to a natural interest in their habits. Through the long habit of observing animals, people began to notice and comment on behavioral similarities between humans and animals. Not only the obvious correlations between monkeys and humans were drawn, but subtler parallels between the sly cleverness of the fox or the combination of apparent foolishness with underlying wisdom of the goose were compared to human personality types.

The fables that arose from these correlations provided object lessons and instruction in an amusing and entertaining form. For instance, perhaps the most enduring tale is of the tortoise and the hare. While the hare seems to be the clear winner of the race before it even starts, it is the steady plodding pace of the tortoise, stressing fidelity to a purpose and calm endurance, that ultimately emerges victorious.

During the Middle Ages, in which metaphor and allegory played such important roles, stories that emphasized the closeness of human and animal behaviors took on additional resonance reflecting Catholic spirituality. Medieval people believed that the "book of nature" could reveal truths about God's plan. More specifically, they believed that God provided lessons there, as in the Bible, to guide human behavior. All of the tools for understanding God's mysterious plan are in the world around us. Note, for example, the Doctrine of Signatures in medicine that held that the color of a plant could provide a clue to its medicinal purpose. It is up to us as God's creations to make it our business to discover the truth revealed in the clues.

Bolstering this belief were various biblical verses, most notably in Job:

But ask the animals, and they will teach you, or the birds of the air, and they will tell you; or speak to the earth, and it will teach you, or let the fish of the sea inform you. Which of all these does not know that the hand of the Lord has done this? In his hand is the life of every creature and the breath of all mankind.

(Job 12:7–10)

Because each animal was believed to embody certain human characteristics, allegories and fables about their interactions with one another provided moral lessons reflecting Christian teachings of proper behavior.

Yet not all animal fables transmitted moral teachings. One of the most famous characters during the Middle Ages was Aesop's Reynard the Fox who breaks several of the Ten Commandments. However, the crafty Reynard not only suffers no consequences, he leaves his usually innocent victims worse off than when he found them. Reynard specifically appears in Chaucer's "The Nun's Priest's Tale," while the generic symbol of the fox is included in the descriptions of some of his characters.

Although Chaucer is not an author especially well known for his animal characters or for employing a great deal of animal symbolism, when he does use it, the allegory is striking and meaningful. In particular for Chaucer, birds are prominent animal symbols, so much so that they are handled in a separate entry. Besides birds, horses, sheep, and dogs are his most important domesticated animal symbols, while the fox, wolf, boar, and hare are prominent wild animals in his works.

See also Birds; Boar; Dog; Fox; Hare; Horse; Sheep; Wolf

FURTHER READING

Rowland, Beryl. *Blind Beasts: Chaucer's Animal World*. Kent, OH: Kent State University Press, 1971.

Salisbury, Joyce E., ed. *The Medieval World of Nature: A Book of Essays*. New York: Garland, 1993.

Strickland, Debra Higgs. *Medieval Bestiaries: Text, Image, Ideology*. New York: Cambridge University Press, 1995.

Telesko, Werner. *The Wisdom of Nature: The Healing Powers and Symbolism of Plants and Animals in the Middle Ages*. New York: Prestel, 2001.

Apollo

The son of Jupiter, Apollo was the god of music, prophecy, medicine, and poetry. His shrine, home of the famous Oracle of Delphi, was probably the most important in ancient Greece, and he was one of the more influential and powerful gods on Olympus.

He figures very prominently in "The Manciple's Tale," which recounts the legend of Apollo's love for Coronis, a mortal woman who betrayed him with another lover. When Apollo's white crow tells him of her infidelity, Apollo kills Coronis but later, in a fit of remorse, punishes the crow by turning its beautiful feathers black and taking away its lovely singing voice.

Apollo also appears briefly in other of Chaucer's works. In "The Franklin's Tale," Aurelias prays to Apollo for help:

He seyde, "Appollo, god and governour
Of every plaunte, herbe, tree, and flour,
That yevest, after thy declinacioun,
To ech of hem his tyme and his seson,
As thyn herberwe chaungeth lowe or heighe,
Lord Phebus, cast thy merciable eighe
On wrecche Aurelie, which that am but lorn.
Lo, lord! My lady hath my deeth ysworn
Withoute gilt, but thy benignytee
Upon my dedly herte have som pitee.
For well I woot, lord Phebus, if yow lest,
Ye may me helpen, save my lady, best.
...
"Youre blisful suster, Lucina the sheene,
That of the see is chief goddesse and queene
...

"Lord Phebus, dooth this miracle for me.
Preye hire she go no faster cours than ye;
I seye, preyeth your suster that she go
No faster cours than ye thise yeres two.
Thanne shal she been evene atte fulle always,
And spryng flood laste bothe nyght and day.
And but she vouche sauf in swich manere
To graunte me my sovereyn lady deere,
Prey hire to synken every rok adoun
Into hir owene dirke regioun
Under the ground, ther Pluto dwelleth inne,
Or nevere mo shal I my lady wynne."

He said, "Apollo, oh god and ruler
Of every plant, herb, tree, and flour
That grows; and who gives to each one
Its time and season, varying by your place—
High or low—in the zodiac
Oh, lord Phoebus, cast your pitying eye
On wretched Aurelius, who is lovelorn.
Listen, lord! My lady has guaranteed my death
Although she knows it not. But please upon
My broken heart have some pity.
For I well know that, if you really wanted to,
You above all, except for my lady, could help me most.
    …
"Your blissful sister, Lucina goddess of the moon
Who is the chief goddess and queen of the sea
    …
"Lord Phoebus, do this miracle for me.
See that your sister not move any faster than you do.
I pray you, ask her to not move faster than you
For the next two years and be always at the full
So that the spring flood lasts all night and day.
And if she does this for me,
To help be obtain my beloved lady
Then ask her also to sink every rock around
Down into the ground all around the region
Where Pluto lives, or I will never win my lady's love."

(*Canterbury Tales,*
"The Franklin's Tale," V (F), 1031–79)

In *The House of Fame,* Chaucer mentions the story of Marsyas, who attempted to best Apollo in a singing contest and was flayed as punishment for losing (*House of Fame,* 1229–32). Finally, Troilus, in the throes of romantic despair, curses Apollo and all the other gods concerned with tender feelings: "'Deth!' he criede; / And in his throwes frenetik and madde, / He corseth Jove, Appollo, and ek Cupide; / He corseth Ceres, Bacus, and Cipride, / His burthe, hymsaf, his fate, and ek nature, / And, save his lady, every creature" (*"Death!" he cried, / and his throes of grief, all frantic and mad, / He cursed Jove, Apollo, and also Cupid / He cursed Ceres, Bacchus, and Venus / As well as the day he was born, his fate, and all of nature / Everything, every creature, except for his lady*) (*Troilus and Criseyde*, Book V, 205–10).

FURTHER READING

Brown, Peter, ed. *A Companion to Chaucer.* Malden, MA: Blackwell, 2002.

Frye, Northrop. *Biblical and Classical Myths: The Mythological Framework of Western Culture.* Buffalo, NY: University of Toronto Press, 2004.

Hansen, William F. *Classical Mythology: A Guide to the Mythical World of the Greeks and Romans.* New York: Oxford University Press, 2005.

Manser, Martin H. *The Facts On File Dictionary of Classical and Biblical Allusions.* New York: Facts On File, 2003.

Morford, Mark P. O. *Classical Mythology.* 7th ed. New York: Oxford University Press, 2003.

Nolan, Barbara. *Chaucer and the Tradition of the Roman Antique.* New York: Cambridge University Press, 1992.

Powell, Barry B. *Classical Myth.* Translated by Herbert M. Howe. 4th ed. Upper Saddle River, NJ: Pearson/Prentice Hall, 2004.

Price, Simon, and Emily Kearns, eds. *The Oxford Dictionary of Classical Myth and Religion.* New York: Oxford University Press, 2003.

Architecture

Medieval architecture evolved directly from the architectural styles of the classical world. Yet, the technological developments and wider influences to which the people of the Middle Ages were exposed meant that the architecture of this period, widely defined, demonstrated the same kind of diversity that was evidenced in other areas of culture. Architecture provides us with an important social barometer because, thanks to the amount of natural resources, time, and physical effort required for their construction and the practical demands of use as well as the very public nature of a building, more than any other art form, architecture reflects the values and concerns of a society.

There are five major periods of style from the Middle Ages and, for various reasons, most architectural planning revolved around the construction of sacred buildings. The first, Early Christian, was the closest stylistically and temporally to the Roman style of architecture. This is especially evident in the design of the basilica, which was adapted to suit the liturgical demands of the Catholic mass. This structure was built in the form of a cross, which provided both symbolic significance as well as a useful floor plan.

The altar occupied the center of the short top arm, the most prominent place of the structure which was visible from all angles. The clergy would be seated within the short side arms, known as the transepts. The congregation would sit in the central hall or nave, so named for the Latin word for ship. The entrance at the foot of the cross was called either the galilee, which symbolized entry into the holy land, or the narthex, which derived from the Latin word for casket. The entire conceptualization of the church was of a vessel that carried the soul forth into the afterlife.

The second architectural period, the Romanesque, was initiated in the court of Charlemagne in the late ninth and early tenth centuries. The so-called Carolingian renaissance sought to re-create the splendor of the Roman Empire and thus sparked

Canterbury Cathedral. Courtesy of Lisa Kirchner.

Museum of the Middle Ages, Paris. Courtesy of Lisa Kirchner.

a new set of architectural styles to this end. Charlemagne's palace and chapel at Aachen reflects all of the new innovations of his time as well as the varied influences. These included both Byzantine and Roman styles. Carolingian style was also characterized by structural improvements in tower building.

Again, the cross-shaped floor plan was utilized almost exclusively, while the choir area expanded in order to accommodate and reflect the rise of the saint cult. More space was needed to accommodate the shrines to various saints' relics housed in individual churches. These shrines, as is evidenced by Canterbury Cathedral, for instance, were an important source of revenue and prestige for churches. Pilgrims traveled from miles around to visit the relics of important saints, hoping that miracles would be performed on their behalf.

While the opening up of the floor plan to wider spaces created a more generous feeling inside the church, it was negated by the limitations of building technology at the time. The style of arched vaults created a need for heavy columns and thick walls—along with massive buttresses—which, combined with a lack of glass (which was often prohibitively expensive), made churches very dimly lit, fortress-like places. The structure, however, reflected the view of the Church's role in society that was current at the time. Because the world was brutal, dominated by war and oppressed by

Buttresses of Chartres Cathedral. Courtesy of Lisa Kirchner.

sin, the Church viewed itself in a militant light, protecting souls from the evil around them in a warrior fashion. Those within its walls could feel that they were securely sheltered from the besieging armies of sin.

The Gothic style, which first emerged in Paris during the early twelfth century, represents the growth of the Romanesque style into a new phase of open spaces and soaring vaults made possible by impressive technological developments. The changes in architecture directly reflected a growing evolution in the role of the Church in society. No longer was the warrior stance popular. The Church had instead, as is evidenced by the cult of the Virgin Mary, reshaped itself as the enlightener, the gate of love and forgiveness, a peaceful shelter from the world's concerns. Thus, the buildings themselves had to reflect this with light, airy construction.

Large windows, thinner support columns, and soaring, pointed arches all characterized this style. The invention of the flying buttress enabled architects to create ever higher, thinner walls, broken up with immense stained glass windows depicting important biblical passages. It is this style that dominated during Chaucer's time and is reflected in the Abbey of St. Denis, as well as the cathedrals at Chartres, Bourges, Reims, Cologne, Wells, Ely, and the Henry VII chapel at Westminster. The final two architectural styles were High Gothic and Rayonant, and they dominated the fifteenth and sixteenth centuries.

Figurine-detailed arch over a doorway at Chartres Cathedral. Courtesy of Lisa Kirchner.

The north door of Chartres Cathedral. Courtesy of Lisa Kirchner.

Stained glass windows at Chartres Cathedral. Courtesy of Lisa Kirchner.

Interestingly, the Gothic style was not actually defined as such until the nineteenth century, when Eugene Emmanuel Viollet-le-Duc classified it as having similar and definable elements: pointed arches, ribbed vaults, and flying buttresses. Of course, any transitional period is gradual, and examples can be pointed to that reflect a number of styles. In addition, many churches and cathedrals, Canterbury included, experienced periodic expansions and renovations that caused their final appearances to be a combination of architectural styles that dominated the particular period to which each phase of construction dates.

See also Castles; Cathedrals; Private Houses

FURTHER READING

Abulafia, David, Michael Franklin, and Miri Rubin, eds. *Church and City, 1000–1500: Essays in Honour of Christopher Brooke.* New York: Cambridge University Press, 1992.

Archer, Lucy. *Architecture in Britain and Ireland, 600–1500.* London: Harvill Press, 1999.

Backhouse, Janet, ed. *The Medieval English Cathedral: Papers in Honour of Pamela Tudor-Craig: Proceedings of the 1998 Harlaxton Symposium.* Donington, Lincolnshire, England: Shaun Tyas, 2003.

Binding, Günther. *Medieval Building Techniques.* Stroud, England Tempus, 2004.

Blick, Sarah, and Rita Tekippe, eds. *Art and Architecture of Late Medieval Pilgrimage in Northern Europe and the British Isles.* Boston: Brill, 2005.

Calkins, Robert G. *Medieval Architecture in Western Europe: From* A.D. *300 to 1500.* New York: Oxford University Press, 1998.

Coldstream, Nicola. *Medieval Architecture.* New York: Oxford University Press, 2002.

Erlande-Brandenburg, Alain. *The Cathedral Builders of the Middle Ages.* Translated by Rosemary Stonehewer. London: Thames and Hudson, 1995.

Gimpel, Jean. *The Cathedral Builders.* Translated by Teresa Waugh. New York: HarperPerennial, 1992.

Hilliam, David. *Castles and Cathedrals: The Great Buildings of Medieval Times.* New York: Rosen, 2004.

Lasansky, D. Medina, and Brian McLaren, eds. *Architecture and Tourism: Perception, Performance and Place.* New York: Berg, 2004.

Laule, Ulrike. *Architecture of the Middle Ages.* Berlin: Feierabend, 2004.

Platt, Colin. *The Architecture of Medieval Britain: A Social History.* New Haven, CT: Yale University Press, 1990.

Simson, Otto Georg von. *The Gothic Cathedral: Origins of Gothic Architecture and the Medieval Concept of Order.* 3rd ed. Princeton, NJ: Princeton University Press, 1988.

Ariadne

The daughter of king Minos and Pasiphae of Crete, Ariadne was in love with Theseus of Athens, who was fated to be sacrificed to the minotaur. To save her love, she helped him escape the labyrinth with the aid of a ball of thread. Theseus killed the minotaur and escaped with Ariadne with the promise to marry her later. Once free on the island of Naxos, however, Theseus cruelly abandoned her. She would be discovered by Bacchus, who, touched by her beauty, claimed her for his own and married her.

Chaucer devotes a biography to Ariadne in *The Legend of Good Women,* a work that the Man of Law mentions in the prologue to his tale (*Canterbury Tales,* "The Man of Law's Tale," II (B[1]), 67).

FURTHER READING

Brown, Peter, ed. *A Companion to Chaucer.* Malden, MA: Blackwell, 2002.

Frye, Northrop. *Biblical and Classical Myths: The Mythological Framework of Western Culture.* Buffalo, NY: University of Toronto Press, 2004.

Hansen, William F. *Classical Mythology: A Guide to the Mythical World of the Greeks and Romans*. New York: Oxford University Press, 2005.

Manser, Martin H. *The Facts On File Dictionary of Classical and Biblical Allusions*. New York: Facts On File, 2003.

Morford, Mark P. O. *Classical Mythology*. 7th ed. New York: Oxford University Press, 2003.

Nolan, Barbara. *Chaucer and the Tradition of the Roman Antique*. New York: Cambridge University Press, 1992.

Powell, Barry B. *Classical Myth*. Translated by Herbert M. Howe. 4th ed. Upper Saddle River, NJ: Pearson/Prentice Hall, 2004.

Price, Simon, and Emily Kearns, eds. *The Oxford Dictionary of Classical Myth and Religion*. New York: Oxford University Press, 2003.

Armor

Som wol ben armed in an haubergeoun,
And in a brestplate and a light gypoun;
And som wol have a paire plates large;
And som wol have a Pruce sheeld or a targe;
Som wol ben armed on his legges weel,
And have an ax, and som a mace of steel—
Ther is no newe gyse that it nas old.

…

Ther maystow seen devisynge of harneys
So unkouth and so riche, and wroght so weel
Of goldsmythrye, of browdynge, and of steel;
The sheeldes brighte, testeres, and trappures,
Gold-hewen helmes, hauberkes, cote-armures;
Lordes in parementz on hir courseres,
Knyghtes of retenue, and eek squieres

…

Duc Theseus leet forth thre steeds brynge,
That trapped were in steel al gliterynge,
And covered with the armes of daun Arcite.
Upon thise steeds, that weren grete and white,
Ther seten folk, of whiche oon baar his sheeld,
Another his spere up on his hondes heeld,
The thridde baar with hym his bowe Turkeys
(Of brend gold was the caas and eek the harneys).

Some were armed in a coat of mail,
Along with a breastplate and a lightweight tunic,
While some others would have a set of heavy plate mail;
And some would have a Prussian shield or a targe;
Some of them would cover their legs well with armor,
And carry an ax, while others would carry a steel mace—
For there is no new fashion that hasn't been old.

...
There you might see such an array of harnesses
So exotic and expensive and made so carefully and well;
So much fancy embroidery, steelwork, and goldsmithery
Of shields brightly polished, and hauberks, trappings,
Helmets of gold, mail, and coats of arms;
Lords in costly robes on fine horses,
Knights of the retinue and their squires.

...

Duke Theseus led forth three steeds
That were covered in glittering steel mail
That was covered with Arcite's coat of arms.
Upon the back of each white horse
Sat a knight, one of which held the dead man's shield,
The other his spear, and the third his Turkish bow
(The harness and quiver of which was trapped with burnished gold).

(*Canterbury Tales,*
"The Knight's Tale," I (A) 2119–25,
2496–2510; 2889–96)

Warfare underwent vast changes over the course of the Middle Ages and was shaped by sweeping technological developments. Because warfare was such an important element of the lives of the nobility, these changes, by extension, altered the social and feudal structure. As methods of fighting were changing during the fourteenth century, the armor that knights wore changed as well to keep pace with new methods of fighting. New pieces and practices were slowly being incorporated to protect knights, those elite members of an increasingly expensive fighting fraternity. The use of crossbows, longbows, and especially cannon meant that armor had to evolve to prevent unnecessarily high injury, maiming, and death rates on the field. In addition, during the late Middle Ages, ceremonial armor for tournaments and court life was beginning to be developed. Although they would not come into full fashion until the following two centuries, changes in materials and manufacture helped to facilitate these innovations in armor and weaponry.

Armor was fashioned by armorers, who were respected artisans of the Middle Ages.

A shield hanging at the Tower of London. Courtesy of Lisa Kirchner.

Armoring tended to be a lucrative family business, and particular techniques were kept as close secrets, preventing competitors from profiteering on the research and development of another craftsman. Armorers were proud of their craft, and they marked each piece with a stamp to identify their work.

Most armor until the fourteenth century was made of iron or leather, with steel becoming increasingly popular by the fifteenth century. Leather was used to reinforce portions of the armor, particularly at the interstices between plates (the bends of the elbow or knees, for example) where the knight's body was only protected by mail and where flexibility was useful. Leather also helped to keep weight down, which was important for preventing fatigue. The average weight of a full suit of armor was 40 pounds. This does not sound like a great deal until one considers the demands of instantly gaining roughly one-quarter to one-third of one's entire body weight, then being required to maintain a high level of physically and psychologically demanding and straining activity while wearing it.

The Full Harness

The full suit of equipment, including undergarments, spurs, sword, and the shield, was called the harness. Underneath the armor was a coat of chain mail, known as a hauberk, which was a tunic of woven links of iron that covered the arms and torso down to the mid-thigh, and sometimes went as far up the body as to cover the head and throat (in a hood-like device known as a coif). The Knight describes the armor of Palamon's soldiers, which is very medieval considering that they are ancient Greeks, "With hym ther wenten knyghtes many on, / Som wol ben armed in an haubergeoun, / And in a brestplate and a light gypoun" (*With him there were many knights / Some were armed in a coat of mail, / Along with a breastplate and a lightweight tunic*) (*Canterbury Tales,* "The Knight's Tale," I (A) 2118–20). Mail was good for protecting against sword slashes but not thrusts. It could often deflect arrows as well. It was flexible and covered areas that might become exposed during fighting as the knight bent and moved to strike or avoid blows.

By the late thirteenth century, the hauberk was sometimes supplanted by a padded *courboille* that was lighter in weight and chafed less. Over the hauberk or *courboille* was the plate mail, which was formed by hammered iron. Between the plates, beginning in the fourteenth century, *lames* were added at points of articulation to further protect the knight while allowing for flexibility and range of motion. *Lames* were made of very thin plates of iron and were placed between the main plates of the harness. To attach individual pieces of armor to each other, bronze buckles and leather straps were used.

Armor was not merely a necessary part of being a knight from the standpoint of physical safety. It was also a very tangible symbol of status and wealth, as "The Knight's Tale" makes clear. When a knight was captured on the battlefield, the higher the quality of his armor, the more likely he would be held for ransom rather than killed.

Opposing armies face each other; the soldiers on the left carry a banner with the fleur-de-lys of France, while the flag of Flanders is seen among those on the right. From the "Chroniques de France et d'Angleterre," ca. 1470. © Erich Lessing / Art Resource, NY.

Not only was the armor in and of itself valuable, but it denoted a higher economic echelon in general. The craftsmanship was of course important, demonstrated in the tooling of the leather and the polish of the plates. Increasingly by the end of the fourteenth century, however, workmanship was highlighted by painting and other forms of decoration to make the armor stand out. By the fifteenth century, in fact, highly polished white armor was the ultimate status symbol.

Horses as well were protected by the use of armor. Until the fourteenth century, war-horses were usually provided with a coat of mail. The practice of armoring horses, protecting one's investment in the most expensive piece of a knight's equipment, led to the development of new bits of armor. The *chamfron*—the faceplate—started to come into fashion during this century, as did the *crinet*, which protected the horse's neck.

Head and Neck

Several layers that served various comfort and defensive functions protected the knight's head. On the outermost layer was a helmet. During the fourteenth century, the most popular type was the *bascinet*, which covered the top of the head and extended down the face to protect the cheeks and the neck. The *bascinet* was relatively lightweight and allowed for a wider range of vision over earlier helmet models. By the 1330s, *bascinets* had removable visors on hinges, which were known as *hunskulls.* This was a feature that later evolved into a rather sophisticated system in which the visor pivoted on its hinges to secure at the back of the helmet. This prevented its being lost in the heat of battle. In addition, the new *bascinet* included an attached mail skirt, known as an *aventail,* which protected the neck.

During the Hundred Years War, another variation of the *bascinet,* known commonly as the *great bascinet,* was developed. The *great bascinet* was distinguished by the modification of the mail *aventail* into a steel *ventail.* The entire helmet offered excellent protection to the head and neck, including a sleek surface that defended against glancing blows.

For bachelor knights and common men-at-arms who could not afford such luxurious head protection, the iron cap known as the *chapel de fer* had to suffice. The *chapel de fer* was little more than an iron cap with a wide brim. No facial protection was gained, although it was excellent for warding off sword blows to the top of the head.

Under the helmet were a couple of layers of further protection and padding. Heavy iron helmets were not the most comfortable form of headgear, and so knights wore padding under the helmet. Until the fourteenth century, knights wore an arming cap; however, increasingly *bascinets* were fitted with a sewn-in lining that was fashioned of linen and stuffed with more cloth or grasses. For further defense of the face and neck, a coif, or mail hood, was worn over the arming cap and under the *bascinet.* Finally, for tournament decoration or for the practical use of battlefield identification by color, helmets were topped off with the *torse,* a cloth that was rolled around the helmet's crown and attached to a cloth decoration.

Upper Body

The torso presented the largest and most vulnerable target on the battlefield. It was imperative that a knight protect himself thoroughly, but protection was complicated by the equally crucial need for mobility. The fourteenth century offered several innovations in accomplishing both of these needs in armor. Late in the century came the *cuirass,* which was formed of two large plates—the breastplate and the backplate—as well as hip protection known as *faulds* and *tassets* (*Canterbury Tales,* "The Knight's Tale," I (A), 2120). The pieces were fitted together with straps and buckles to allow for full range of motion. By 1360, the one-piece breastplate was in general widespread use as its unbroken surface presented a sleek defense against blows and arrows. Also around mid-century, the top of the breastplate included a stop rib that created a bump at the neck, preventing the tip of a sword or lance from sliding straight up into the knight's throat. Finishing off the outer protection of the torso were the *faulds,* which were steel hoops that attached to the breastplate. The *faulds* were designed to protect the upper hips, lower back, and stomach. Below the *faulds* were the *tassets,* which covered the lower hips.

Like knightly headgear, protection of the torso featured several layers. Beneath the outer mail would be either the hauberk or the *courboille.* The *courboille* was perhaps the more comfortable choice because it was padded. However, the hauberk, made entirely of mail and covering the body down to the upper thighs, remained popular well into the fourteenth century because of its ability to protect parts of the body exposed by joints between plates. The *gambeson,* or arming coat, was a kind of padded coat that could be worn either as light armor or as padding beneath the plate mail. *Gambesons* were quilted and stuffed with linen or grass. They laced up the front.

Over the top of the armor a knight would wear a surcoat, which was emblazoned with heraldic devices (*Canterbury Tales,* General Prologue, I (A), 2120). This served the very important function of identifying a knight on the battlefield, where chaos reigned and knights were sometimes separated from the standard bearer. Chaucer's Knight wears a dirty tunic over his mail rather than a surcoat, demonstrating either his modesty or his poverty: "Of fustian he wered a gypon / Al bismotered with his habergeon, / For he was late ycome from his viage, / And wente for to doon his pilgrymage" (*He wore a gypon made of common fustian / Which was all stained by his coat of mail / Because he was just come back from fighting / And traveled straight to his pilgrimage*) (*Canterbury Tales,* General Prologue, I (A), 75–78).

Arms

Because fighting depends upon upper body strength and mobility, a knight's arms were the most important part of his body offensively. They were also the hardest to protect defensively. Articulated armor left vulnerable parts potentially open to exposure. Known collectively as the arm harness, the components that went into protecting the arms demonstrate a complex system that increasingly maximized agility and protection.

At the top was the *spaulder,* a fourteenth-century development that covered the shoulder point and continued down the upper arm in a series of plates known as *lames.* At the elbow was fitted the *couter,* which evolved from being a single dish-shaped plate to two or three articulated *lames.* The *couter* attached to the *vambrace,* which was a fourteenth-century innovation. The *vambrace* was a tubular piece of leather or iron that fitted over the forearm over the hauberk.

Archers wore a specialized guard over the forearm to prevent chafing, known as a bracer (*Canterbury Tales,* General Prologue, I (A), 111). Protecting the wrist and hand was the gauntlet, designed specifically to protect the hands. Beginning early in the fourteenth century, armorers began to fashion very small plates and attached them to leather for articulated movement in the fingers. At the wrist was a flared cuff that was sometimes decorated with engravings.

Lower Body

The knight's legs had to allow him to sit on his war-horse and, should he be unseated, defend himself and move freely about the battlefield on foot. Again, the emphasis was on defense and flexibility. The leg harness in particular underwent big changes over the course of the fourteenth century, developing from mail *chausses* into a fully articulated system that allowed the knight free range of mobility. On the thighs were *cuisses,* made initially from leather or quilted linen, but eventually from plate armor. Over the knee was the *poleyn,* attached on both sides to allow for free movement of the joint. *Greaves* or *shynbalds* covered the lower leg, flaring at the ankle and ending with the *sabatons,* which fitted over the feet. The *sabatons* as well were articulated to allow the knight maximum flexibility to ensure proper balance.

See also Hundred Years War; Knight

FURTHER READING

Barker, Juliet R. V. *The Tournament in England, 1100–1400.* Wolfeboro, NH: Boydell Press, 1986.

Bell, Adrian R. *War and the Soldier in the Fourteenth Century.* Rochester, NY: Boydell Press, 2004.

De Pisan, Christine. *The Book of Deeds of Arms and of Chivalry.* Translated by Sumner Willard. Edited by Charity Cannon Willard. University Park: Pennsylvania State University Press, 1999.

Dressler, Rachel Ann. *Of Armor and Men in Medieval England: The Chivalric Rhetoric of Three English Knights' Effigies.* Burlington, VT: Ashgate, 2004.

Hilliam, David. *Medieval Weapons and Warfare: Armies and Combat in Medieval Times.* New York: Rosen, 2004.

Jones, Terry. *Chaucer's Knight: The Portrait of a Medieval Mercenary.* Baton Rouge: Louisiana State University Press, 1980.

Nicolle, David, ed. *A Companion to Medieval Arms and Armour.* Rochester, NY: Boydell Press, 2002.

Oakeshott, R. Ewart. *The Archaeology of Weapons: Arms and Armour from Prehistory to the Age of Chivalry.* Rochester, NY: Boydell Press, 1994.

———. *A Knight and His Armor.* 2nd ed. Chester Springs, PA: Dufour Editions, 1999.

Thordeman, Bengt. *Armour from the Battle of Wisby, 1361.* In collaboration with Poul Nörlund and Bo E. Ingelmark. New ed. Union City, CA: Chivalry Bookshelf, 2002.

Astrolabe

Now fleeth Venus unto Cilenios tour
With voide cours for fere of Phebus lyght—
Alas—and ther ne hath she no socour,

...

Now wol I speke of Mars, furious and wod.

...

He passeth but o steyre in dayes two.
But nathelesse, for al his hevy armure,
He foloweth her that is his lyves cure

...

That, while that Venus weping made her mone,
Cilenius, rydinge in his chevache,
Fro Venus valaunse myghte his paleys se,
And Venus he salueth and doth chere,
And her receyveth as his frend ful dere.

Now Venus flees into her tour through Gemini
And made her course for fear of Phoebus's light
However, there she had no comfort.

...

Now I will describe Mars, who was furious and heartsick.

...

He passed only a star in two days' time
But despite that, for all of the heavy armor he wore,
He followed her who is the cure of his life's sorrow.

...

And while Venus, weeping, made her plea
Gemini, riding past in his carriage
From Venus's home might he see his palace
And he saluted her and bid her good cheer,
And received her as his very dear friend.

("The Complaint of Mars," 113–54).

An astrolabe is an ancient device that is used for calculating the movement of the planets, the sun, and the stars. It was one of the most basic tools of the medieval astronomer. It could be used at night to determine the time and could accurately calculate such astronomical events as sunrise, sunset, and the movement of the zodiac.

The astrolabe itself was quite simple in design, no more than a two-dimensional model of the sky. Its main part was a hollow disk, known as the *mater*, which was fitted with flat plates called *tympans*. Around the rim of the *mater* were etched lines for hours or degrees of arc. Each *tympan* was designed for a specific latitude and was etched with lines of altitude and azimuth. Above all of it was the *rete*, which was a rotating frame representing the ecliptic and pointers for the positions of stars. The astronomer would rotate the *rete*, moving the stars and ecliptic over the coordinates shown on the *tympan*. A 360° rotation equaled one day. On the other side of the *mater* were other scales for calculations, including the conversion of time and days of the month.

A miniature of Boethius teaching students, 1385. Courtesy of the Glasgow University Library.

Mastery of the astrolabe was rather tricky, and Chaucer's skill, demonstrated both in his frequent references to astrological time in his poetry and in his *Treatise on the Astrolabe,* is an impressive display of knowledge for someone whose interest in astronomy was never more than a hobby. For instance, in "The Complaint of Mars," Chaucer includes a lengthy description of planetary motion that could only have been accurately described through the use of equipment such as the astrolabe. In this poem, Chaucer has cleverly combined the planetary movements with the chase of romance, personifying the planets as both heavenly bodies and the pagan deities they represent.

An astrolabe. Courtesy of Corbis.

See also Astrology and Astronomy

FURTHER READING

Brown, Peter, ed. *A Companion to Chaucer.* Malden, MA: Blackwell, 2002.

Curry, Patrick, ed. *Astrology, Science, and Society: Historical Essays.* Wolfeboro, NH: Boydell Press, 1987.

Kibre, Pearl. *Studies in Medieval Science: Alchemy, Astrology, Mathematics, and Medicine.* London: Hambledon Press, 1984.

Osborn, Marijane. *Time and the Astrolabe in the* "Canterbury Tales." Norman: University of Oklahoma Press, 2002.

Page, Sophie. *Astrology in Medieval Manuscripts.* London: British Library, 2002.

Astrology and Astronomy

...
But al his fantasye
Was turned for to lerne astrologye,
And koude a certeyn of conclusiouns,
To demen by interrogaciouns,
If that men asked hym, in certain houres
Whan that men sholde have droghte or elles shoures,
Or if men asked hym what shoulde bifalle
Of every thyng ...
His Almageste, and bookes grete and smale,
His astrelabie, longynge for his art,

...
But all of his mind and curiosity
Was turned toward the mastery of astrology
And he could with a great deal of certainty
Accurate down to the hour based on his experiments
In answer to questions from men as to whether there
Would be drought or flooding.
Or if men asked him what should happen in the future
His most prized possessions were his books, especially
Ptolemy's Treatise on astrology, and his astrolabe.

(*Canterbury Tales,*
"The Miller's Tale," I (A), 3191–96, 3208–09)

The motion of the heavens played a critical role in the everyday lives of medieval people. Although they would not have the benefit of a telescope until its invention by Galileo Galilei in 1610, there was much in the sky that was visible to the naked eye of the medieval astronomer. In a world that was often capricious and unstable, the predictable movement of the stars and planets seemed to provide some kind of guidance, if not

Prognostication: A clergyman ("Jupiter") blessing a farmer ("Sagitarius") tilling his soil; "Mars" in armor is radiating beams upon them, 1484. Courtesy of the Library of Congress.

completely reliable explanations for disease, natural disasters, and even political upheaval.

During the Middle Ages, people viewed the skies as the macrocosm that reflected the microcosm of the world of men. While this belief had its roots in classical paganism, medieval Christianity inspired a concurrent belief in the stars as evidence of God's actions and intentions. Thus, the hierarchy of the pagan gods and goddesses was meshed with the Christian heavenly hierarchy of angels, archangels, seraphim, and the trinity.

Planetary and stellar alignments could indicate favorable or malign conditions for travel, marriage, war, business ventures, medical procedures, or birth. In Chaucer's works, this deeply held belief is apparent, as is his considerable expertise in matters astrological. In Chaucer's time, there was not a clear delineation between astronomy, which we consider today to be a scientific field closely connected with physics, and astrology, the province of fortune-tellers, psychics, and newspaper horoscopes. The separate terms, however, did serve to subtly differentiate between astronomy as the study of the heavens and astrology as "applied astronomy." The connection of astrological signs to many important aspects of life led to its being an important element in furthering other areas of inquiry such as natural sciences, medicine, and navigation.

Understanding of the heavens was one of the marks of an educated man of the medieval period. Chaucer's Doctour of Phisik, to be discussed later, used astrology to diagnose patients. In "The Miller's Tale," which is perhaps Chaucer's most astrologically dependent narrative, filled as it is with popular superstitions and beliefs about the active role of the heavens in daily life, one of the first things mentioned about the scholar is that he studies astrology. Of course, it is through his mastery of things astrological that he "discovers" the coming flood that he uses to cuckold the Carpenter.

"Now John," quod Nicholas, "I wol nat lye;
I have yfounde in my astrologye,
As I have looked in the moone bright,
That now a Monday next, at quarter nyght,
Shal falle a reyn, and that so wilde and wood

That half so greet was nevere Noes flood.
This world," he seyde, "in lasse than an hour
Shal al be dreynt, so hidous is the shour.
Thus shal mankynde drenche, and lese hir lyf."

"Now John," said Nicholas, "I would not lie to you;
I have found through my astrological research,
While looking at the bright moon,
That next Monday shortly after midnight,
There will fall a rain that will be so wild and drenching
That it will make Noah's flood look like a passing shower.
This world," he said, "in under an hour
Will be drenched through, so hideous will this rain be.
And in this way mankind will all drown and lose its life."

(*Canterbury Tales,*
"The Miller's Tale," I (A), 3513–21)

The Ptolemaic System

Fourteenth-century astronomy relied on a modified version of the geocentric Ptolemaic system. This system was the theory of the second-century Greek astronomer Claudius Ptolemaeus, better known as Ptolemy. Ptolemaic astronomy, at its simplest, maintains that the Earth is the center of the universe. In actuality, the theory was more complex, recognizing that other heavenly bodies orbit points that in turn orbit the Earth. In order to achieve this complex epicentric system, it was believed that surrounding the Earth were nine concentric rotating spheres, each of which contained a particular heavenly body. Moving outward from the Earth were the moon, Mercury, Venus, the sun, Mars, Jupiter, Saturn, the stars, and finally *Primum Mobile*, which was thought to control the movement of the other eight spheres

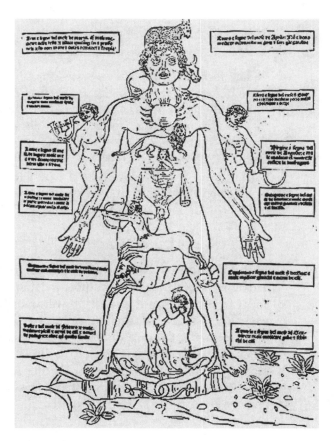

A fifteenth-century illustration of "Zodiac Man" by Joannes de Ketham. Courtesy of the National Library of Medicine.

(*Canterbury Tales,* "The Man of Law's Tale," II (B¹), 295–307). In *Troilus and Criseyde,* Chaucer refers to the Third Heaven in relation to love, as this is the sphere inhabited by Venus:

O blisful light of which the bemes clere
Adorneth al the thridde heven faire!
O sonnes lief, O Joves doughter deere,
Plesance of love, O goodly debonaire,
In gintil hertes ay redy to repaire!
O veray cause of heele and of gladnesse,
Iheryed by thy myght and thi goodnesse!

Oh blissful light from which clear beams
Light the beautiful third heaven!
Oh sun's beloved, Jove's dearest daughter,
The pleasure of love, the happiness of bliss,
In gentle hearts are ready to enter!
Oh very cause of joy and gladness,
Praised both for your strength and your goodness!

(*Troilus and Criseyde,* Book III, 1–7)

The motion of the spheres was one of the beautiful mysteries of the universe because it was thought to create the "music of the spheres," inaudible to human ears (*Parliament of Fowls,* 59–63). The perfection of each sphere's rotation, numerical in its precision, connected medieval music to numbers theory. To the medieval mind, the universe was vast, but its borders were finite, predetermined by the creator. It was also bathed in celestial light, and light, of course, symbolized God's love. Night, in turn, was a product of shadows cast by planets crossing paths. In keeping with the macro/micro model, divine love was a mirror to human love.

The Power of the Planets

By dividing the sky into sections, known as zodiacal houses, medieval astrologers comfortably predicted the outcome of events both long and short term. Although divination was considered sinful because it interfered with free will, the numerical precision in the functioning of the universe only seemed to indicate God's larger plan, the comprehension of which was apparently not considered to be on the same plane with tarot card reading and crystal ball gazing. While the Catholic Church did not officially tolerate such activities, astrologers and sympathetic Church philosophers were able to skirt the issue by claiming that one could practice free will with regard to a predicted fate and change it through good Christian behavior. In other words, God provides us with signs and it is up to us to read them. Throughout Chaucer's works, we see the opinion that a man's fate was written in the stars and works with Fortune to determine our destinies: "Were it by destynee or by aventure, / Were it by influence or by nature, / Or constellacion, that in swich estaat / The hevene stood that tyme forunaat / Was for to putte a bille of Venus werkes" (*Whether it was by destiny or coincidence / By God's influence or by nature / or by the constellations, standing in their positions / that heaven at that time blessed anyone who wanted to plead / With a woman to play Venus's game*) (*Canterbury Tales*, "The Merchant's Tale," IV (E), 1967–71; see also *Canterbury Tales*, "The Man of Law's Tale," II (B¹), 190–203; *House of Fame*, Book II, 935–50, 991–1011).

The zodiacal signs resided in the eighth sphere where the stars were. Using the annual path of the sun as the foundational belt, called the ecliptic, the zodiac signs formed 12 "houses" along that belt through which each planet passed. Each planet, as well as each sign, had particular qualities that were enhanced or diminished as the planet moved through each zodiacal house (*A Treatise on the Astrolabe*, Book I, 63–77, Book II, 30–68). For instance, aggressive Mars was known to cause war. If it were passing through Aries, then a military conflict could be eminent. In "The Man of Law's Tale," Custace's ill-fated voyage is foretold by the planetary alignments (*Canterbury Tales*, "The Man of Law's Tale," II (B¹), 295–3008). Pandarus plans to visit his niece on Troilus's behalf when the moon is favorable for journeys and business (*Troilus and Criseyde*, Book II, 74–75). Later, Calkas predicts the Greek victory by means of astrological signs, and Criseyde declares herself to be born under a bad constellation.

"On peril of my lif, I shal nat lye;
Appollo hath me told it feithfully;
I have ek founde it be astronomye.
By sort, and by augurye ek, trewely,
And dar wel say, the tyme is faste by
That fire and flaumbe on al the town shal sprede,
And thus shal Troie torne to ashen dede.

…

"Allas," quod she, "out of this regioun
I, woful wrecche and infortuned wight,
And born in corsed constellacioun,
Moot goon and thus departen fro my knyght!"

*"On peril of my life, I will not lie to you
Apollo has told me in good faith
And I have since found it is true through astronomy
Through research and observation, truly
And I hardly dare to speak it, that the time is
Coming fast when fire and flame will engulf this town
And Troy will be reduced to dust and death.*

…

> *"Alas," she said, "out of this place*
> *I, sad and woeful woman that I am*
> *And born under a cursed constellation,*
> *Must go away, leaving my beloved knight behind!"*

(*Troilus and Criseyde*, Book IV, 113–19, 743–46)

Hypermnestra's fate and personality both are subject to the rule of the stars in *The Legend of Good Women* (*Legend of Good Women*, 2484–99). In the short poem, "L'Envoy de Chaucer a Scogan," Chaucer blames his friend for the disarray of the planets and the effects this will have on everyone ("L'Envoy de Chaucer a Scogan," 3–12).

Days of the week were also tied to the stars and were believed to have individually specific characteristics based on which sign, constellation, or planet ruled them. Friday, Chaucer tells us, is Venus's day. Hence it is unpredictable, unlucky, fickle, and generally subject to bad weather:

Right as the Friday, soothly for to telle,
Now it shyneth, now it reyneth faste,
Right so kan geery Venus overcaste
The hertes of hir folk; right as hir day
Is gereful, right so chaungeth she array.
Selde is the Friday al the wowke ylike

Just like a Friday, if the truth be known
Now the sun shines, now it pours down raining
So can changeable Venus sadden
The hearts of her followers; just like her day
Is fickle, so is she.
Seldom is any Friday like another.

(*Canterbury Tales*,
"The Knight's Tale," I (A), 1534–39)

See also Canterbury Tales, "The Nun's Priest's Tale," VII, 3341–54.

The zodiac was not only used to predict the outcome of events, but it was also used to pinpoint a precise time in the past. Chaucer quite frequently uses this method of providing a specific time for the action he describes. We know that the Canterbury pilgrims set out on or about April 18, as he tells us "Whan that Aprill with his shoures soote / ... and the yonge sonne / Hath in the Ram his half cours yronne" (*When April with his sweet showers / ... and the young sun / had run half of the course through Aries*) (*Canterbury Tales*, General Prologue, I (A), 1, 7–8). In other passages, Chaucer provides the date simply by the description of where the sun was in its passage in the zodiac (*Canterbury Tales*, "The Squire's Tale," V

(F), 48–51, 263–65, 386; *Canterbury Tales*, "The Franklin's Tale," V (F), 1248; *Canterbury Tales*, "The Nun's Priest's Tale," VII, 3194–95; *Canterbury Tales*, "The Parson's Tale," X (I), 2–11; *Troilus and Criseyde*, Book II, 50–56: *Troilus and Criseyde*, Book IV, 1590–96; *Troilus and Criseyde*, Book V, 1016–22; *Legend of Good Women*, 113–15). In "The Merchant's Tale" and *Troilus and Criseyde*, the passage of days is told by the moon's movements through the zodiac (*Canterbury Tales*, "The Merchant's Tale," IV (E), 1885–87, 2222–24; *Troilus and Criseyde*, Book III, 624–26). *Troilus and Criseyde* even refers to telling time by Lucifer, the morning star (*Troilus and Criseyde*, Book III, 1415–20).

Chauntecleer the rooster of "The Nun's Priest's Tale," is able to tell the passage of time instinctually by the sun's passage through the equinoctial circle and thus knows when to crow: "By nature he knew ech ascencioun / Of the equynoxial in thilke toun; / For whan degrees fiftene weren ascended, / Thanne crew he that it myghte nat been amended" (*He naturally knew each ascension / Of the equinoctial circle in his town ; / And its movement by each 15 degrees / Then he crowed on the hour with great precision*) (*Canterbury Tales*, "The Nun's Priest's Tale," VII, 2855–58). Chaucer describes the Corona Borealis as Adriane of Athens's crown and says "in the signe of Taurus men may se / The stones of hire corone shyne clere" (*In the sign of Taurus men can see / the stones of Adriane's corona shining clearly*) (*Legend of Good Women*, 2223–24). The ability, through the mastery of complex equipment like the astrolabe and the *volvelle*, to compute such equations took a great deal of training and effort.

"The Franklin's Tale" makes it clear, however, that there were certain unscrupulous types who used astrology to bad ends, employing it for magical purposes. At his sympathetic brother's urging, love-sick Aurelius employs an astrologer-magician to win over Dorigen (*Canterbury Tales*, "The Franklin's Tale," V (F), 119–50).

Astrology and Medicine

Not only did the planets have the ability to influence events, but they played a critical role in medieval medicine because it was believed that planetary motion affected not only the entire human body but also that individual planets influenced specific body parts. Surgeries were carefully planned when possible to coincide with the most favorable planetary alignment, and injuries were despaired of healing should they occur under a "bad star."

Bloodletting in particular was closely tied to signs of the zodiac. Physicians were advised against letting blood to cure an ailment in a particular body part when the zodiac was in that part's sign because its blood flow could be too forceful. For example, bleeding to treat an ailing abdomen should not be undertaken in Virgo, while pains in the calves should not be treated by bloodletting in Aquarius. Of course, the four humors were believed to be tied to planetary movements as well.

Perhaps the most curious connection between medieval medicine and astrology is the habit of some physicians of diagnosing based on astrological conditions. Chaucer's Doctour of Phisik, we are told, "was grounded in astronomye" (*Canterbury Tales,* General Prologue, I (A), 414). It was not uncommon for doctors to make diagnoses at a distance, sometimes merely looking at a patient's urine without even interviewing the patient. To make an astrological diagnosis, the physician would note the patient's name, birth date, and sex and use number theory to create a value for the patient's vital statistics. When compared with astronomical conditions, a mathematically determined diagnosis could be reached.

BLOODLETTING	
Sign	*Body Part*
Aries	Head
Taurus	Neck
Gemini	Chest
Cancer	Lungs
Leo	Stomach
Virgo	Abdomen
Libra	Lower Abdomen
Scorpio	Penis and Testicles
Sagittarius	Thighs
Capricorn	Knees
Aquarius	Calves
Pisces	Ankles

See also Alchemy; Astrolabe; Fortune; Four Humors; Medicine; Physician

FURTHER READING

Brown, Peter, ed. *A Companion to Chaucer.* Malden, MA: Blackwell, 2002.

Curry, Patrick, ed. *Astrology, Science, and Society: Historical Essays.* Wolfeboro, NH: Boydell Press, 1987.

Kibre, Pearl. *Studies in Medieval Science: Alchemy, Astrology, Mathematics, and Medicine.* London: Hambledon Press, 1984.

Page, Sophie. *Astrology in Medieval Manuscripts.* London: British Library, 2002.

B

Bacchus

The son of Zeus and Semele, Bacchus/Dionysos was the Greek god of wine and fertility. His cult was one of the more popular throughout Greece and beyond, perhaps in part because celebrations in his honor included drunkenness and uninhibited group sex. Bacchus appears in "The Merchant's Tale," where Chaucer refers to him during the wedding of January and May, implying that the groom needed a bit of help to stiffen his courage: "Bacus the wyn hem shynketh al aboute, / And Venus laugheth upon every wight, / For Januarie was bicome hir knight / And wolde bothe assayen his corage / In libertee, and eek in mariage" (*Bacchus poured the wine all around / And Venus laughed and smiled upon every man / Because January had become her knight / And would test his courage / In marriage as he had when he was free*) (*Canterbury Tales*, "The Merchant's Tale," IV (E), 1722–26).

FURTHER READING

Brown, Peter, ed. *A Companion to Chaucer*. Malden, MA: Blackwell, 2002.

Frye, Northrop. *Biblical and Classical Myths: The Mythological Framework of Western Culture*. Buffalo, NY: University of Toronto Press, 2004.

Hansen, William F. *Classical Mythology: A Guide to the Mythical World of the Greeks and Romans*. New York: Oxford University Press, 2005.

Manser, Martin H. *The Facts On File Dictionary of Classical and Biblical Allusions.* New York: Facts On File, 2003.

Morford, Mark P. O. *Classical Mythology.* 7th ed. New York: Oxford University Press, 2003.

Nolan, Barbara. *Chaucer and the Tradition of the Roman Antique.* New York: Cambridge University Press, 1992.

Powell, Barry B. *Classical Myth.* Translated by Herbert M. Howe. 4th ed. Upper Saddle River, NJ: Pearson/Prentice Hall, 2004.

Price, Simon, and Emily Kearns, eds. *The Oxford Dictionary of Classical Myth and Religion.* New York: Oxford University Press, 2003.

Baptism

Baptism symbolized one's entry into the Christian community, and, because that community holds that we are all born with original sin, the ritual was intended to cleanse the newborn infant of this burden from the start. By the beginning of the twelfth century, it was generally believed that the unbaptized were not saved; thus, many parents were consumed with worry—in a time of high infant mortality rates—that their children might be consigned to Purgatory (or worse) for eternity.

Midwives were permitted to perform unofficial rites if a baby seemed sickly or if there was to be a substantial lag between birth and the official church ceremony. By the beginning of the twelfth century, however, the Church was increasingly encouraging parents to eschew the amateur work of the midwives and instead bring the baby to the church as soon as possible, preferably the day of birth.

The party would meet the priest at the church door, the mother left behind to recuperate from the birth. Before entering the church, the priest would ask the sex of the child and whether it had already been baptized. The godparents would be tested on their knowledge of basic prayers, and then prior to anointing at the font, the priest would place a small quantity of salt on the baby's tongue to symbolize taking in wisdom and expelling evil. At the font, the child would be anointed, immersed, named, and then wrapped in a christening gown of white linen.

As is still the case, the rite of baptism provided the child with his or her official name, so that entrance into the Catholic community was completed and symbolized by a publicly voiced identity. Three godparents would be chosen for the child: one of the opposite sex, and two of the same. The child was generally christened with the name of the principal godparent of the same sex. Godparents were expected to be people of spiritually responsible character who would instruct the child in prayers, morals, and virtues. They could be blood relatives, friends, or lay clergy.

However, people who were related by godparentage only and not by blood were still forbidden to marry each other, demonstrating the close spiritual relationship that this duty entailed. The word "gossip" or "god-sib," in fact, originally meant someone who was related by godparentage. It ultimately came to mean any close friend, one with whom one would share information of a delicate or secret nature.

See also Religion

FURTHER READING

Britnell, Richard, ed. *Daily Life in the Late Middle Ages.* Stroud, England: Sutton, 1998.

Finucane, Ronald C. *Miracles and Pilgrims: Popular Beliefs in Medieval England.* New York: St. Martin's Press, 1995.

French, Katherine L. *The People of the Parish: Community Life in a Late Medieval English Diocese.* Philadelphia: University of Pennsylvania Press, 2001.

Gies, Frances, and Joseph Gies. *Women in the Middle Ages.* New York: Harper, 1978.

Hanawalt, Barbara. *Growing Up in Medieval London: The Experience of Childhood in History.* New York: Oxford University Press, 1993.

Heywood, Colin. *A History of Childhood: Children and Childhood in the West from Medieval to Modern Times.* Malden, MA: Blackwell, 2001.

Bath

A good WIF was ther OF biside BATHE,
But she was somdel deef, and that was scathe.
Of clooth-makyng she hadde swich an haunt
She passed hem of Ypres and of Gaunt.

A good wife was there from the town next to Bath
She was rather deaf, which is a great pity.
She had such a skill at making cloth
That she surpassed the weavers of Ypres and Ghent.

(*Canterbury Tales,*
General Prologue, I (A), 445–48).

Bath, located in southwestern England, began its history as a Roman spa because of its natural hot springs. It survived the Viking invasions and became a major cathedral city after the Norman Conquest. By Chaucer's time, Bath's role had changed to an industrial city dominant in the wool trade. The invention of a mechanical fuller, propelled by water power, enabled English wool producers to make cloth themselves rather than exporting it to Flanders. Grain mills along the Avon were adapted to full cloth, and the cottage industry of spinning and weaving boomed, bringing industry into the rural villages as well as the cities.

Many of these new cloth makers became quite wealthy. The Wife of Bath, of course, is Chaucer's representative. She, along with the Merchant and the Franklin, represent the new rising middle class.

The Wyf of Bathes' prologue

Here endith the ffraunklepns tale
And folowith the prologe of the Wyf of Bathe

E xperience though none auctorite
Were in this worlde is right ynough for me
To speke of wo that is in mariage
But lordes sithen I twelue yere was of age
Thanked be god that is eternalle onlyue
Husbondes at the chirche dore haue I had fyue
If I so ofte myght haue wedded be
And al were worthy men in theire degre
But me was tolde nat longe a go y wys
That sithen crist went nauer but onys
To weddyng in the Cane of galilie
That by the same ensample taught he me
That I ne wedded shulde be but onys
Loo he whiche a sharpe worde for the nones
Beside a welle Jesus god and man

f ij

A woodcut of the Wife of Bath from a fifteenth-century edition of *The Canterbury Tales.* Courtesy of the Glasgow University Library.

See also Wool

FURTHER READING

Attreed, Lorraine Christine. *The King's Towns: Identity and Survival in Late Medieval English Boroughs.* New York: P. Lang, 2001.

Britnell, R. H. *The Commercialisation of English Society, 1000–1500.* 2nd ed. New York: Manchester University Press, 1996.

Childress, Diana. *Chaucer's England.* North Haven, CT: Linnet Books, 2000.

Clare, John D., ed. *Fourteenth-Century Towns.* San Diego: Harcourt Brace Jovanovich, 1993.

Belmarye. See Morocco

Birds

Among all of the animals that Chaucer mentions in his works, birds are perhaps the most important. Not only are they the chief characters in his *Parliament of Fowls,* but an eagle is his guide in *The House of Fame,* and two of *The Canterbury Tales*—"The Nun's Priest's Tale" and "The Manciple's Tale"—feature birds as the focus of the plot. Birds were important allegorical symbols during the Middle Ages. Since the beginning of written history, we can trace humans' fascination with birds, the envy of their ability to fly that is reflected in the story of Icarus and Daedalus. Not only were wild and domesticated birds an important source of food, whether it be eggs or meat, but they were enduring windows into the imaginative life of humanity. During the Middle Ages, as with other animals, the symbolism of birds was a complex merger of ancient pagan and Christian allegory.

See also Animals; Crow; Cuckoo; Dove; Eagle; Falcon; Goose; Rooster and Hen

FURTHER READING

Rowland, Beryl. *Blind Beasts: Chaucer's Animal World*. Kent, OH: Kent State University Press, 1971.

Salisbury, Joyce E., ed. *The Medieval World of Nature: A Book of Essays*. New York: Garland, 1993.

Strickland, Debra Higgs. *Medieval Bestiaries: Text, Image, Ideology*. New York: Cambridge University Press, 1995.

Telesko, Werner. *The Wisdom of Nature: The Healing Powers and Symbolism of Plants and Animals in the Middle Ages*. New York: Prestel, 2001.

Birth

Birth in the Middle Ages was simultaneously one of the most natural parts of life and one of the most dangerous. The arrival of a baby into a family—the fulfillment of the sole official purpose of marriage—was an occasion of great joy. However, infant mortality rates were high, and the danger to the mother from complications or subsequent infections was quite likely. This resulted in a fair amount of anxiety around the impending arrival of children.

Aristocratic women were treated with extreme care as they neared their delivery dates, often being sent to their lying-in room a month or more before the expected birth. In Chaucer's time, the almost exclusive domination of midwives in the birthing chamber was beginning to be challenged by male doctors in the urban centers. However, in much of England, the process of birth remained almost exclusively a female-dominated occasion, with a physician only summoned should surgery be deemed absolutely necessary.

Midwives were competent, respected, and experienced, by and large, although there are court records indicating that when something went wrong with a birth, the midwife often bore the legal responsibility and suspicions of the bereaved couple. She would typically be assisted in the birth by whatever young aspiring midwives she was training. In addition to the midwife's staff, female relatives and friends of the mother would be present in the chamber. The father was never included, and the superstition died hard in rural areas that men actually defiled the birth chamber.

Water was heated over the fire in the chamber to bathe the mother and the infant. In fact, high standards of hygiene, by medieval definitions, were maintained. Of course, the average person during this time did not understand the concepts of bacteria and other germs and how they might precisely be transmitted; thus, a high incidence of childbed fever and other internal infections occurred despite the practice of midwives of washing their hands before delivering babies. Even allowing for a quick wash-up, dirt and bacteria would remain beneath the midwife's fingernails, only to be introduced into the woman's birth canal when she reached in to retrieve the baby.

Unlike the typical supine position of women today, medieval women gave birth either sitting upright or squatting, allowing simple gravity to aid the mother with the pushing and contractions. The mother's belly and thighs would be rubbed with various concoctions that were believed to aid with the pains of delivery. She might be anointed with oil of roses or given a magnet to hold. Some medical manuals recommended feeding the mother powdered ivory, vinegar and sugar, or eagle's dung. If labor lasted for what was considered to be a long time, windows and drawers were opened throughout the house, symbolizing the opening of the womb.

Once the child was born, the midwife would cut the umbilical cord and assist the infant with its first breaths. This sometimes required clearing its face and mouth of mucus. She would then bathe the baby in water or a combination of salt, olive oil, and rose petals. Honey was sometimes rubbed onto the roof of the baby's mouth to help stimulate its appetite. Once cleaned, the newborn would be wrapped in linen and placed in a dark corner so as not to strain its eyes. The parents would hope that the baby would survive not only its first days, but its first years. Child mortality rates were high until the age of five in a world lacking immunizations against common childhood diseases.

See also Religion

FURTHER READING

Britnell, Richard, ed. *Daily Life in the Late Middle Ages.* Stroud, England: Sutton, 1998.

Finucane, Ronald C. *Miracles and Pilgrims: Popular Beliefs in Medieval England.* New York: St. Martin's Press, 1995.

French, Katherine L. *The People of the Parish: Community Life in a Late Medieval English Diocese.* Philadelphia: University of Pennsylvania Press, 2001.

Gies, Frances, and Joseph Gies. *Women in the Middle Ages.* New York: Harper, 1978.

Hanawalt, Barbara. *Growing Up in Medieval London: The Experience of Childhood in History.* New York: Oxford University Press, 1993.

Heywood, Colin. *A History of Childhood: Children and Childhood in the West from Medieval to Modern Times.* Malden, MA: Blackwell, 2001.

Black Death

The years that the Black Death fell across Europe have long been accepted as pivotal ones in history. In the plague's wake, no aspect of society escaped unscathed. The economy, along with the population, was decimated. The feudal hierarchy and the Church that supported it were both shaken to their foundations. Europe emerged on the other side of this flea-borne pestilence a different place, in which long-accepted notions of truth were now in question and money, not promises, provided the means of purchasing a man's labor and loyalty. Although the Black Death does not seem to

A religious procession to protect against the plague; from a fourteenth-century publication. © Bibliothèque nationale de France.

have influenced Chaucer's writings extensively—not in the way that Boccaccio's writings were influenced, for example—Chaucer was born into a world undergoing transformation and reached adulthood in the post-plague era. Thus, an understanding of the Black Death in context becomes important in re-creating Chaucer's world.

The Cause

The Black Death ravaged Europe for four years, beginning in Cyprus in December 1347, and spreading north to Italy. The disease worked its way northward, afflicting urban and rural areas alike. Cities were the hardest hit, presumably because of unsanitary conditions and population density. In any given area, between one-quarter and one-half of the population was lost to plague. No social class was exempted, even though the wealthy had better access to both medical treatment and travel in order to escape from plague-infested areas.

The Black Death has long been connected specifically to the black rat (*Rattus rattus*) and to the particular flea (*Xenopsylla cheopsis*) that preferred to feed upon it rather than to its rodent cousins so common around medieval households, the brown rat (*Rattus norvegicus*) and the house mouse (*Mus musculus*). As the theories go, infected black rats on Genoese trade ships left China, where bubonic plague had been endemic since the tenth century. Once the traders and their deadly cargo disembarked, fleas left their rodent hosts for humans. Because of its many trade ports, Italy was hardest hit. The disease spread north as far as Scandinavia, roughly following trade routes.

Although the predominant form of plague—the bubonic, scientifically named *Yersinia Pestis*—is generally believed both to have given the Black

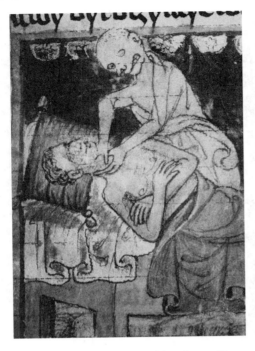

Death strangling a victim of the plague. From the codex called the *Clementinum Collection of Tracts* by Thomas of Stitny, 1376. © Werner Forman / Art Resource, NY.

Death its macabre moniker and to have claimed the most victims, it was apparently not the only form of plague that constituted the Black Death. The bubonic, according to long-held theories of the spread of the disease, was joined by the pneumonic and septicaemic plagues. These two forms of the plague may have generated greater panic because neither left discernable marks on the victim and their rapid incubation period and ease of transmission (in the case of the pneumonic plague) gave rise to the famous anecdotes of victims lying down apparently healthy and never rising in the morning.

The name Black Death, so common to us today, did not come into use until sixteenth-century Danish and Swedish chroniclers coined the term. The emphasis was not, as has generally been believed, on the black color of the buboes on victims' necks, thighs, and torsos, but on its presence as something dark and dreadful.

The Cure

Medieval medicine was ill equipped to deal with the epidemic. Europe's leading physician, Gentile da Foligno, believed the sickness to be the result of poisoned air, perhaps produced by planetary motions. His general advice to patients was to leave the area if possible. If travel was not an option, one should attempt to thoroughly cleanse the air at home and near the face with aromatic herbs. Moderate daily exercise and foods that balance the humors might also protect from disease, a piece of advice that might improve general health and the ability to fight off infections, making it one of the more sound remedies or preventions of the time. Other general treatments included the ever-popular bloodletting to balance the four humors as well as other more exotic "cures" such as snakeskin or precious gems ground into powders and drunk in a potion. Da Foligno (whom the Black Death would claim in June 1348) swore by emeralds because they were said to crack a toad's eyes.

Firsthand accounts of the plague evoke disturbing images of bodies layered in mass graves like ingredients in lasagna and of family ties severed by fear of infection:

> The mortality in Siena began in May. It was a cruel and horrible thing.... It seemed that almost everyone became stupefied seeing the pain. It is impossible for the human tongue to recount the awful truth. Indeed, one who did not see such horribleness can be called blessed. The victims died almost immediately. They would swell beneath the armpits and in the groin, and fall over while talking. Father abandoned child, wife husband, one brother another; for this illness seemed to strike through breath and sight. And so they died. None could be found to bury the dead for money or friendship. Members of a household brought their dead to a ditch as best they could, without priest, without divine offices. In many places in Siena great pits were dug and piled deep with the multitude of dead. And they died by the hundreds, both day and night, and all were thrown in those ditches and covered with earth. And as soon as those ditches were filled, more were dug. I, Agnolo di Tura ... buried my five children with my own hands.... And so many died that all believed it was the end of the world. (from the *Journal of Agnolo di Tura of Siena*, np)

The Effect

Post-plague life presented deep changes and challenges to the socioeconomic and religious structures of Europe. Villages were depleted of inhabitants and the agriculturally dominated society, so dependent on a labor force, faced a paucity of healthy workers. Peasants found themselves in a position of relative power and were able to bargain for more rights and real wages. Improvements in long-term status and rising expectations in the standard of living dominated the lower echelons of society. They were willing to fight and die to protect the gains that the Black Death enabled them to make. When kings attempted to reassert the earlier status quo through heavy taxation, as was the case in England in 1381, the peasants would revolt in retaliation.

Noble landlords, troubled by this assault on their liquid assets (as well as their social position) sought legal redress in the form of wage caps. More importantly, in an effort to limit the number of peasants they were forced to employ, many nobles converted the use of their lands to the less labor-intensive rearing of livestock, especially sheep. While the long-term repercussions for England led to its becoming first the leader in raw wool production and later a dominant force in finished cloth, the cracks in the stability of the long-standing feudal system were evident. The high mortality rate among the aristocracy during the plague further eroded a once apparently unassailable social supremacy. The belief in the ability of the Church to protect its faithful wavered in the face of correspondingly high mortality rates among its clergy and the unwillingness of many priests to administer last rites for fear of contamination.

The long years of intense depression and the aftershock of great and sudden loss of population, combined with a need to understand how to treat or prevent such problems in the future, led to the intellectual sea change known as the Renaissance. Art and funerary practices during the years surrounding the Black Death were dominated by dark images of death and decay. The specter of Death, riding a white horse with scythe in hand, or skulls crawling with worms became pervasive in medieval society. However, the influx of wealth once trade reasserted itself led to a cultural rebirth that embraced beauty and light with almost pathological fervor. Intellectual and philosophical focus began to shift toward exploration of the value and glory of the individual and away from the glory of God. Finally, medicine and technology started to make strides forward to explore the human body more closely to determine its functions and weaknesses.

Reassessment

As in most historical studies, these long-accepted notions of the plague's cause and effect have recently come under scrutiny that may require extensive revisions to our understanding of the Black Death and its times. This evidence, combined with a reevaluation of the symptoms and spread of the Black Death, has led historians and scientists to question whether it was really plague. Findings of the Indian Plague Commission in the first quarter of the twentieth century indicate very different patterns in modern bubonic plague than are chronicled in medieval records of the Black Death. The commission discovered that buboes do not generally cause pain, although the buboes of Black Death victims were reported by chroniclers as being very painful. Furthermore, the plague usually renders its victims lethargic rather than wild with delirium, as many victims of the Black Death became in the throes of fever. More telling are the natural factors governing general patterns of the plague and its spread. Bubonic plague, because it is spread by rat fleas, follows a seasonal cyclic pattern, with most deaths occurring in warmer weather, coinciding with the breeding cycle of the flea. Yet the Black Death killed year round. Furthermore, outbreaks are more likely to follow good harvests rather than periods of famine as an excess of grain leads to larger rat and, by extension, flea populations.

Historians generally have pointed to the famine that predated the Black Death as a factor in the weakening of the population that made it more susceptible. But the plague could not have thrived in periods of scarcity. To further undermine the connection between rats, fleas, and the Black Death is the dearth of archival evidence of an epizootic in rats predating the emergence of the plague. "Humans, in the classic bubonic epidemiology, can contract the disease only from a dying rodent; unless the rodents die, the human population remains untouched" (Herlihy, 26). There are no accounts in which large numbers of dead rats, or rats exhibiting the "drunken dance" of plague, are mentioned. The single source that mentions rats,

Nicephorus Gregoras's account of the Black Death in the Aegean Islands, also mentions the death of large numbers of dogs, horses, and birds, all of which have a natural immunity to plague. Perhaps most damning of all is that humans neither possess nor can acquire an immunity to *Yersinia pestis*. Therefore, the rapid decline in the Black Death's onslaught is unaccountable if it was, in fact, plague. What the disease actually was may remain one of history's great unsolved mysteries.

As for the socioeconomic repercussions of the Black Death, long-held conclusions have recently come under scrutiny as well. While it is certainly true that the massive death tolls cast a general existential malaise over Europe and the economic expectations of the peasant class were heightened significantly, newly examined evidence points toward forces already in motion to change the social framework of Europe. One historian has described the effects of the Black Death (as well as the famines of 1315–17) as "more purgative than toxic" (Platt, 1) because there was a great deal of surplus population by the start of the fourteenth century.

Economically and socially, the feudal system was already showing signs of obsolescence. Improved standards of living in the peasantry and the shift toward urbanization were slowly but surely changing the shape of the third estate. Meanwhile, the use of gunpowder in warfare, as well as the increased dependence in England on common foot soldiers, was making inroads into the position and purpose of the second estate. The plague hastened the effects of these changes. Europe was entering a more modern world, and it got there sooner because of the Black Death—a disease that we might never be able to identify reliably.

See also Astrology and Astronomy; Four Humors; Medicine; Physician

FURTHER READING

Aberth, John. *From the Brink of the Apocalypse*. New York: Routledge, 2001.

Attreed, Lorraine Christine. *The King's Towns: Identity and Survival in Late Medieval English Boroughs*. New York: P. Lang, 2001.

Campbell, Bruce M. S., ed. *Before the Black Death: Studies in the "Crisis" of the Early Fourteenth Century*. New York: Manchester University Press, 1991.

Cantor, Norman. *In the Wake of the Plague*. New York: Free Press, 2001.

Clare, John D., ed. *Fourteenth-Century Towns*. San Diego: Harcourt Brace Jovanovich, 1993.

French, Roger, Jon Arrizabalaga, Andrew Cunningham, and Luis García-Ballester, eds. *Medicine from the Black Death to the French Disease*. Aldershot, England: Ashgate, 1998.

Herlihy, David. *The Black Death and the Transformation of the West*. Introduction by Samuel K. Cohn, Jr. Cambridge, MA: Harvard University Press, 1997.

Huppert, George. *After the Black Death*. Bloomington: Indiana University Press, 1986.

Platt, Colin. *King Death: The Black Death and Its Aftermath in Late-Medieval England*. Toronto: University of Toronto Press, 1996.

Ziegler, Philip. *The Black Death*. Gloucestershire, England: Sutton, 1998.

Blanche, Duchess of Lancaster

Blanche, the youngest daughter of Henry of Lancaster, was born ca. 1341. In 1359, she married John of Gaunt, third son of Edward III and Philippa of Hainault. It was through Blanche that Gaunt would become Duke of Lancaster, taking the title upon the death of her father. She would bear John three children: Philippa, Elizabeth, and Henry of Bolingbroke. The latter would become King Henry IV upon Richard II's abdication of the throne.

In September 1368, Blanche died suddenly of the plague. Although John of Gaunt would go on to marry twice again, he would be buried beside his first wife upon his own death in 1399, attesting to the legend that theirs was essentially a love match. Chaucer's *The Book of the Duchess* was supposedly written for Gaunt in response to his grief at Blanche's untimely passing. The many references to the lost lady as "white" and a reference in *The Legend of Good Women* to another poem called "the Deeth of Blaunche the Duchesse" are strong evidence for this conclusion (*Legend of Good Women*, F, 418).

See also John of Gaunt

FURTHER READING

Ainsworth, Peter F. *Jean Froissart and the Fabric of History: Truth, Myth, and Fiction in the* "Chroniques." New York: Oxford University Press, 1990.

Barber, Richard. *Edward Prince of Wales and Aquitaine.* Woodbridge, Suffolk, England: Boydell and Brewer, 1996.

Bevan, Bryan. *Edward III: Monarch of Chivalry.* London: Rubicon Press, 1992.

Fraser, Antonia, ed. *The Lives of the Kings and Queens of England.* Rev. ed. Berkeley: University of California Press, 1998.

Boar

The boar, or wild pig, was known for aggression and belligerence. Its dangerous tusks—razor sharp and capable of killing an inattentive hunter—and bristly spine adorned an animal that was as imposing as it was unattractive. It was also known to be ruthless, vigilant, athletic, and unpredictable. These characteristics made the boar one of the more popular heraldic devices, perhaps most famously used by Richard III. Chaucer evokes the boar in heraldic guise, placing it upon the shield of Sir Thopas, apparently indicating his prowess in battle: "His sheeld was al of gold so reed, / And therinne was a bores heed, / A charbocle bisyde; / And there he swoor on ale and breed / How that the geaunt shal be deed" (*His shield was of a gold so red / and upon it was a great boar's head / And a carbuncle besides; / And there he swore upon ale and bread / That the giant would soon be dead*) (*Canterbury Tales*, "The Tale of Sir Thopas," VII, 869–73). Since the entire tale is rather ridiculous, and Chaucer is begged by Harry Bailly to stop, the reader is left with some ambiguity about what the boar's head symbolizes.

On the other hand, there is nothing ambiguous about the wife's comparison of her husband to a boar in "The Summoner's Tale": "Though I hym wrye a-nyght and make hym warm, / and over hym leye my leg outher myn arm, / He groneth lyk oure boor, lith in oure sty" (*Even though I lie with him at night and warm him / and cover him with my leg and arm / he still groans like our boar, who lies in our sty.*) (*Canterbury Tales,* "The Summoner's Tale," III (D), 1827–9). Later in the tale, it is the cuckolding friar who is compared to a boar, gnashing his teeth and staring wildly (*Canterbury Tales,* "The Summoner's Tale," III (D), 2156–64). In each instance, the man characterized by the boar embodies the wild, unpredictable nature of the boar, conjuring images of a temperamental and disheveled creature wallowing in mud and grunting unattractively.

FURTHER READING

Rowland, Beryl. *Blind Beasts: Chaucer's Animal World*. Kent, OH: Kent State University Press, 1971.

Salisbury, Joyce E., ed. *The Medieval World of Nature: A Book of Essays*. New York: Garland, 1993.

Strickland, Debra Higgs. *Medieval Bestiaries: Text, Image, Ideology*. New York: Cambridge University Press, 1995.

Telesko, Werner. *The Wisdom of Nature: The Healing Powers and Symbolism of Plants and Animals in the Middle Ages*. New York: Prestel, 2001.

Boccaccio

Giovanni Boccaccio, one of Chaucer's most important poetic influences, was born June 16, 1313. Like Chaucer, he was from a solid middle-class background, his father a Florentine banker, and worked most of his life in law and finance. He was apprenticed to the bank in Naples of which his father was the head in 1327. After six uninspired years, young Giovanni convinced his father to allow him to study law instead. His attraction to the legal profession was equally uninspired, but it did enable him to make important contacts with other scholars, especially prominent secular humanists.

It was these contacts that brought him to his true vocation, poetry. In 1349, he started work on the *Decameron,* the most famous of his works that inspired the structure of Chaucer's *The Canterbury Tales* as well as some of the individual tales. He completed the work in 1352, and revisited it in 1370 and 1371 to rewrite and revise it. It is this later version that has survived to the present day. The *Decameron* was written in response to the Black Death and chronicles the journey of three men and seven women who attempt to escape the plague in Florence. To entertain each other during the journey, they tell one another tales of (mostly) romance, much as Chaucer's pilgrims would entertain one another on their journey to Canterbury.

An illustration from Boccaccio's *Le livre des cas des nobles et illustres hommes*, ca.1470. © Bibliothèque nationale de France.

Boccaccio is also the author of *Filostrato* (ca. 1340), which provided the source for *Troilus and Criseyde,* and *Tesieda delle nozze di Emilia* (ca. 1341), which inspired Chaucer's "The Knight's Tale." In addition, he was a close friend of Petrarch's and would be the first person to lecture on the works of Dante.

Boccaccio's final years were plagued with poor health, contributed to by his obesity. He died December 21, 1375.

FURTHER READING

Edwards, Robert. *Chaucer and Boccaccio: Antiquity and Modernity.* New York: Palgrave, 2002.

Boethius

Allas! I wepynge, am constreyned to bygynnen vers of sorwful matere, that whilom in florysschyng studie made delitable ditees. For lo, rendynge muses of poetes enditen to me thynges to ben written, and drery vers of wretchidnesse weten my face with verray teres. At the leeste, no drede ne myghte overcomen tho muses, that thei ne were felawes, and folwyden my wey.

Alas! Weeping bitterly, I am compelled to begin sad verses, I who in better circumstances made beautiful and happy songs. For hear me, the poetic muses urge me to write down things that are dreary and the product of my personal wretchedness, while my face is wet with tears. At the very least, I pray that no sorrow or dread will overcome the muses, who follow and urge me on my way.

(Boece, Incipit Liber Boecii de Consolacione Philosophie, 1–9)

Anicius Manlius Severinus Boethius (480–524) was born near Rome to a wealthy noble family that was distantly related to Olybrius, emperor of Rome from April to November 472 (the Roman Empire fell to the Germans in 476). Boethius was orphaned at about the age of seven and was taken into the household of the wealthy and powerful Symmachus.

Boethius married Symmachus's daughter and, thanks to his powerful connections, embarked on a senatorial career. The intellectual advantages he was given as a part of Symmachus's household also enabled Boethius to become arguably the best-educated Roman of his time, his command of Greek distinguishing him as the foremost translator and commentator on Platonic philosophy.

Politically—and unfortunately for him—Boethius was a throwback to an earlier age. His devotion to civil service was such that it cost him his life. He served a term as consul in 510 and later, as *magister officiorum*—the head of all government and court services—under the Ostrogothic king Theodoric.

It was Theodoric's tumultuous career that brought about Boethius's downfall. During the fifth century, the Roman Empire, now split into halves, had increasingly been harassed by a succession of Germanic tribes. Eventually, Odoacer, a half-Hun mercenary, deposed the Western Roman emperor, Romulus Augustus, and returned the imperial regalia to Emperor Zeno in Constantinople. Odoacer claimed he would act as Zeno's regent but quickly seized power for himself, and the lands were lost to the Eastern Empire.

In retaliation, Zeno sent the Ostrogoths into Italy. The Ostrogoths, under Theodoric the Great (493–526), had been attacking Constantinople for some time, making life difficult for Zeno. The emperor negotiated a deal with Theodoric to convince him to turn his attentions elsewhere: bring Odoacer to heel and Theodoric would be Zeno's deputy. Theodoric successfully killed Odoacer and promptly set himself up as ruler of Italy in 493. Despite this, he maintained an uneasy alliance with Constantinople until the reign of Zeno's successor Justin (r. 519–527), when the two rulers had a falling out. Boethius, suspected of being sympathetic to the emperor's religious opinions (Theodoric was an Arian, a movement that was considered heresy by the Catholic Church as well as the Eastern Orthodox Church) and condemned for defending the rights of the Senate against the emperor, was executed in 525.

Boethius's *Consolation of Philosophy* was written during his year-long imprisonment awaiting trial and execution. It is modeled on the Roman form of Menippean satire, which blends prose and verse. The book is a conversation between Boethius and Lady Philosophy, who attempts to lead Boethius to the conclusion that happiness must come from inside himself and not from material success. If he follows this advice, Dame Fortune cannot take anything away from him. Boethius's discussion attempts to answer religious questions in a purely secular, philosophical fashion, bringing faith and reason into harmony. He addresses questions of free will, predestination, virtue, and justice and attempts to reveal why goodness is no guarantee of success while evil behavior does not condemn one to failure.

It is impossible to overestimate Boethius's influence on Chaucer. Not only did Chaucer translate the *Consolation* into Middle English, but many of his concepts and characters are direct references to Boethius's work. Nature in the *Parliament of Fowls* is the literary daughter of Lady Philosophy. Furthermore, Boethius's use of Dame Fortune and his emphasis on patience and steadfastness find their way into all of Chaucer's works.

See also Fortune; Philosophy

FURTHER READING

Marenbon, John. *Boethius*. New York: Oxford University Press, 2003.
Minnis, A. J. *Chaucer's Boece and the Medieval Tradition of Boethius*. Rochester, NY: D. S. Brewer, 1993.

Bruges

One of Flanders's most important cities, Bruges was founded in the ninth century by Viking invaders. The name comes from the Scandinavian word for "harbor." By the thirteenth century, Bruges had become an important port for international trade as the headquarters of the Hanseatic League, dominating the wool and linen textile market in particular. British wool producers would ship their product to Flanders, where it would be woven into cloth, then resold. However, in the fourteenth century, the tide was turning. The English had started producing their own cloth, creating a cottage industry that would become vital to the English economy over the subsequent centuries. Bruges responded by expanding its trading role beyond the cloth market. It would eventually become, in essence, the warehouse of northern Europe, storing and clearing exotic luxury goods.

Bruges figures prominently in "The Shipman's Tale" as the business destination of the merchant. While he is away, the monk, Brother John, cuckolds him with the merchant's young lusty wife. In addition, as a nod to Bruges's position as a maker of fine cloth, Chaucer mentions that Sir Thopas's hose come from "Brugges" (*Canterbury Tales*, "The Shipman's Tale," VII, 733).

See also Fashion; Ypres

FURTHER READING

Attreed, Lorraine Christine. *The King's Towns: Identity and Survival in Late Medieval English Boroughs*. New York: P. Lang, 2001.

Britnell, R. H. *The Commercialisation of English Society, 1000–1500*. 2nd ed. New York: Manchester University Press, 1996.

Clare, John D., ed. *Fourteenth-Century Towns*. San Diego: Harcourt Brace Jovanovich, 1993.

Brugges. See Bruges

Burgundy

Renowned for both Dijon mustard and its wine, Burgundy was a rising star on the European horizon in Chaucer's day. The Duchy was originally a kingdom (also called Arles) that had been formed after the Carolingian Empire was divided in 843. It had its roots in the migrations of the Burgundii, Scandinavians who came to the Roman Empire during the early fifth century and settled in southeastern France. It would be conquered by the Merovingians during the sixth century and eventually absorbed into the Carolingian Empire under Charles Martel in the eighth century. After the death of Charlemagne, when the empire was partitioned, the land between the Sarne and the Jura became the Kingdom of Burgundy under Emperor Lothair. The duchy of Burgundy was created at the same time, comprising the lands west of the Sarne ruled by Charles the Bald.

The kingdom underwent several changes in boundaries over successive generations, and remained a bone of contention between its French rulers and German Holy Roman Emperors. In 1032, when Rudolf III died without issue, it passed into German hands. Yet it remained unruly and, over the course of the following centuries, it slowly, by bits and pieces, passed into the hands of the French.

Meanwhile, the duchy of Burgundy became the foundational area for the Capetian dynasty, of which the ill-fated Louis XVI was a descendant. The Capetian house was founded by Hugh Capet in 1032 and the family ruled there until 1361. With the death of Phillip of Rouvres, Capetian control ended and the duchy passed to John II of France, known as John the Good. John II transferred the duchy to his son Philip the Bold in 1363, founding the Valois-Bourgogne line. Under Philip and his successors, Burgundy's territory expanded to include the modern day Netherlands, Belgium, and Luxembourg, as well as vast territories in France. Burgundy also allied with England against France in the Hundred Years War.

See also Hundred Years War

FURTHER READING

Attreed, Lorraine Christine. *The King's Towns: Identity and Survival in Late Medieval English Boroughs*. New York: P. Lang, 2001.

Britnell, R. H. *The Commercialisation of English Society, 1000–1500*. 2nd ed. New York: Manchester University Press, 1996.

Childress, Diana. *Chaucer's England*. North Haven, CT: Linnet Books, 2000.

Clare, John D., ed. *Fourteenth-Century Towns*. San Diego: Harcourt Brace Jovanovich, 1993.

Vernier, Richard. *The Flower of Chivalry: Bertrand Du Guesclin and the Hundred Years War*. Rochester, NY: D. S. Brewer, 2003.

Wright, Nicholas. *Knights and Peasants: The Hundred Years War in the French Countryside*. Rochester, NY: Boydell Press, 1998.

Business and Commerce

A MARCHANT was ther with a forked berd,
In mottelee, and hye on horse he sat;
Upon his heed a Flaundryssh bever hat,
His bootes clasped faire and fetisly.
...
Hir coverchiefs ful fyne weren of ground;
I dorste swere they weyeden ten pound
That on a Sonday weren upon hir heed.
Hir hosen weren of fyn scarlet reed,
Ful streite yteyd, and shoes ful moyste and newe.

There was a Merchant with a forked beard,
Dressed in motley, and sitting high on a fine horse.
He wore on his head a beaver hat made in Flanders,
And his boots were of the highest fashion.
...
Her kerchiefs were finely woven of ground
There were so many that she wore every Sunday upon her head,
I would have sworn they weighed ten pounds.
Her stockings were of a fine scarlet red
Tied very straight and fashionable, and her shoes were
Of the latest fashion and made of the best leather.

(*Canterbury Tales,*
General Prologue, I (A), 270–74, 453–57)

The history of medieval trade has been divided by historians roughly into two periods of development. The earlier period, lasting from the fifth until the eleventh century, was a time when trade comprised a tiny and mostly insignificant role in the economy of Europe. The second period, lasting through the High Middle Ages, from the twelfth to the fifteenth century, indicated an entirely different world, when trade became the most important facet of medieval economics. It was aided by the rise of urban centers and the development of new technologies such as improved shipbuilding and changes in coinage that helped smooth the progress of trade. In turn, the acceleration of the economy also accelerated the development of cities and the creation of new technologies so that a circular, symbiotic relationship existed between these various facets of medieval economic life.

A woodcut of a Medieval book collector from a fifteenth-century manuscript. Courtesy of the Library of Congress.

In the early Middle Ages, western Europe was a sparsely populated, fairly impoverished area, only marginally adapted for farming and much less concerned with any kind of advanced developments such as trade and commerce. The invasions of Germanic tribes during the fifth and sixth centuries only further exacerbated a movement toward subsistence and regressive, disconnected rural villages. By the eighth century, in fact, the use of coin had all but died out in western Europe.

Beginning at the end of Charlemagne's reign and accelerating into the eleventh century, trade became an integral and vital part of the European landscape. Several societal factors enabled this to occur. First, the unstable political conditions that had plagued Europe for so long were finally brought under control as kings and religious leaders were able to enforce their authority in a real sense. Stability led to greater safety in moving goods and currency. The beginning of the Crusades also enabled people to not only improve methods of transport, but also exposed them to new markets and sources for luxury goods. Finally, the population of Europe began to expand, creating an interest in and the ability to develop larger towns and cities.

As trade expanded, merchants developed the means to conduct international finance. Instead of passing sacks of silver or gold coins, which were often of varying currencies depending on the country of origin, merchants substituted letters of exchange. To facilitate these transactions, banks began to appear at the end of the twelfth century, first in northern Italy and then across the rest of Europe.

Perhaps the most important development was the spirit of financial cooperation that led to the creation of formal partnerships and other means of raising investment capital. Like limited partnerships today, investors pooled their resources to fund bigger projects. Often the partnership consisted of an active or general partner or partners who took an active role in managing the enterprise, and a group of silent partners who merely invested capital. Contracts were drawn up, giving legal backing and assuring the participation of each member.

On the practical side, developments in travel methods as well as the growth of centralized fairs meant that merchants had set places at which they could sell their wares, places that were more easily reached by improvements in the building of roads. The fairs were staggered across Europe to ensure practically a 12-month cycle. By Chaucer's time, the fairs had passed their prime, but they had provided the idea that it might be profitable to travel further and longer to increase profitability. Many merchants established permanent offices in foreign cities and created elaborate systems of partnerships to hedge against a volatile international market.

In every country, the increased availability of luxury or exotic goods meant an increased demand for them. Larger cities meant an ever-increasing need for the everyday goods that are not producible in an urban setting, such as food. This meant the growth of rural markets and regular town markets for grocery shopping. In addition, the ease of moving goods meant that luxury goods were no longer the exclusive provenance of the aristocracy. As one writer has commented, "By Chaucer's day, a prosperous Londoner might expect to wear a gown made from Flemish cloth, tinted with French dye, trimmed in Russian fur, shoes of Spanish leather, wine from Bordeaux, fish from Scandinavia, fishoil from Iceland, apples from Normandy, salt from Brittany, sugar from Sicily, and spices from Mediterranean, on a table made from Irish boards set with Venetian glassware, silver mined near Prague." Indeed, Chaucer's Merchant and the outlandish clothes of the Wife of Bath, reflecting her wide travels and prosperity, both reflect this.

For England, wool proved to be a better cash crop than grain, and it was through the development of the wool trade that England would rise to economic prominence in a post-Renaissance world. It created a thriving cottage industry that would also foreshadow England's domination in later centuries when the Industrial Revolution occurred.

See also Cities, Towns, and Villages; Fashion; Merchant; Money

FURTHER READING

Backman, Clifford R. *The Worlds of Medieval Europe*. New York: Oxford University Press, 2003.

Bisson, Lillian M. *Chaucer and the Late Medieval World*. New York: St. Martin's Press, 1998.

Boitani, Piero, and Jill Mann. *The Cambridge Chaucer Companion*. New York: Cambridge University Press, 1986.

Britnell, R. H. *The Commercialisation of English Society, 1000–1500*. 2nd ed. New York: Manchester University Press, 1996.

Brown, Peter, ed. *A Companion to Chaucer.* Malden, MA: Blackwell, 2002.

Dyer, Christopher. *Making a Living in the Middle Ages: The People of Britain 850–1520.* New Haven, CT: Yale University Press, 2002.

Frugoni, Chiara. *A Day in a Medieval City.* Introduction by Arsenio Frugoni. Translated by William McCuaig. Chicago: University of Chicago Press, 2005.

Le Goff, Jacques. *Medieval Callings.* Translated by Lydia G. Cochrane. Chicago: University of Chicago Press, 1980.

———. *Time, Work, and Culture in the Middle Ages.* Translated by Arthur Goldhammer. Chicago: University of Chicago Press, 1980.

Lerer, Seth, ed. *The Yale Companion to Chaucer.* New Haven, CT: Yale University Press, 2006.

Liddy, Christian D. *War, Politics and Finance in Late Medieval English Towns: Bristol, York and the Crown, 1350–1400.* Woodbridge, Suffolk, England: Boydell Press, 2005.

Lilley, Keith D. *Urban Life in the Middle Ages, 1000–1450.* New York: Palgrave, 2002.

Masschaele, James. *Peasants, Merchants, and Markets: Inland Trade in Medieval England, 1150–1350.* New York: St. Martin's Press, 1997.

Nicholas, David. *The Growth of the Medieval City: From Late Antiquity to the Early Fourteenth Century.* New York: Longman, 1997.

———. *The Later Medieval City, 1300–1500.* New York: Longman, 1997.

———. *Urban Europe, 1100–1700.* New York: Palgrave Macmillan, 2003.

C

Calendar

The progress of the medieval calendar held far greater significance than perhaps it does today. Certainly, we mark the passage of the seasons and the various holidays throughout the year. In the Middle Ages, the number of holidays that had to be celebrated were vital to salvation (as well as mental well-being as days off), and the importance of planting or harvesting at an appropriate time of year were equally vital to survival. Moveable holidays, such as Easter, were the subject of strict and careful calculations.

Medieval Europe used the Julian calendar, which had been developed by Julius Caesar and provides the basis, with some adjustments, for our calendar today. The Julian calendar is based on the number of days—365.25—that it takes for the sun to return to an exact position in the sky at noon. The number of months and days in those months are fairly arbitrarily set, and the occurrence of leap year every forth year is meant to offset the quarter day differential.

The beginning of the year, in Chaucer's day, was March 25, Annunciation Day, which also roughly coincided with the planting of spring crops. The Romans, however, had calculated January 1 as the first day of the year, as we do today.

The activities that were connected with each month reflect the heavy dominance in medieval Europe of the agricultural world, activities that were reflected in Books of Hours of the time. The winter months were characterized by maintenance activities such as repairing buildings and hedges. By

An illumination of the visit of the Three Magi from a medieval *Book of Hours*. © Bibliothèque nationale de France.

February, the ground was soft enough to be plowed in preparation for the spring crops, all of which had to be sown by Annunciation Day. These crops included grains such as barley and oats and important protein sources such as beans and peas.

March was passed in planting these crops. April required further plowing, for the summer crops and for the fallow fields, as well as the start of dairy work. June was taken up with sheep shearing and the hay harvest by the end of the month. July was a busy month, dominated almost entirely by the extensive hay harvest, which provided warmth and food for livestock over the cold winter months. August was perhaps the busiest month of the year, with the end of hay harvest and the start of the involved task of grain harvest. Grains were threshed, and the straw was gathered and bound for use in baskets, rugs, and roof thatching.

By September, the weather was beginning to cool and many days were spent indoors continuing to thresh the grain; good days allowed fruit and other crops to be picked. In October, another round of plowing ensued in preparation for the winter crops of rye and wheat, the seeds for which had to be planted by the end of November. Excess livestock were slaughtered and preserved also by the end of November.

The importance of the calendar and the flow of time are subtly evident in Chaucer's works. He typically calculates time by astrology, referencing the zodiac sign through which the sun is passing. For instance, he says of Chauntecleer the rooster, "By nature he knew ech ascencioun / Of the equynoxial in thilke toun; / For whan degrees fifteen weren ascended, / Thanne crew he that it myghte nat been amended" (*He naturally knew each ascension / Of the equinoctial circle in his town; / And its movement by each 15 degrees / Then he crowed on the hour with great precision*) (*Canterbury Tales,* "The Nun's Priest's Tale," VII, 2855–58). We know that the Canterbury pilgrims set out on or about April 18, as he tells us "Whan that Aprill with his shoures soote / … and the yonge sonne / Hath in the Ram his half cours yronne" (*When April with his sweet showers / ... and the young sun / had run half of the course through Aries*) (*Canterbury Tales*, General Prologue, I (A), 1, 7–8).

In other passages, Chaucer provides the date simply by the description of where the sun was in its passage in the zodiac (*Canterbury Tales*, "The Squire's Tale," V (F), 48–51, 263–65, 386; *Canterbury Tales*, "The Franklin's Tale," V (F), 1248; *Canterbury Tales*, "The Nun's Priest's Tale," VII, 3194–95; *Canterbury Tales*, "The Parson's Tale," XI, 2–11; *Troilus and Criseyde*, Book II, 50–56: *Troilus and Criseyde*, Book IV, 1590–96; *Troilus and Criseyde*, Book V, 1016–22; *Legend of Good Women*, 113–15).

See also Astrology and Astronomy; Daily Life; Holidays and Holy Days

FURTHER READING

Britnell, Richard, ed. *Daily Life in the Late Middle Ages.* Stroud, England: Sutton, 1998.

Brown, Peter, ed. *A Companion to Chaucer.* Malden, MA: Blackwell, 2002.

Caliope

The muse of epic poetry, Caliope was often called upon by writers for inspiration and assistance. She appears notably in Chaucer's *The House of Fame*, where she and her eight sister muses gather around Fame's throne:

So song the myghty Muse, she
That cleped ys Caliope,
And hir eighte sustren eke,
That in her face semen meke;
And ever mo, eternally,
They songe of Fame, as thoo herd y:
"Heryed be thou and thy name,
Goddesse of Renoun or of Fame!"

So sang the mighty Muse, she
Who is named Caliope
And her eight sisters as well
Who in the face of her seem meek
And forever, eternally,
They sing of Fame, as we have heard:
"Heralded be Fame and her name,
Goddess of Renoun!!"

(*House of Fame*, Book III, 1399–1406)

Chaucer also calls upon both Caliope and Venus in the opening lines Book III of *Troilus and Criseyde* to describe the joy of the new lovers:

Caliope, thi vois be now present,
For now is nede: sestow noght my destresse,
How I mot telle anonright the gladnesse
Of Troilus, to Venus heryinge?
To which gladnesse, who nede hath, God hym brynge!

Caliope, lift up your voice now,
When it is most needed: Do you not see my distress,
For how can I be up to the task of telling of the happiness
Of Troilus, in Venus's hearing?
And of such happiness, whoever needs it, let God bring it to him!

(*Troilus and Criseyde*, Book III, 45–49)

FURTHER READING

Brown, Peter, ed. *A Companion to Chaucer.* Malden, MA: Blackwell, 2002.

Frye, Northrop. *Biblical and Classical Myths: The Mythological Framework of Western Culture.* Buffalo: University of Toronto Press, 2004.

Hansen, William F. *Classical Mythology: A Guide to the Mythical World of the Greeks and Romans.* New York: Oxford University Press, 2005.

Manser, Martin H. *The Facts On File Dictionary of Classical and Biblical Allusions.* New York: Facts On File, 2003.

Morford, Mark P. O. *Classical Mythology.* 7th ed. New York: Oxford University Press, 2003.

Nolan, Barbara. *Chaucer and the Tradition of the Roman Antique.* New York: Cambridge University Press, 1992.

Powell, Barry B. *Classical Myth.* Translated by Herbert M. Howe. 4th ed. Upper Saddle River, NJ: Pearson/Prentice Hall, 2004.

Price, Simon, and Emily Kearns, eds. *The Oxford Dictionary of Classical Myth and Religion.* New York: Oxford University Press, 2003.

Cambridge

And nameliche ther was a greet collegge
Men clepen the Soler Halle at Cantebregge;
. . .

Thanne were ther yonge povre scolers two,
That dwelten in this halle, of which I seye.
Testif they were, and lusty for to pleye,
And, oonly for hire myrthe and revelrye,
Upon the wardeyn bisily they crye
To yeve hem leve, but a litel stounde,
To goon to mille and seen hir corn ygrounde;

And namely there was a great college
That men called the Solar hall at Cambridge

...

There were two poor young scholars
Who lived at this hall, of which I have spoken.
They were constrained by study and ready for any amusement
And so, they went to the warden to ask for leave
So that they could see if the Miller would try to cheat them.
They swore that he could not and both were willing
To gamble anything on that statement.

(*Canterbury Tales,*
"The Reeve's Tale," I (A), 3989–4008)

Located in central England on the Cam River, the town of Cambridge is best known for its university, which is the second oldest in England after Oxford. Cambridge appears to have first been a Roman military outpost and later became an important site for trade between England and the Continent. It was chartered in 1207, and the university was recognized by Pope John XXII as a place of study in 1318. The university expanded at an impressive rate, adding five new colleges during the fourteenth century.

The students John and Alan from "The Reeve's Tale" are taking a holiday from their Cambridge studies when they play a prank on the miller, rewarding his hospitality by sleeping with his wife and daughter.

FURTHER READING

Attreed, Lorraine Christine. *The King's Towns: Identity and Survival in Late Medieval English Boroughs.* New York: P. Lang, 2001.

Britnell, R. H. *The Commercialisation of English Society, 1000–1500.* 2nd ed. New York: Manchester University Press, 1996.

Childress, Diana. *Chaucer's England.* North Haven, CT: Linnet Books, 2000.

Clare, John D., ed. *Fourteenth-Century Towns.* San Diego: Harcourt Brace Jovanovich, 1993.

Bridge of Sighs in Cambridge, England, ca. 1900. Courtesy of the Library of Congress.

Cantebregge. *See* Cambridge

Canterbury

Located on the River Stour in the county of Kent in rural southeast England, Canterbury is most notable for its famous cathedral, the ultimate destination for the pilgrims of *The Canterbury Tales.* In the Middle Ages, it was also England's most i mportant spiritual center, and the Archbishop of Canterbury was the country's preeminent prelate.

The first Archbishop was St. Augustine, who was sent by Pope Gregory the Great as a missionary in 579. He arrived on the coast of the kingdom of Kent and was almost immediately given a church by King Æthelbert, who wanted a place of worship for his Christian wife Bertha. In 998, the cathedral community was dedicated to the Rule of St. Benedict. The community of Benedictines continued to live there until the dissolution of the monastery under Henry VIII in 1540.

The original Saxon church of St. Augustine was destroyed by a fire in 1067, but rebuilding began shortly afterward by the Norman conquerors in 1070. Subsequent generations added elements to the cathedral, in keeping with the prevailing styles of the day, until its completion in 1503. Its highest point stands 235 feet.

Canterbury cathedral façade. Courtesy of Lisa Kirchner.

A detail of the cathedral portal. Courtesy of Lisa Kirchner.

Canterbury city wall. Courtesy of Lisa Kirchner.

Canterbury became a popular pilgrimage destination in the twelfth century as thousands of the faithful traveled to view the tomb of St. Thomas à Becket, the archbishop who was murdered in the cathedral in 1170. His shrine was completed in 1220, only to be destroyed in 1538. Other prominent archbishops include Thomas Cranmer, who, as the driving force behind Henry VIII's break with Rome, compiled the first two prayer books and established the liturgy of the Anglican Church. The cathedral also houses the tombs of Henry IV, his wife Joan of Navarre, and Edward of Woodstock, the Black Prince.

Canterbury city, houses, and the cathedral. Courtesy of Lisa Kirchner.

See also Pilgrimage; St. Augustine; St. Benedict; Thomas à Becket

FURTHER READING

Butler, John R. *The Quest for Becket's Bones: The Mystery of the Relics of St Thomas Becket of Canterbury.* New Haven, CT: Yale University Press, 1995.

Collinson, Patrick, Nigel Ramsay, and Margaret Sparks, eds. *A History of Canterbury Cathedral.* New York: Oxford University Press, 1995.

Lyle, Marjorie. *Canterbury: 2000 Years of History.* Rev. ed. Stroud, England: Tempus, 2002.

Michael, M. A. *Stained Glass of Canterbury Cathedral.* London: Scala, 2004.

Cassandra

The unfortunate daughter of King Priam and Hecuba of Troy, Cassandra was also the sister of Troilus, Hector, Deiphebus, and Paris. Apollo rewarded her with the gift of prophecy when she agreed to become his lover. When she changed her mind, however, and backed out of the relationship, Apollo punished her by preventing anyone from believing her. It was her sad fate to foretell the fall of Troy, but to be powerless to make anyone heed her warnings.

After the fall, Cassandra was enslaved by Agamemnon and, ultimately, murdered with him by his vengeful wife Clytemnestra. In *Troilus and Criseyde*, her broken-hearted brother Troilus asks her to interpret his dream:

For which he for Siblle his suster sente,
That called was Cassandre ek al about,
And al his drem he tolde hire er he stente,
And hire bisoughte assoilen hym the doute
Of the stronge boor with tustkes stoute;
And fynaly, withinne a litel stounde,
Cassandre hym gan right thus his drem expounde.

For which he sent for his sister Cassandra
Who was a Sybil,
And he told her his dream before he lost his nerve,
And asked her to explain to him the meaning
Of the fierce boar with huge tusks;
And finally, after a little while to think,
Cassandra became to tell him what his dream meant.

(*Troilus and Criseyde*, Book V, 1450–1540)

In *The Book of the Duchesse*, the Black Knight proclaims that his sorrow outstrips any Cassandra might have felt at the fall of Troy (*Book of the Duchess*, 1246).

FURTHER READING

Brown, Peter, ed. *A Companion to Chaucer.* Malden, MA: Blackwell, 2002.
Frye, Northrop. *Biblical and Classical Myths: The Mythological Framework of Western Culture.* Buffalo, NY: University of Toronto Press, 2004.
Hansen, William F. *Classical Mythology: A Guide to the Mythical World of the Greeks and Romans.* New York: Oxford University Press, 2005.
Manser, Martin H. *The Facts On File Dictionary of Classical and Biblical Allusions.* New York: Facts On File, 2003.
Morford, Mark P. O. *Classical Mythology.* 7th ed. New York: Oxford University Press, 2003.
Nolan, Barbara. *Chaucer and the Tradition of the Roman Antique.* New York: Cambridge University Press, 1992.
Powell, Barry B. *Classical Myth.* Translated by Herbert M. Howe. 4th ed. Upper Saddle River, NJ: Pearson/Prentice Hall, 2004.
Price, Simon, and Emily Kearns, eds. *The Oxford Dictionary of Classical Myth and Religion.* New York: Oxford University Press, 2003.

Castles

Castles are perhaps the single most recognizable feature of the Middle Ages. They are symbolic of our romanticized notions of the life of noble knights,

Ludlow Castle in Shropshire, England. Courtesy of the Library of Congress.

fair maidens, and lavish stone edifices behind the walls of which everyone was treated with courtesy and socially prescribed deference. The reality is somewhat different, and the development of castles came from very practical concerns. The earliest castles were of very simple wooden construction and reflected the need of early towns for defense against increasingly advanced forms of weapons. The first were surrounded by wooden fences called palisades, which were built above ditches to make scaling them more difficult for invading forces.

Later, as the feudal system evolved, the motte and bailey castle developed. The motte—a mound—housed a tower. Around the tower was built a palisade, and around the motte was dug a deep ditch that was sometimes filled with water or with sharp spikes. Around the ditch was constructed the bailey, or stone or earth wall. From a defensive standpoint, the height of the motte was a key element. Height meant that soldiers could spy an enemy force from further away; in addition, high walls were not only difficult to climb, but also more difficult to fire arrows into.

With the Crusades came new advanced weapon technologies, which rendered the motte and bailey construction obsolete. Wood, in short supply by the eleventh century, was vulnerable to the large, sometimes flaming projectiles hurled by trebuchets and catapults. Stone was necessary for the best protection from outside enemies. Castle builders quickly adapted their techniques to accommodate this new requirement for durable and fireproof stone.

A typical Norman castle in Canterbury. Courtesy of Lisa Kirchner.

Stone castles, however, were not without their own vulnerabilities, as unlucky nobles soon realized. Since walls could be undermined and thus easily collapsed, simply building a stone tower was not enough. Combining the older idea of the bailey with the new stone towers, castles of the twelfth and thirteenth centuries were built with layers of defensive protection. They were placed inside deep ditches called moats and were only approachable across a long drawbridge. If an attacker tried to fill or cross the moat, he could be stopped from the top of the castle's walls. At the door, should the enemy manage to make it past the gatehouse and across the drawbridge, was a metal gate, which was raised by a system of pulleys and known as a portcullis.

Inside a castle an entire world thrived. Because the idea of a castle was to survive a prolonged siege, the community inside had to be as close to self-sufficiency as possible. Castles often housed extensive kitchens and storerooms, armories, stables, chapels, as well as the living quarters of those who called it their home. There were also training grounds for knights. The primary feature of the castle interior was the great hall, which functioned as a banquet area, a main gathering place for all of the castle's inhabitants, and a meeting hall for political guests. All business of an official nature took place in the great hall.

By Chaucer's day, the time of the great castles was passing, with nobles and kings building large manor houses instead, sprawling homes more suited to living than defense, although certainly castles would dominate the landscape for centuries to come.

See also Cathedrals; Private Houses

FURTHER READING

Corfis, Ivy A., and Michael Wolfe, eds. *The Medieval City under Siege*. Rochester, NY: Boydell Press, 1995.
Hilliam, David. *Castles and Cathedrals: The Great Buildings of Medieval Times*. New York: Rosen, 2004.
Laule, Ulrike. *Architecture of the Middle Ages*. Berlin: Feierabend, 2004.
Lever, Jill, and John Harris. *Illustrated Dictionary of Architecture, 800–1914*. 2nd ed. Boston: Faber and Faber, 1993.

Cataloigne. See Catalonia

Catalonia

And alle that used clarion
In Cataloigne and Aragon,
That in her tyme famous were
To lerne, saugh I trumpe there.

And I saw Catalonia and Aragon
That were famous at one time,
Where Fame had blown her trumpet once,
But now their day was done.

(*House of Fame*, 1247–50)

Catalonia, part of the Aragonese empire in the Middle Ages, became a crucial region in the eleventh and twelfth centuries thanks to the role its capital, Barcelona, played as a trading port. By the late twelfth century, it had become nearly as important as Venice or Genoa. It was conquered by Jaume I of Aragon in the thirteenth century and continued to rise in importance as the Aragonese empire expanded. However, it became apparent during the fourteenth century that the empire had overextended itself, resulting in economic, social, and political crises that eventually erupted into civil war by the mid-fifteenth century.

Catalonia is mentioned as one of the places seen by the dreamer in *The House of Fame*.

FURTHER READING

Labarge, Margaret Wade. *Medieval Travellers*. New York: Norton, 1983.
Nicholas, David. *The Growth of the Medieval City: From Late Antiquity to the Early Fourteenth Century*. New York: Longman, 1997.
———. *The Later Medieval City, 1300–1500*. New York: Longman, 1997.
———. *Urban Europe, 1100–1700*. New York: Palgrave Macmillan, 2003.
Verdon, Jean. *Travel in the Middle Ages*. Notre Dame, IN: University of Notre Dame Press, 2003.

Cathedrals

The earliest Catholic churches were constructed on the former sites of pagan temples, providing new converts with a familiar locale in which to practice an unfamiliar religion. Each church, in order to be officially approved to hold a mass, had to be equipped with an altar. However, there was not much difference between a purpose-built church and a building connected to a residence that was used for worship. Cathedrals, on the other hand, were far more elaborate expressions of the power and glory of the Church. These soaring edifices have come to be some of the most recognizable symbols, after castles, of the Middle Ages.

Cathedrals, by definitions, are the homes of bishops. Masses could be performed there, certainly, as in any church, but the cathedral represented the central or main place of worship for a particular diocese. Although they did not need to be larger or more elaborate than any church (and some wealthy churches were quite elaborate indeed), they typically were. Usually built and designed by bishops, cathedrals represented the pinnacle of technological developments in architecture as well as prevailing attitudes and conceptions of Christian worship.

Symbolically, every aspect of a cathedral was important. Their very construction and ornamentation was intended to remind the visitor of God's glory and actual presence. The more fanciful the cathedral's design—the

Chartres Cathedral. Courtesy of Lisa Kirchner.

Notre Dame Cathedral. Courtesy of Lisa Kirchner.

thinner and higher the walls and the more light that flowed in through improbably huge windows—the more the visitor was intended to be awe-struck by the power of God. Not only was the power of God represented in cathedral design, but increasing reverence of saint cults and the Virgin Mary came to have their place as well.

Increased need to venerate saintly relics and open them up to the many visitors who came to view them and, sometimes, be healed by them, re-quired increasingly large portions of the floor plan to be devoted to the display of reliquaries. The Virgin was symbolized and venerated through the addition of the rose window above the entrance of a cathedral, an addi-tion first included at St. Denis. As the church changed its focus from being a fortress against evil to a softer focus on illumination and forgiveness, the intercession of figures like Mary and the saints, as well as increased light, all combined to represent the church's purpose.

Cathedrals were also the most conspicuous repositories of Church wealth. Nobles who sought some insurance of their ultimate salvation made opulent gifts of golden crucifixes or candlesticks to their local cathe-dral or, more practically, spent vast sums on commissioning special win-dows or fixtures within the church itself. Canterbury, as the preeminent cathedral in Britain, enjoyed many lavish gifts as well as the distinction of being, until Chaucer's time, the primary pilgrimage destination in the British Isles.

Notre Dame Cathedral butresses. Courtesy of Lisa Kirchner.

A closer look at the portal figurines at Notre Dame Cathedral. Courtesy of Lisa Kirchner.

See also Architecture; Canterbury

FURTHER READING

Abulafia, David, Michael Franklin, and Miri Rubin, eds. *Church and City, 1000–1500: Essays in Honour of Christopher Brooke*. New York: Cambridge University Press, 1992.

Archer, Lucy. *Architecture in Britain and Ireland, 600–1500*. London: Harvill Press, 1999.

Backhouse, Janet, ed. *The Medieval English Cathedral: Papers in Honour of Pamela Tudor-Craig: Proceedings of the 1998 Harlaxton Symposium*. Donington, Lincolnshire, England: Shaun Tyas, 2003.

Binding, Günther. *Medieval Building Techniques*. Stroud, England: Tempus, 2004.

Blick, Sarah, and Rita Tekippe, eds. *Art and Architecture of Late Medieval Pilgrimage in Northern Europe and the British Isles*. Boston: Brill, 2005.

Calkins, Robert G. *Medieval Architecture in Western Europe: From A.D. 300 to 1500*. New York: Oxford University Press, 1998.

Coldstream, Nicola. *Medieval Architecture*. New York: Oxford University Press, 2002.

Collinson, Patrick, Nigel Ramsay, and Margaret Sparks, eds. *A History of Canterbury Cathedral*. New York: Oxford University Press, 1995.

Erlande-Brandenburg, Alain. *The Cathedral Builders of the Middle Ages*. Translated by Rosemary Stonehewer. London: Thames and Hudson, 1995.

Gimpel, Jean. *The Cathedral Builders*. Translated by Teresa Waugh. New York: HarperPerennial, 1992.

Hilliam, David. *Castles and Cathedrals: The Great Buildings of Medieval Times*. New York: Rosen, 2004.

Lasansky, D. Medina, and Brian McLaren, eds. *Architecture and Tourism: Perception, Performance and Place*. New York: Berg, 2004.

Laule, Ulrike. *Architecture of the Middle Ages*. Berlin: Feierabend, 2004.

Lyle, Marjorie. *Canterbury: 2000 Years of History*. Rev. ed. Stroud, England: Tempus, 2002.

Michael, M. A. *Stained Glass of Canterbury Cathedral*. London: Scala, 2004.

Platt, Colin. *The Architecture of Medieval Britain: A Social History*. New Haven, CT: Yale University Press, 1990.

Simson, Otto Georg von. *The Gothic Cathedral: Origins of Gothic Architecture and the Medieval Concept of Order*. 3rd ed. Princeton, NJ: Princeton University Press, 1988.

Childhood

Childhood in the Middle Ages was interpreted far differently than it is today. There was no conception of adolescence and, for all intents and purposes, the period between ages 7 and 14 was an important rehearsal for the adult world, which would be entered after the fourteenth birthday. Children, quite understandably given the harsh realities of life in the Middle Ages, were required to grow up much faster and to take on responsibilities at a far younger age than they have been at perhaps any other time in history.

Infancy lasted officially for the first seven years, at which point the child would increasingly take on the responsibilities of adulthood and participation in adult society. Noble boys would begin training for knighthood, learning skills such as riding and increasingly difficult combat techniques. They also entered tutoring to gain the formal education necessary for the increasingly complex and demanding adult world they would inhabit someday.

Noble girls learned the skills they would need for managing their husbands' households as well as "finishing" in decorative skills such as music, embroidery, and perhaps tapestry weaving. For peasants, their education comprised such skills as their place in society dictated. Peasant boys began to learn to hunt, farm, herd or fish, and girls learned to cook, spin, wash and repair clothing, and heal.

At age 14, children entered adulthood as junior members of society. While they were expected to act as fully functioning adults, there were still some restrictions on their participation. For instance, boys were still not completely physically developed, so were not really required to take on the heaviest or most demanding tasks until they turned 21. They also did not attain the official age of inheritance until 21. Girls, on the other hand, could inherit property by the age of 16 if they were married. They also could marry as early as 12 (14 for boys), and were expected to take on the same tasks as adult women at age 14.

Thus, the period we now label adolescence, when the child begins to mature into the adult in a radically shifting spectrum of emotional and physical development, was partially recognized in the slower physical development of boys, but remained a relatively unknown territory for girls, who were expected to mature at a faster rate than their brothers.

See also Birth

FURTHER READING

Britnell, Richard, ed. *Daily Life in the Late Middle Ages.* Stroud, England: Sutton, 1998.

French, Katherine L. *The People of the Parish: Community Life in a Late Medieval English Diocese.* Philadelphia: University of Pennsylvania Press, 2001.

Gies, Frances, and Joseph Gies. *Women in the Middle Ages.* New York: Harper, 1978.

Hanawalt, Barbara. *Growing Up in Medieval London: The Experience of Childhood in History.* New York: Oxford University Press, 1993.

Heywood, Colin. *A History of Childhood: Children and Childhood in the West from Medieval to Modern Times.* Malden, MA: Blackwell, 2001.

Chivalry

A KNYGHT ther was, and that a worthy man,
That fro the tyme that he first bigan

To riden out, he loved chivalrie,
Trouthe and honour, fredom and curteisie.
Ful worthy was he in his lordes werre,
And therto hadde he riden, no man ferre,
As wel in cristendom as in hethenesse,
And evere honoured for his worthynesse;
. . .

With hym ther was his sone, a yong SQUIER,
A lovyere and a lusty bacheler,
With lokkes crulle as they were leyd in presse.
. . .

And he hadde been somtyme in chyvachie
In Flaundres, in Artoys, and Pycardie,
And born hym weel, as of so litel space,
In hope to stonden in his lady grace.
Embrouded was he, as it were a meede
Al ful of fresshe floures, white and reede.
Syngynge he was, or floytynge, al the day;
He was as fresh as is the month of May.

There was a Knight, a worthy man
Who from the beginning of his career of campaigning,
Loved chivalry, honor and truth, freedom and courtesy.
He fought bravely in his lord's service
And had ridden far to serve him
Throughout Christendom as well as the pagan lands
And he was always honored for his bravery.
. . .

With him he had his son, a young Squire,
Who was a lover and a high-spirited bachelor
With hair so curly it seemed they had been pressed.
. . .

He had spent some time doing chivalric deeds,
In Flanders, Artois, and Picardy
And he had born himself well, in so little time
In the hopes of winning his lady's favor.
His clothes were richly embroidered, like those of a maid,
With flowers of red and white.
He sang all of the time and played the flute all day long
He was as fresh as the month of May.

(*Canterbury Tales,*
General Prologue, I (A), 43–100)

The concept of chivalry is closely bound to the perception of knight-hood, nobility, and *gentilesse*. The word "chivalry" comes from the French *chevalerie,* which derives from *chevalier* (knight) and ultimately from the Latin *caballus* (horse). In practice, it embodies the ideal virtues that a knight

Tiel se tendra p̄ fol qui ore se tient p̄ sage. e n tote la comp̄
pour diolomen est sur le lorz enbuschees. S iparz ne si nai

A fourteenth-century depiction of the Battle of Gaugamèles. © Bibliothèque nationale de France.

should represent. Because knights were essentially warriors, with rather brutal warrior ethics and behaviors, society and especially the Catholic Church sought to civilize them.

As the title of knight evolved to signify a social elite, their manners evolved to conform as well. Knights transformed themselves into Christian soldiers who were bound to defend society, treat women with honor and deference, and honor and serve their lord. Courtly love—the unrequited passion of a bachelor knight for a married aristocratic woman whom he would serve—was another civilizing element of the knightly code of chivalry. By doing great deeds in her name, the knight would seek honor and glory, not unnecessary brutality and bloodshed.

The code of chivalry was essentially developed as a kind of social self-defense. The earliest knights developed from the Carolingian cavalry, fierce warriors whose place in the military did not depend on social caste. As independent landowners, they owed no great allegiance to any leader, and so worked primarily for their own betterment. "They were a threat to Church and peasant alike."

Realizing the need for fighting men in society, but also wanting to have tame fighting men, the Church sought to curb their more dangerous tendencies by instituting a code of behavior by which a noble knight should abide. The notion appealed to the proud nature of these men, to whom honor and glory were nearly as appealing as wealth and power.

To emphasize this focus, knighthood eventually was conferred through a ceremony supervised by a priest, beginning with spiritual and physical cleansing and ending with a dubbing and the kiss of peace. Becoming a knight was a transformative experience. With the advent of the Crusades, the role of the knight as the defender of the Church was made explicit. Knights were soldiers for God, defending the Holy Land from its infidel invaders.

As the Middle Ages progressed, the role of the knight further evolved until it reached its zenith and decline. Gunpowder and archery eventually broke the dominance of mounted cavalry, a development made clear in the battle of Agincourt of 1415. From this point forward, chivalry became increasingly a ceremonial and romanticized notion, embodied in tournaments and, eventually, the ideal of the Renaissance Man.

Chaucer's description of the Knight in the General Prologue of *The Canterbury Tales* appears to be a light parody of the epitome of battlefield chivalry that he claims the Knight to be, while the Squire embodies the other side of the chivalric ideal, courtly love. This theme of love is also continued in the tales of both men: the Knight's focuses on unrequited love from afar for which noble men must vie on the field of arms, and the Squire's focuses on sentimentalism and high adventure.

See also Gentilesse; Knight; Squire

FURTHER READING

Ainsworth, Peter F. *Jean Froissart and the Fabric of History: Truth, Myth, and Fiction in the* "Chroniques." New York: Oxford University Press, 1990.

Alexander, Jonathan, and Paul Binski, eds. *Age of Chivalry: Art in Plantagenet England, 1200–1400.* London: Royal Academy of Arts in association with Weidenfeld and Nicholson, 1987.

Barber, Richard. *The Reign of Chivalry.* Rochester, NY: Boydell Press, 2005.

Barker, Juliet R. V. *The Tournament in England, 1100–1400.* Wolfeboro, NH: Boydell Press, 1986.

Broughton, Bradford B. *Dictionary of Medieval Knighthood and Chivalry. Concepts and Terms.* Westport, CT: Greenwood Press, 1986.

Bumke, Joachim. *Courtly Culture.* New York: Overlook Press, 2000.

Chickering, Howell, and Thomas H. Seiler, eds. *The Study of Chivalry: Resources and Approaches.* Kalamazoo: Medieval Institute Publications, Western Michigan University, 1988.

De Pisan, Christine. *The Book of Deeds of Arms and of Chivalry.* Translated by Sumner Willard. Edited by Charity Cannon Willard. University Park: Pennsylvania State University Press, 1999.

Jones, Terry. *Chaucer's Knight: The Portrait of a Medieval Mercenary.* Baton Rouge: Louisiana State University Press, 1980.

Kaeuper, Richard W. *Chivalry and Violence in Medieval Europe.* New York: Oxford University Press, 1999.

Laing, Lloyd Robert. *Medieval Britain: The Age of Chivalry.* New York: St. Martin's Press, 1996.

Trim, D.J.B., ed. *The Chivalric Ethos and the Development of Military Professionalism.* Boston: Brill, 2003.

Church. *See* Religion

Cities, Towns, and Villages

As at any other period of human history, medieval people, for reasons of interdependence and the desire for companionship as well as other concerns, organized themselves into villages, towns, or cities. It was the rare soul who lived in a rural area, completely apart. These unusual men were known as hermits and were generally sought out as holy.

For the rest of society, residences were arranged in clusters of varying degrees of organization. By definition, a city housed at least 5,000 people (and in order to be official, a city had to have a cathedral), while a town was comprised of 1,000–5,000 inhabitants. Anything less was defined as a village, which could theoretically be made up of just a few families. By the start of the fourteenth century, it is estimated that between 10 and 15 percent of Europe's total population lived in towns or cities.

Despite their small size, villages housed the most people across Europe. Villages fell into two categories: nucleated and extended. The nucleated village was by far the most popular form, with all of the houses clustered around a central crossroads, providing easy access to all of the amenities required by the inhabitants, such as a church, perhaps a mill, and certain artisanal shops as were required. Extended villages were comprised of houses strung out along a particular road.

Cities were, by virtue of their larger populations and focus on urban activities such as trade, the most complex of these places. They were typically walled completely to protect the inhabitants from outside invaders, much as a castle was. If a city lacked a cathedral, it might still be considered to be a city unofficially, but was technically only a burg, a term that originally meant "fortress" because early burgs or boroughs developed under the walls of a lord's castle.

Eventually, the burghers would wall in their town, and the growing urban center would eventually be comprised of a wider-ranging fortress with the castle at the center, situated on a hill. When all of the space within the walls was filled, people would move to the suburbs just outside the walls, which in turn would eventually be enclosed. This pattern of building would continue until the Black Death decimated the population at a time when new forms of warfare made protective walls essentially obsolete.

Within cities and towns, there were many artisans and craftsmen who, in order to protect their body of knowledge and their rights, organized themselves into guilds. Guilds controlled such vital elements of a trade as membership, apprenticeship, standards of production, and pricing. Often guild masters became highly influential and wealthy men within their towns, and, as society began to democratize during Chaucer's time, they were able to rise to positions of power. With the growth and increased sophistication of trade and investing during this time, wealthy guildsmen were able to capitalize and increase their standing and influence through investing in banking and trading concerns.

Cities provided their inhabitants with intellectual stimulation as well as wider access and exposure to diverse material and luxury goods. However, despite their seeming benefits, cities also had their drawbacks. As the Black Death demonstrates, they were particularly susceptible to disease. Cities were also quite vulnerable to fire, because most houses were constructed of wood.

Finally, sanitation was a concern that would not be properly addressed until well into the nineteenth century. Concentration of population meant concentration of waste. Garbage and animal waste piled up in the streets, and the ability to clean it depended on both the labor and the water supply, the second of which could be severely limited depending on how much was available in the wells. In order to manage waste, carts were employed to transport it to the rural areas each night. Yet the streets remained sometimes distressingly dirty breeding grounds for disease and vermin.

Although Chaucer was a product of the most thriving urban center in England, we do not get a real flavor for daily life within a city in any of his works. His eye for detail seems to have been more keenly focused on the human show around him rather than his urban landscape.

See also Architecture; Business and Commerce

FURTHER READING

Abulafia, David, Michael Franklin, and Miri Rubin, eds. *Church and City, 1000–1500: Essays in Honour of Christopher Brooke.* New York: Cambridge University Press, 1992.

Britnell, R. H. *The Commercialisation of English Society, 1000–1500.* 2nd ed. New York: Manchester University Press, 1996.

Britnell, Richard, ed. *Daily Life in the Late Middle Ages.* Stroud, England: Sutton, 1998.

Carlin, Martha. *Medieval Southwark.* Rio Grande, OH: Hambledon Press, 1996.

Corfis, Ivy A., and Michael Wolfe, eds. *The Medieval City under Siege.* Rochester, NY: Boydell Press, 1995.

Frugoni, Chiara. *A Day in a Medieval City.* Introduction by Arsenio Frugoni. Translated by William McCuaig. Chicago: University of Chicago Press, 2005.

Hanawalt, Barbara A., ed. *Chaucer's England: Literature in Historical Context.* Minneapolis: University of Minnesota Press, 1992.

———. *Growing Up in Medieval London: The Experience of Childhood in History.* New York: Oxford University Press, 1993.

Lilley, Keith D. *Urban Life in the Middle Ages, 1000–1450.* New York: Palgrave, 2002.

Nicholas, David. *The Growth of the Medieval City: From Late Antiquity to the Early Fourteenth Century.* New York: Longman, 1997.

———. *The Later Medieval City, 1300–1500.* New York: Longman, 1997.
———. *Urban Europe, 1100–1700.* New York: Palgrave Macmillan, 2003.

Clerk

A CLERK ther was of Oxenford also,
That unto logyk hadde longe ygo.
As leene was his hors as is a rake,
And he nas nat right fat, I undertake,
But looked holwe, and therto sobrely.
Ful thredbare was his overeste courtepy,
For he hadde geten hym yet no benefice,
Ne was so worldly for to have office.
For hym was levere have at his beddes heed
Twenty bookes, clad in blak or reed,
Of Aristotle and his philosophie
Than robes riche, or fithele, or gay sautrie.
But al be that he was a philosophre.
Yet hadde he but litel gold in cofre;
But al that he myghte of his freendes hente,
On bookes and on lernynge he it spente,
And bisily gan for the soules preye
Of hem that yaf hym wherwith to scoleye.
Of studie took he moost cure and moost heede.

There was a scholar from Oxford too,
Who was studying logic, but had not taken his degree.
His horse was as lean as a rake,
And the scholar himself was not fat either, let me tell you.
He looked hollow and, because of it, serious and sober.
His overcoat was threadbare
Because he had not yet gotten himself an income,
Being too devoted to study to find an office.
For he would much rather have at the head of his bed
Twenty books, bound in black or red leather,
By Aristotle and his philosophy
Than to have rich robes, or a fiddle, or even a beautiful psaltery.
Although he was a man of science,
He had little in the way of money in his coffers;
All that he did get by the help of friends he spent freely
On books and learning
And he would pray for their souls in return
For enabling him to continue to go to school.
He was completely devoted to his studies, which were all he cared about.

(*Canterbury Tales,*
General Prologue, I (A), 285–303)

The Clerkes tale of Oxenforde

t Here is in the west syde of Itayle
Doun at the rute of Vesulus the colde
A lusty playn habundannt of vptayle
Where many a toun and toure thou mayst behold
That founded were in tyme of faders olde
And many a nother delytable sight
And Saluces this noble countre hight

A Marktes somtyme lord was of that londe
As were his worthy elders him bifore
And obeysaunt ay redy to his honde
Were alle his tieges bothe lasse and more
Thus in delyte he lyued and hath doo pore
Beloued and drabbe through fauoure of fortune
Bothe of his lordes and eke of his comune

Therwith he was to speke of lynage
The gentylleft y born of Lumbardy
A fayre parson a strong and pong of age
And ful of honoure and of curtefye

A woodcut of the Clerk from a fifteenth-century edition of *The Canterbury Tales*. Courtesy of the Glasgow University Library.

Chaucer provides us with several portraits of students from his time, the most fully formed of which is the Clerk. While the Oxford students from "The Reeve's Tale" are light-minded and seemingly only really interested in having a holiday from school work, and Nicholas from "The Miller's Tale" is equally concerned with seducing his landlord's wife, the Clerk is the portrait of the serious student who is more interested in the life of the mind, perhaps, than with the life around him.

His clothing is threadbare, as he obviously spends what little money he possesses on books, not clothes or possessions. Although his age is indeterminate, he has studied logic for a long time and teaches, which implies that he at least has a bachelor's degree. His career plans are uncertain, because he seems to not be directed toward an ecclesiastical post, as was the norm at that time. His character is serious and morally upright, yet not in a preaching way. He is quiet and shy and only speaks when it becomes necessary.

And yet, there seems to be more to him than meets the eye. His Envoy is quite cynical and almost proto-feminist, implying a much deeper understanding of the real world and human nature than his portrait in the General Prologue implied. He is also pleasingly acerbic and gives an indication that he might be more intellectually combative than his shy nature implies.

In short, the Clerk seems to indicate the development of a new kind of university student during Chaucer's time, one who is taking a degree for intellectual development and not for the pursuit of a Church position, a development that further illustrates the kind of modernization and democratization that is apparent in many of Chaucer's other characters.

See also Education; Philosophy

FURTHER READING

Astell, Ann W. *Chaucer and the Universe of Learning.* Ithaca, NY: Cornell University Press, 1996.

Brown, Peter, ed. *A Companion to Chaucer.* Malden, MA: Blackwell, 2002.

Gray, Douglas, ed. *The Oxford Companion to Chaucer.* New York: Oxford University Press, 2003.

Jeffery, Paul. *The Collegiate Churches of England and Wales.* London: Robert Hale, 2004.

King, Margot, H., and Wesley M. Stevens, eds. *Saints, Scholars, and Heroes: Studies in Medieval Culture in Honor of Charles W. Jones.* Collegeville, MN: Hill Monastic Manuscript Library, Saint John's Abbey and University, 1979.

Kircher, Timothy. *The Poet's Wisdom: The Humanists, the Church, and the Formation of Philosophy in the Early Renaissance.* Boston: Brill, 2006.

MacDonald, Alasdair A., and Michael W. Twonmey, eds. *Schooling and Society: The Ordering and Reordering of Knowledge in the Western Middle Ages.* Dudley, MA: Peeters, 2004.

Courtly Love

"Nay, God forbede a lovere shulde chaunge!"
The turtle seyde, and wex for shame al red,
"Though that his lady everemore be sraunge,
Yit lat hym serve hire ever, til he be ded.
Forsothe, I preyse nat the goses red;
For, though she deyede, I wolde non other make;
I wol ben hires, til that the deth me take."

"No, God forbid that a lover should change his mind!"
The turtledove said, and then blushed deeply for shame,
"Even if his lady should always remain a stranger to him,
Still let him serve her forever, until the day he dies.
Therefore, I cannot agree with the Goose's advice;
For, although my lady might be dead, I could not love another;
I will be hers until death finally takes me."

(*Parliament of Fowls*, 582–88)

L'amour courtois, or courtly love, is the modern term coined to describe the code and philosophy governing tender relations during the High Middle Ages. The precise source of the code is unclear, although many have speculated, including C. S. Lewis, that it evolved out of Platonic theory combined with Ovid's *Ars Amatoria* (*Art of Love*). Whatever its source, courtly love developed in the twelfth century in Provençal, at the courts of Marie de France and her famous mother, Eleanor of Aquitaine. The structure of feudal society, with its emphasis on chivalric behavior and noble intentions, nearly guaranteed that it would spread throughout Europe.

In the most basic structure of courtly love, a miserable lover pines for a woman who is, for varying reasons, apparently unobtainable. Although the lover is a brave and accomplished knight, falling in love renders him an emotional and physical wreck. He suffers from a feeling of great helplessness, loss of appetite, and inability to sleep. He sometimes collapses into a trembling and weeping heap, unable to control his emotional distress. He spends all of his time questioning his own self-worth and pondering the nature of love.

Eventually, he gains enough confidence to approach his lady love, at which point, there can be several potential resolutions. If the woman is married—and quite often the object of courtly love was a married woman—then she will remain unobtainable. However, she may bestow a favor upon the lover, who will now become strictly platonic although still worshipful, and allow him to serve her. If she is unattached, then she can either reject him outright or agree to accept his overtures. If she rejects him, the lover may call her cruel, but he will certainly also be crushed by her rejection, and the pain of his unrequited love will nearly ruin him.

If she accepts his attentions, the lady must be delicate. She cannot give in to him too quickly, lest she be called easy. Her most respectable course is to agree to spend time with him and to give him a "favor"—perhaps a ribbon or handkerchief that he can display on his helmet or sleeve. She must also agree to vows of secrecy and total faithfulness. In either case—rejection or acceptance—the lady is the dominant partner in this delicate dance, a position she will enjoy until she is married and becomes submissive.

Courtly love appears in many of Chaucer's works. The most obvious example of the courtly lover's suffering appears in *Troilus and Criseyde,* in which the aloof and nearly misogynistic Troilus becomes Criseyde's hopeless and suffering worshipper, only to be cruelly rejected by her apparent faithlessness by the end of the poem.

"The Franklin's Tale" tackles the issue of the married woman's role in the courtly love triangle, with the virtuous Dorigen fending off the persistent attentions of her lover Aurelius. In *The Parliament of Fowls,* the turtledove argues for courtly love conventions (*Parliament of Fowls,* 582–88).

"The Miller's Tale" and "The Merchant's Tale" both take a comic twist to the conventions of courtly love. "The Merchant's Tale" mocks the notion of the young knight wooing the unobtainable woman by having an old man foolishly imagine himself to be in the throes of cripplingly powerful love. "The Miller's Tale" pokes unrelenting fun at the figure of the inappropriate lover, Absolon, who is the fourth member of the story's love triangle of Alison, her husband John, and their young boarder Nicholas, a position that makes Absolon completely irrelevant. So ridiculous is he made to appear in his courting of Alison that he becomes the tale's punchline by unsuspectingly kissing a part of Alison that he did not expect:

This Absolon gan wype his mouth ful drie.
Derk was the nyght as pich, or as the cole,
And at the window out she putte hir hole,
And Absolon, hym fil no bet ne wers,
Fut with his mouth he kiste hir naked ers
Ful savourly, er he were war of this.

Abak he stirte, and thoughte it was amys,
For wel he wiste a womman hath no berd.
He felte a thing al rough and long yherd.

Then Absolon began to wipe his lips completely dry.
The night was as dark as pitch or as coal
And out of the window she put her hole,
And poor Absolon, completely unaware
With his mouth kissed her naked ass
Passionately, before he was aware of what was happening
He pulled back and thought something might be strange,
Because he knew that a woman has no beard,
Although he had felt something rough with long hair.

(*Canterbury Tales,*
"The Miller's Tale," I (A), 3730–38)

See also Chivalry; Marriage

FURTHER READING

Allen, Peter L. *The Art of Love: Amatory Fiction from Ovid to the* "Romance of the Rose." Philadelphia: University of Pennsylvania Press, 1992.

Barber, Richard. *The Reign of Chivalry.* Rochester, NY: Boydell Press, 2005.

Bumke, Joachim. *Courtly Culture.* New York: Overlook Press, 2000.

Burnley, J. D. *Courtliness and Literature in Medieval England.* New York: Longman, 1998.

Cantor, Norman. *The Civilization of the Middle Ages.* Rev. ed. New York: Harper Collins, 1993.

Duby, Georges. *Love and Marriage in the Middle* Ages. Translated by Jane Dunnett. Chicago: University of Chicago Press, 1988; reprinted in translation 1994.

Hallissy, Margaret. *Clean Maids, True Wives, Steadfast Widows: Chaucer's Women and Medieval Codes of Conduct.* Westport, CT: Greenwood Press, 1993.

Miller, Mark. *Philosophical Chaucer: Love, Sex, and Agency in the* "Canterbury Tales." New York: Cambridge University Press, 2004.

Porter, Pamela J. *Courtly Love in Medieval Manuscripts.* Toronto: University of Toronto Press, 2003.

Smith, Warren S., ed. *Satiric Advice on Women and Marriage: From Plautus to Chaucer.* Ann Arbor: University of Michigan Press, 2005.

Crow

My sone, thenk on the crowe, a Goddes name!
My sone, keep wel thy tonge, and keep thy freend.
A wikked tonge is worse than a feend;
My sone, from a feend men may hem blesse.
My sone, God of his endelees goodnesse

Walled a tonge with teeth and lippes eke,
For man sholde hym avyse what he speeke.
My sone, ful ofte, for to muche speche
Hath many a man been spilt, as clerkes teche,
But for litel speche avysely
Is no man shent, to speke generally.
My sone, thy tonge soldestow restreyne
At alle tymes.

My son, think of the crow, in God's name!
My son, hold your tongue and keep your friend.
A wicked tongue is worse than any devil;
My son, because at least you can cross yourself.
My son, God in his endless wisdom and goodness
Made walls for a tongue with teeth and lips,
So that a man should think twice before he speaks.
Too many times, my son, a man has been brought down
By saying too much, or so the monks tell us.
For never is it a bad idea to say too little.
So, my son, restrain your tongue from wanton speech
At all times.

(*Canterbury Tales,*
"The Manciple's Tale," 318–30)

Like doves, crows mate for life and are monogamous. However, it is rare to find one connected with romance in the manner of a turtledove. More often, crows are noted for their intelligence, a belief that they can predict the future, and for their habit of dining on the dead. With their sharp beaks and sharp eyes, crows often seem to know more than a bird should, while their black coloring and taste for carrion imbued them with certain devilish connotations during the Middle Ages.

It is the native intelligence of the crow that Chaucer references in "The Manciple's Tale," in which a snow white crow belongs to Phoebus Apollo. The crow was able to "countrefete the speche of every man / He koude, whan he sholde telle a tale" (*Mimic the speech of any man / Whenever he was telling a story*) (*Canterbury Tales,* "The Manciple's Tale," 134–5). Phoebus also had an adulterous wife, and the crow attempts to help his master by revealing the cuckoldry in his own home. In a fit of rage, Phoebus murders his wife. Then, in an equally passionate fit of remorse, he blames the crow for his own actions. As punishment for the crow's loose tongue, Phoebus takes away the bird's ability to talk and sing, and then replaces his beautiful white feathers with black ones. The moral of the story?

"My sone, thenk on the crowe, a Goddes name!
My sone, keep wel thy tonge, and keep thy freend."

"My son, think of the crow, in God's name!
My son, hold your tongue and keep your friend."

See also Animals; Birds

FURTHER READING

Rowland, Beryl. *Blind Beasts: Chaucer's Animal World*. Kent, OH: Kent State University Press, 1971.

Salisbury, Joyce E., ed. *The Medieval World of Nature: A Book of Essays*. New York: Garland, 1993.

Strickland, Debra Higgs. *Medieval Bestiaries: Text, Image, Ideology*. New York: Cambridge University Press, 1995.

Telesko, Werner. *The Wisdom of Nature: The Healing Powers and Symbolism of Plants and Animals in the Middle Ages*. New York: Prestel, 2001.

Cuckoo

"Ye, have the glotoun fild inow his puanche,
Thanne are we wel!" seyde the merlioun;
"Thow mortherere of the heysoge on the braunche
That broughte the forth, thow reufullest glotoun!
Lyve thow soleyn, wormes corupcioun,
For no fors is of lak of thy nature!
Go, lewed be thow whil the world may dure!"

"Yes, if the glutton has now filled up his belly,
then we are well!" said the merlin;
"You murderer of the hedge sparrow on the branch
That hatched you, you pitiful glutton!
Live you alone, worm's corruption,
Because nothing is beyond your bad nature!
Go on, be wicked while the world can endure you!"

(*Parliament of Fowls*, 610–16)

In the bird world, the cuckoo alone seems to represent no positive characteristics. It is described as wicked and ill-mannered. Most of the negative reputation of the cuckoo stems from its habit of laying eggs in other birds' nests. This, of course, makes it a thief and a home-wrecker, as it were. From this connotation grew the use of the cuckoo as the symbol of cuckoldry—another man bringing his own "goods" into another man's domestic life by sleeping with his wife.

Chaucer uses the cuckoo in *The Parliament of Fowls* in the original sense, calling it merely "unkynde" for laying its eggs in another birds' nest (*Par-*

liament of Fowls, 358). Yet, Chaucer is never one to let a double entendre slip past him, and he creates a dialogue between the noble merlin who seems to feel his lineage is threatened by the cuckoo. The connotation is obvious: a bird that can slip eggs into one's nest unnoticed can go far in sullying the dynastic line in much the same way an undetected male lover can get a woman pregnant while she passes the child off as her husband's.

See also Animals; Birds

FURTHER READING

Rowland, Beryl. *Blind Beasts: Chaucer's Animal World.* Kent, OH: Kent State University Press, 1971.

Salisbury, Joyce E., ed. *The Medieval World of Nature: A Book of Essays.* New York: Garland, 1993.

Strickland, Debra Higgs. *Medieval Bestiaries: Text, Image, Ideology.* New York: Cambridge University Press, 1995.

Telesko, Werner. *The Wisdom of Nature: The Healing Powers and Symbolism of Plants and Animals in the Middle Ages.* New York: Prestel, 2001.

D

Daedalus

Ne eke the wrechche Dedalus,
Ne his child, nyce Ykarus,
That fleigh so highe that the hete
Hys wynges malt, and he fel wete
In myd the see, and ther he dreynte,
For whom was maked moch compleynte.
  …
Tho gan I forth with hym to goon
Out of the castel, soth to seye.
Tho saugh y stonde in a valeye,
Under the castel, faste by,
An hous, that Domus Dedaly,
That Laboryntus cleped ys,
Nas mad so wonderlych, ywis,
Ne half so queyntelych ywrought.
And ever mo, as swyft as thought,
This queynte hous aboute wente,
That never mo hyt stille stente.

See the wretched Daedalus
And his son, the noble Icarus,

Daedalus

Who flew so high that the heat of the sun
Melted his wings
And he fell to earth in the middle of the sea
And there he was drowned
Much to his father's everlasting grief.
...

And I ventured for with him to go
Out of the castle, in order to see more.
There I saw in the valley
Beneath the castle, nearby
A house, the House of Daedalus
To which the labyrinth led
It was made so wonderingly, I saw,
Designed to be in constant motion
Changing its shape as quickly as thought does
This quaint little house twisted in the wind
And was never still or silent.

(*House of Fame*, 919–24; 1916–26)

Daedalus was an engineer and a craftsman in classical Greek myth. His talent gained him great prestige, but also was the cause of his downfall. The god Poseidon gave King Minos of Crete a beautiful white bull, which he intended Minos to sacrifice in his honor. Instead, Minos kept the bull for himself. Enraged, Poseidon decided to punish Minos by making his wife, Pasiphae, fall madly in love with the bull.

Pasiphae's desire was so overwhelming that she convinced Daedalus to fashion a wooden cow that she could climb inside in order to mate with the bull. She became pregnant and gave birth to Asterius the Minotaur. Minos, unaware of Daedalus's complicity in enabling the bestial union, asked the engineer to build a complex labyrinth to imprison Asterius. Eventually the truth came out and Minos exacted his revenge on Daedalus by imprisoning him in a tower with his son, Icarus.

Not being able to escape by sea, Daedalus contrived a means for the two to escape, building wings of feathers and wax for them both. Warning his son not to fly too close to the sun, lest the heat melt the wax, Daedalus and Icarus took flight. The boy, entranced by the experience of flying, drifted too high, his wings fell apart, and he plummeted to Earth. His father eventually found his body and, cursing his own ingenuity, buried the body, traveled to Sicily, and built a temple to Apollo where he hung up his own wings forever.

The story of Daedalus's flight from Crete appears in *The House of Fame* and the goddess Fama's house of pastel wicker whirling in the sky evokes an image of a bird cage that reminds us that those who seek fame are apt to fly too high and fall from their own overreaching pride, despite their exquisite talents.

See also Allusions, Classical; Fame

FURTHER READING

Brown, Peter, ed. *A Companion to Chaucer.* Malden, MA: Blackwell, 2002.

Frye, Northrop. *Biblical and Classical Myths: The Mythological Framework of Western Culture.* Buffalo, NY: University of Toronto Press, 2004.

Hansen, William F. *Classical Mythology: A Guide to the Mythical World of the Greeks and Romans.* New York: Oxford University Press, 2005.

Manser, Martin H. *The Facts On File Dictionary of Classical and Biblical Allusions.* New York: Facts On File, 2003.

Morford, Mark P. O. *Classical Mythology.* 7th ed. New York: Oxford University Press, 2003.

Nolan, Barbara. *Chaucer and the Tradition of the Roman Antique.* New York: Cambridge University Press, 1992.

Powell, Barry B. *Classical Myth.* Translated by Herbert M. Howe. 4th ed. Upper Saddle River, NJ: Pearson/Prentice Hall, 2004.

Price, Simon, and Emily Kearns, eds. *The Oxford Dictionary of Classical Myth and Religion.* New York: Oxford University Press, 2003.

Daily Life

A povre wydwe, somdeel stape in age,
Was whilom dwellyng in a narwe cotage,
Biside a grove, stondynge in a dale.
This wydwe, of which I tell yow my tale,
Syn thilke day that she was last a wyf
In pacience ladde a ful symple lyf,
For litel was hir catel and hir rente
By housbondrie of swich as God hire sente
She foonde hirself and eek hir doghtren two.
Thre large sowes hadde she, and namo,
Three keen, and eek a sheep that highte Malle.
Ful sooty was hire bour and eek hir halle,
In which she eet ful many a sklendre meel.
Of poynaunt sauce hir neded never a deel.
No deyntee morsel passed thurgh hir throte;
Hir diete was accordant to hir cote.
Repleccioun ne made hire nevere sik;
Attempree diete was al hir phisik,
And exercise, and hertes suffisaunce,
The goute lette hire nothyng for to daunce,
N'apoplexie shente nat hir heed.
No wyn ne drank she, neither whit ne reed;
Hir bord was served moost with whit and blak—
Milk and broun breed, in which she foond no lak,

Seynd bacoun, and somtyme an ey or tweye,
For she was, as it were, a maner deye.

A poor widow, well advanced in age,
Lived in a narrow little cottage,
In the middle of a dale, beside a grove of trees.
This widow, of whom I tell my tale,
Ever since the last day that she was a wife
Had lived a good and simple life.
She had few needs, and only a little money for her rent
And by careful husbandry she made the most of what God sent her
To take care of herself and her two daughters.
She had three large sows, as well as
Three cows and a sheep named Moll.
Her bedroom and her hall were both thick with soot,
For there she had eaten many a tiny meal.
She never needed piquant sauces on her food
And no delicate morsel ever passed her lips
Her diet was like the place she lived, simple,
So she never suffered from eating too much.
A temperate diet was her only medicine,
Along with exercise and a happy heart.
Gout never stopped her from dancing
And apoplexy never hurt her head.
She never drank wine, neither white nor red.
Her board was mostly served with white and black—
Milk and brown bread, which she never lacked
Some bacon and sometimes an egg or two;
Because she was, above all, a dairy woman.

(*Canterbury Tales,*
"The Nun's Priest's Tale," VII, 2821–46)

For the average medieval peasant, life was dictated by the passage of the seasons and the daily boundaries imposed by the rising and setting of the sun and the overarching structure provided by the Church. The summer and fall were the busiest times of the year, with harvest time coming in August and continuing into September, and the fall occupied with planting the winter crop and slaughtering and preserving meat for the coming months. The other seasons were occupied with other plantings, frequent plowing, sheep shearing and lambing, dairy responsibilities, and the repair and maintenance of buildings and hedges.

Throughout all of these times, the calendar was punctuated with feast days, or holidays, that bound a village in some common activity. The three most important holidays were Christmas, Easter, and Pentecost, which occurred 50 days after Easter. In addition, there were a number of saints' days that were celebrated to varying extent throughout the year. These days provided a welcome break in the calendar and a chance for village camaraderie.

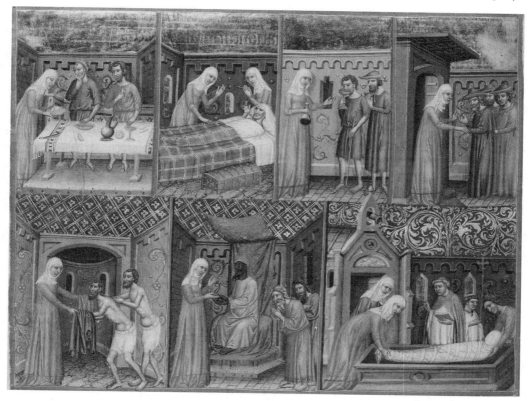

Scenes from a fifteenth-century manuscript of daily life; a woman setting the table for two poor men, visiting a patient, giving a drink to two prisoners, accommodating travelers, giving away clothing, repurchasing prisoners, and burying a corpse. © Bibliothèque nationale de France.

The typical peasant rose at or before dawn. He or she would rise, say a quick prayer, and wash face and hands. A light breakfast was optional, and some waited several hours to have a break in the fields. The midday meal, called dinner, consisted mainly of bread and cheese. Bread was the staple of peasant diets, and it was of the rough variety, not the refined white bread of the nobility.

The hours were long, usually sunrise to sunset, and peasants were in the fields in rain or shine not only to make sure the harvest would sustain the family throughout the winter but also to cover the rent to the overlord. Those who did not work as farmers also put in long hours at their particular trades, such as millers or blacksmiths.

The sun dictated the length of each day, as candles, even tallow, were expensive. Therefore, peasants made use of every moment of daylight to accomplish their necessary tasks. Bells were the closest thing to a clock that they experienced in their lives. The work week began on Monday, with Friday set aside for religious penance, symbolized by the prohibition of any meat other than fish.

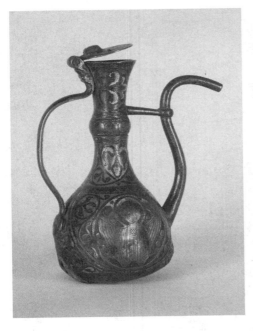

Late-eighteenth-century copper burette. © Bibliothèque nationale de France.

Sunday was to be spent in enforced leisure, with church services in the morning followed by a mass later that day. Everyone in the village was expected to attend. While many believed that any nonreligious activity during the rest of the day was wicked, many spent their one day off having fun.

The home of the average peasant was simple—a wood frame filled with wattle and daub, or rubble and straw, covered in clay. Roofs were almost always thatched, although in some areas, slate was possible. If a family was very poor, the cottage was a single room; however, cottages usually had two rooms—one for cooking and the other for everything else. This afforded the family members little privacy, which meant that activities that we disguise behind closed doors were performed in front of the entire family. In cold weather, the need to remain near the centrally located fire meant even less privacy as the family crowded around the sole heat source.

The only work of Chaucer's that provides a glimpse into the life of a peasant is "The Nun's Priest's Tale," in which the widow's simple life is described (*Canterbury Tales,* "The Nun's Priest's Tale," VII, 2821–46).

See also Calendar; Private Houses

Masons building a tower while nobels watch; from the Isabella Breviary, presented to Queen Isabella of Spain by Francisco de Roias, ca. 1497. © Erich Lessing / Art Resource, NY.

FURTHER READING

Bowden, Muriel. *A Reader's Guide to Geoffrey Chaucer.* Syracuse, NY: Syracuse University Press, 2001.

Brewer, Derek. *Chaucer and His World.* Cambridge: D. S. Brewer, 1978; reprinted 1992.

Britnell, Richard, ed. *Daily Life in the Late Middle Ages.* Stroud, England: Sutton, 1998.

DeWindt, Edwin Brezette, ed. *The Salt of Common Life: Individuality and Choice in the Medieval Town, Countryside, and Church: Essays Presented to J. Ambrose Raftis.* Kalamazoo: Medieval Institute Publications, Western Michigan University, 1995.

Duby, Georges. *The Three Orders: Feudal Society Imagined.* Translated by Arthur Goldhammer. Chicago: University of Chicago Press, 1980; reprinted 1982.

Dyer, Christopher. *Making a Living in the Middle Ages: The People of Britain 850–1520.* New Haven, CT: Yale University Press, 2002.

French, Katherine L. *The People of the Parish: Community Life in a Late Medieval English Diocese.* Philadelphia: University of Pennsylvania Press, 2001.

Masschaele, James. *Peasants, Merchants, and Markets: Inland Trade in Medieval England, 1150–1350.* New York: St. Martin's Press, 1997.

Morgan, Gwyneth. *Life in a Medieval Village.* New York: Cambridge University Press, 1975.

Power, Eileen. *Medieval People.* New York: Barnes and Noble, 1924; reprinted 1968.

Singman, Jeffrey L., and Will McLean. *Daily Life in Chaucer's England.* Westport, CT: Greenwood Press, 1995.

Daniel

During the Babylonian captivity of the Jews, Daniel (Old Testament) acted as adviser to both the Jews and the foreign kings who ruled until the reign of Cyrus the Great. Daniel had possibly been castrated in Nebuchadnezzar's court. His most famous moment is when he was cast into a lions' den for praying to God at a time when making requests from anyone but Darius was prohibited. When Daniel emerged unharmed, he gained new respect for the god of the Israelites. He is mentioned several times in *The Canterbury Tales,* usually in reference to the idea that God watches out for the faithful.

Such is the case with "The Man of Law's Tale." Daniel's story was mentioned in "The Monk's Tale" and "The Parson's Tale," both times in reference to dreams.

FURTHER READING

Brown, Peter, ed. *A Companion to Chaucer.* Malden, MA: Blackwell, 2002.

Frye, Northrop. *Biblical and Classical Myths: The Mythological Framework of Western Culture.* Buffalo, NY: University of Toronto Press, 2004.

Manser, Martin H. *The Facts On File Dictionary of Classical and Biblical Allusions.* New York: Facts On File, 2003.

Daphne

The daughter of Peneus, Daphne was pursued by Apollo, whom she did not desire. When it became apparent that he would finally capture her against her will, she prayed frantically to Diana, who turned her into a laurel tree. In honor of her, Apollo adopted the laurel as one of his personal symbols.

Daphne is mentioned in "The Knight's Tale"; her story is depicted on the walls of Diana's temple, where Emily prays before the tournament that will decide who will win her hand in marriage. Emily prays not to marry at all. In *Troilus and Criseyde*, Troilus appeals to Apollo based on his love of Daphne, to help him with the love of Criseyde: "O Phebus, think whan Dane hireselven shette / Under the bark, and laurer wax for drede; / Yet for hire lov, O help now at this nede!" (*O Phoebus, think about when Diana shut your love / under the bark of the tree / If only for that love, please help me now in my time of need!*) (*Troilus and Criseyde*, Book III, 726–28).

FURTHER READING

Brown, Peter, ed. *A Companion to Chaucer.* Malden, MA: Blackwell, 2002.

Frye, Northrop. *Biblical and Classical Myths: The Mythological Framework of Western Culture.* Buffalo, NY: University of Toronto Press, 2004.

Hansen, William F. *Classical Mythology: A Guide to the Mythical World of the Greeks and Romans.* New York: Oxford University Press, 2005.

Manser, Martin H. *The Facts On File Dictionary of Classical and Biblical Allusions.* New York: Facts On File, 2003.

Morford, Mark P. O. *Classical Mythology.* 7th ed. New York: Oxford University Press, 2003.

Nolan, Barbara. *Chaucer and the Tradition of the Roman Antique.* New York: Cambridge University Press, 1992.

Powell, Barry B. *Classical Myth.* Translated by Herbert M. Howe. 4th ed. Upper Saddle River, NJ: Pearson/Prentice Hall, 2004.

Price, Simon, and Emily Kearns, eds. *The Oxford Dictionary of Classical Myth and Religion.* New York: Oxford University Press, 2003.

Deianira

The daughter of King Oeneus of Calydon and Queen Althea, Deianira was loved by both Hercules and the river god Achelous. As the result of a wrestling match in which Achelous took the form of a centaur, Hercules won her hand in marriage.

Once, when the couple was traveling, the centaur Nessus fell in lust with Deianira and tried to kidnap her. Hercules killed him with a poisoned arrow, and, in his dying moments, Nessus gave Deianira his robe, stained with his poisoned blood. He told her that it would reawaken Hercules's love for her should he ever stray in his affections. Eventually, Deianira feared that Hercules had abandoned her for the love of another and she sent him the robe as a gift. Although the poisoned robe did not kill him, it caused him such pain that he killed himself. Deianira, distressed by what she had done out of jealousy and insecurity, committed suicide as well.

Deianira receives differing treatments in Chaucer. She is one of the wicked wives in the Wife of Bath's husband's book (*Canterbury Tales,* "The Wife of Bath's Tale," Book III (D), 725–26). However, in most of Chaucer's works, she is either characterized as unaware or completely blameless because Hercules betrayed her first. She is included in Hercules's biography in "The Monk's Tale":

A lemman hadde this noble champoiun,
That highte Dianira, fressh as May;
And as thise clerkes maken mencioun,
She hath hym sent a sherte, fressh and gay.
Allas, this sherte—allas and weylaway!—
Envenymed was so subtilly withalle
That er that he had wered it half a day
It made his flessh al from his bones falle.
But natheless somme clerkes hire excusen
By oon that highte Nessus, that it maked.
Be as be may, I wol hire noght accusen.

A lady love had this noble champion
Whose name was Deianira. She was as fresh as May.
And as many monks mention in books,
She sent him a beautiful shirt, embroidered and lovely.
Alas, this terrible shirt—tragically—
Was saturated with poison, subtley
So that after he had worn it half a day
It made all of his skin peel away from his body.
But despite that many monks excuse her of guilt
Because the wicked man Nessus tricked her with the shirt.
No matter what she did, I cannot accuse her of wrongdoing.

(*Canterbury Tales,*
"The Monk's Tale," VIII, 2119–26)

The prologue to "The Man of Law's Tale" mentions Deianira as one of women from *The Legend of Good Women.* However, she has no story in that work.

FURTHER READING

Brown, Peter, ed. *A Companion to Chaucer.* Malden, MA: Blackwell, 2002.
Frye, Northrop. *Biblical and Classical Myths: The Mythological Framework of Western Culture.* Buffalo, NY: University of Toronto Press, 2004.
Hansen, William F. *Classical Mythology: A Guide to the Mythical World of the Greeks and Romans.* New York: Oxford University Press, 2005.
Manser, Martin H. *The Facts On File Dictionary of Classical and Biblical Allusions.* New York: Facts On File, 2003.

Morford, Mark P. O. *Classical Mythology*. 7th ed. New York: Oxford University Press, 2003.

Nolan, Barbara. *Chaucer and the Tradition of the Roman Antique*. New York: Cambridge University Press, 1992.

Powell, Barry B. *Classical Myth*. Translated by Herbert M. Howe. 4th ed. Upper Saddle River, NJ: Pearson/Prentice Hall, 2004.

Price, Simon, and Emily Kearns, eds. *The Oxford Dictionary of Classical Myth and Religion*. New York: Oxford University Press, 2003.

Demophon

The son of Theseus of Athens and Phaedra, Demophon fought for Greece in the siege of Troy. He rescued his grandmother, who had been taken as a slave when Helen was kidnapped. On his return voyage to Athens, Demophon was shipwrecked on Rhodope, where its queen Phyllis—who was in love with him—gave him money and supplies. When he left to return home, it was with the promise that they would marry. However, once home, he forgot his vows and the heartbroken Phyllis hanged herself in despair.

Demophon is mentioned in both *The House of Fame* and *The Legend of Good Women*, both times in regard to his betrayal of Phyllis:

======================

Loo Demophon, duk of Athenys,
How he forswor hym ful falsly,
And traysed Phillis wikkidly,
That kynges doghtre was of Trace,
And falsly gan hys terme pace;
And when she wiste that he was fals,
She heng hirself ryght be the hals,
For he had doon hir such untrouthe.
Loo, was not this a woo and routhe?

See Demophon, the Duke of Athens,
And how he swore his love falsely
And wickedly treated Phyllis,
The king of Thrace's daughter,
And let the time pass when
He had promised to send for her.
And when she realized that he was false
She hanged herself right in the palace halls,
For he had lied to her.
Indeed, was this not tragic and awful?

(*House of Fame*, 388–96)

======================

The narrator in *The Book of the Duchess* also mentions Demophon when he tells the Black Knight that, if he kills himself, he will be damned just as Phyllis was.

FURTHER READING

Brown, Peter, ed. *A Companion to Chaucer.* Malden, MA: Blackwell, 2002.

Frye, Northrop. *Biblical and Classical Myths: The Mythological Framework of Western Culture.* Buffalo, NY: University of Toronto Press, 2004.

Hansen, William F. *Classical Mythology: A Guide to the Mythical World of the Greeks and Romans.* New York: Oxford University Press, 2005.

Manser, Martin H. *The Facts On File Dictionary of Classical and Biblical Allusions.* New York: Facts On File, 2003.

Morford, Mark P. O. *Classical Mythology.* 7th ed. New York: Oxford University Press, 2003.

Nolan, Barbara. *Chaucer and the Tradition of the Roman Antique.* New York: Cambridge University Press, 1992.

Powell, Barry B. *Classical Myth.* Translated by Herbert M. Howe. 4th ed. Upper Saddle River, NJ: Pearson/Prentice Hall, 2004.

Price, Simon, and Emily Kearns, eds. *The Oxford Dictionary of Classical Myth and Religion.* New York: Oxford University Press, 2003.

Dentistry. *See* Medicine

Disease. *See* Medicine

Dog

Man's best friend was a symbol, in the Middle Ages as now, of loyalty and fidelity. Dogs appeared on effigies of noblemen, lying faithfully at the feet of their masters for eternity. Increasingly, during the late medieval period, as the rising middle class took on the trappings of nobility, dogs of the wealthy gentry became equally powerful symbols of power and riches. The greyhound, in particular, was a popular medieval canine symbol of the noble life-style, because the dogs were not only devoted but also expensive and useful for hunting—all attributes that were important to the aristocracy.

Chaucer provides readers with a pointed clue to the character of the monk when he writes: "Grehounds he hadde as swifte as fowel in flight; / Of prikyng and of huntyng for the hare / Was al his lust, for no cost wolde he spare" (*He had greyhounds who were as swift as an eagle in flight / which he used for hunting hares / Hunting was his consuming passion, and he would spare no cost on his hobby*) (*Canterbury Tales,* General Prologue, I (A), 190–92). This reference, in fact, is the first to dogs in vernacular English literature.

Interestingly, greyhounds were never associated with women. Instead, as is the case of the Prioress, lapdogs, symbols of domestic faithfulness, were a woman's natural companions. The Prioress lavishes an unseemly degree of attention on her little dogs, demonstrating that her priorities are misplaced: "Of smale houndes hadde she that she fedde / With rosted flessh, or milk and wastel-breed. / But soore wepte she if oon of hem were deed, / Or if men smoot it with a yerde smerte" (*A few small dogs she kept, which she fed / on roasted meat and milk and fine white bread / and she would weep bitterly if one of them died / or if a man kicked or hit one*) (*Canterbury Tales,* General Prologue, I (A), 146–49). Chaucer continues by making it clear that her soft heart where her dogs are concerned is an attribute more suited to court life than the convent, where pets are essentially forbidden.

FURTHER READING

Rowland, Beryl. *Blind Beasts: Chaucer's Animal World.* Kent, OH: Kent State University Press, 1971.

Salisbury, Joyce E., ed. *The Medieval World of Nature: A Book of Essays.* New York: Garland, 1993.

Strickland, Debra Higgs. *Medieval Bestiaries: Text, Image, Ideology.* New York: Cambridge University Press, 1995.

Telesko, Werner. *The Wisdom of Nature: The Healing Powers and Symbolism of Plants and Animals in the Middle Ages.* New York: Prestel, 2001.

Dove

The dove is perhaps the most Christian of animal symbols, along with the lamb. It not only is the bringer of safety and peace in the ark story, sent to find land and bringing an olive branch back, it also represents the Holy Spirit, as God took the form of a dove to appear before Christ at his baptism.

In a broader context, gentle seed-eating doves are considered symbols of kindness and placidity. Their mournful call invests them with an aura of calm melancholy. And the habit of doves of choosing a single mate for life has connected them to romantic love, as they are in *The Parliament of Fowls:*

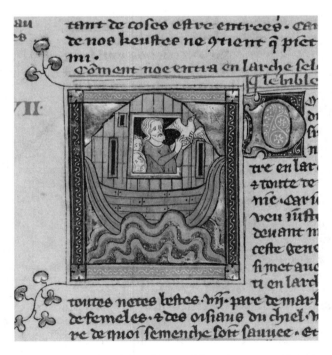

Noah releases the dove, from a fifteenth-century French manuscript. © Bibliothèque nationale de France.

"Nay, God forbede a lovere shulde chaunge!"
The turtle seyde, and wex for shame al red,
"Though that his lady everemore be straunge,
Yit lat him serve hire ever, til he be ded."

"No, God forbid that a lover should change his mind!"
The turtledove said, and then blushed deeply for shame,
"Even if his lady should always remain a stranger to him,
Still let him serve her forever, until the day he dies."

(*Parliament of Fowls*, 582–85)

See also Animals; Birds

Further Reading

Rowland, Beryl. *Blind Beasts: Chaucer's Animal World.* Kent, OH: Kent State University Press, 1971.

Salisbury, Joyce E., ed. *The Medieval World of Nature: A Book of Essays.* New York: Garland, 1993.

Strickland, Debra Higgs. *Medieval Bestiaries: Text, Image, Ideology.* New York: Cambridge University Press, 1995.

Telesko, Werner. *The Wisdom of Nature: The Healing Powers and Symbolism of Plants and Animals in the Middle Ages.* New York: Prestel, 2001.

Dreams

For which he for Sibille his suster sente,
That called was Cassandre ek al about,
And al his drem he tolde hire er he stente,
And hire bisoughte assoilen hym the doute
Of the stronge boor with tuskes stoute;
And fynaly, withinne a litel stounde,
Cassandre hym gan right thus his drem expounde:

For which he sent for his sister Cassandra
Who was a Sybil,
And he told her his dream before he lost his nerve,
And asked her to explain to him the meaning
Of the fierce boar with huge tusks;
And finally, after a little while to think,
Cassandra became to tell him what his dream meant.

(*Troilus and Criseyde*, Book V, 1450–1540)

Dreams in the Middle Ages were generally considered to be possible messages from another world, either the supernatural realm of God, or the next life. For the dreamer, the thought that God might be communicating with him or her was flattering, yet stressful at the same time. The Bible demonstrated that dreams were often prophecies of impending danger—it was rare that a dream foretold good news or happy events. However, comfort could be taken from the implications of predestination that were contained in the prophetic dream. If a dream could foretell the future, then both the dream and the event it predicted had to have been known and controlled by a God who was omniscient.

Dreams are a key element and framing device in Chaucer's works. *The House of Fame, The Book of the Duchess,* and *The Parliament of Fowls* all begin with a narrator who reads a book that inspires a dream that encompasses the plot of the poem. Dreams also play important roles in the narrative flow of his other works. In *Troilus and Criseyde,* for instance, Troilus asks his sister Cassandra to interpret his dream (*Troilus and Criseyde,* Book V, 1450–1540).

One of the more amusing uses of dreams in Chaucer is the debate between Chauntecleer and his wife Pertelote over the nature of his dreams. While she believes that dreams are simply a psychological symptom of a humoral imbalance, Chauntecleer maintains that they are prophecies:

as touching daun Catoun,
That hath of wysdom swich a greet renoun,
Though that he bad no dremes for to drede,
By God, men may in olde books rede
Of many a man moore of auctorite
Than evere Caton was, so moot I thee,
That al the revers seyn of this experience
That dremes been significaciouns
As well of joye as of tribuloacouns
That folk enduren in this lif present.

As touching upon Cato,
Who has such great reknown as a wise man
Although he may have said that bad dreams are nothing to dread,
Nevertheless, men may read in old books
Of many men of more authority
Than ever Cato was on this subject, so your point is moot,
As they all say the opposite
That dreams are significant signs
Of happiness to come as well as trouble
That people endure in their daily lives.

(*Canterbury Tales,*
"The Nun's Priest's Tale," VII, 2882–3171)

See also Allegory and Dream Visions; Allusions, Biblical; Allusions, Classical

FURTHER READING

Bowden, Muriel. *A Reader's Guide to Geoffrey Chaucer.* Syracuse, NY: Syracuse University Press, 2001.

Brown, Peter, ed. *A Companion to Chaucer.* Malden, MA: Blackwell, 2002.

Gray, Douglas, ed. *The Oxford Companion to Chaucer.* New York: Oxford University Press, 2003.

Lerer, Seth, ed. *The Yale Companion to Chaucer.* New Haven, CT: Yale University Press, 2006.

St. John, Michael. *Chaucer's Dream Visions: Courtliness and Individual Identity.* Burlington, VT: Ashgate, 2000.

Drink. *See* Food

E

Eagle

===============

"Soun ys noght but eyr ybroken;
And every speche that ys spoken,
Lowd or pryvee, foul or fair,
In his substaunce ys but air;
For as flaumbe ys but lyghted smoke,
Ryght soo soun ys air ybroke.
But this may be in many wyse,
Of which I wil the twoo devyse,
As soun that cometh of pipe or harpe.
For whan a pipe is blowen sharpe
The air ys twyst with violence
And rent—loo, thys ys my sentence.
Eke whan men harpe-strynges smyte,
Whether hyt e moche or lyte,
Loo, with the strok the ayr tobreketh;
And ryght so breketh it when men speketh."

"Sound is nothing but air broken
And every speech that is made,
Loud or private, beautiful or lewd,
Is at its foundation, merely air.

Just as flames are only lighted smoke,
Thus is sound merely air broken and disturbed.
But this might be in many ways,
Two of which I will explain,
Just as when sound comes out of a pipe or a harpe.
For when a pipe is blown sharply
The air is twisted with violence
And torn asunder—yes, this is what I mean.
And when a man strikes the harp strings
Whether he does it hard or lightly,
With this stroke the air is broken
And thus it is like when men speak.

(*House of Fame,* Book II, 765–80)

In medieval bestiaries, the eagle is said to be able to stare into the sun without blinking, emphasizing its sharp eye. In Christian symbolism, the eagle is said to possess the ability to gaze unflinchingly into the divine light of God. The eagle is also said in old age to have the ability to regenerate itself, much like a phoenix, flying up into the sun and burning its wings, then plunging into water, emerging young and whole. These stories demonstrate a certain purity about the eagle. It is a bird of prey, yet it is noble like a human hunter rather than rapacious like a wolf.

None of Chaucer's works appear to reflect the usual symbolism of the eagle. However, he does characterize it as a noble and wise bird, one that is the worthiest of all avians. In *The House of Fame,* the dreamer travels in the claws of a golden eagle, a rather chatty guide who might represent Philosophy. High above the world, the poet contemplates the fleeting nature of Fame and the effect of rumor on long-standing reputation (see above).

In *The Parliament of Fowls,* three tercel eagles appear before a court of mixed birds on Valentine's Day, vying for the hand (talon?) of the beautiful formel eagle. Although many of the birds weigh in, providing advice to the female as to which of the males she should choose, in the end she asks the Goddess of Nature for one year to decide and the court is adjourned.

See also Animals; Birds; Wolf

FURTHER READING

Rowland, Beryl. *Blind Beasts: Chaucer's Animal World.* Kent, OH: Kent State University Press, 1971.

Salisbury, Joyce E., ed. *The Medieval World of Nature: A Book of Essays.* New York: Garland, 1993.

Strickland, Debra Higgs. *Medieval Bestiaries: Text, Image, Ideology.* New York: Cambridge University Press, 1995.

Telesko, Werner. *The Wisdom of Nature: The Healing Powers and Symbolism of Plants and Animals in the Middle Ages.* New York: Prestel, 2001.

Echo

Echo used her powers of chatter to distract Hera/Juno while Jupiter/Zeus seduced some of her fellow nymphs. Hera punished the beautiful Echo by preventing her from ever speaking unless spoken to first. Echo fell into unrequited love for the self-absorbed Narcissus, eventually pining away until she became nothing but a voice. In "The Clerk's Tale," her story is mentioned as a cautionary parable:

Folweth Ekko, that holdeth no silence,
But evere answereth at the countretaille.
Beth nat bidaffed for youre innocence,
But sharply taak on yow the governaille.
Emprenteth wel this lessoun in youre mynde,
For commune profit sith it may availle.

Be like Echo, and never keep silent,
Forever counter his every statement,
And never keep quiet and innocent,
But instead sharply rebuff him and take the upper hand.
Imprint this lesson well on your mind
Because it will very likely profit you some day.

(*Canterbury Tales,*
"The Clerk's Tale," IV (E), 1189–94)

In "The Franklin's Tale," Aurelius compares his situation to that of Echo when she hopelessly loved Narcissus (*Canterbury Tales,* "The Franklin's Tale," V (F), 949–52). In *The Book of the Duchess,* the negative consequences of Echo's love for Narcissus are mentioned to the Black Knight to help him recover from his grief: "And Ecquo died for Narcisus / Nolde nat love hir, and ryght thus / Hath many another foly doon" (*And Echo died for love of Narcissus, / Who did not love her back, and so you see / How many a folly leads to another*) (*Book of the Duchess,* 735–37).

FURTHER READING

Brown, Peter, ed. *A Companion to Chaucer.* Malden, MA: Blackwell, 2002.

Frye, Northrop. *Biblical and Classical Myths: The Mythological Framework of Western Culture.* Buffalo, NY: University of Toronto Press, 2004.

Hansen, William F. *Classical Mythology: A Guide to the Mythical World of the Greeks and Romans.* New York: Oxford University Press, 2005.

Manser, Martin H. *The Facts On File Dictionary of Classical and Biblical Allusions.* New York: Facts On File, 2003.

Morford, Mark P. O. *Classical Mythology.* 7th ed. New York: Oxford University Press, 2003.

Nolan, Barbara. *Chaucer and the Tradition of the Roman Antique*. New York: Cambridge University Press, 1992.

Powell, Barry B. *Classical Myth*. Translated by Herbert M. Howe. 4th ed. Upper Saddle River, NJ: Pearson/Prentice Hall, 2004.

Price, Simon, and Emily Kearns, eds. *The Oxford Dictionary of Classical Myth and Religion*. New York: Oxford University Press, 2003.

Education

A CLERK ther was of Oxenford also,
That unto logyk hadde longe ygo.
As leene was his hors as is a rake,
And he nas right fat, I undertake,
But looked holwe, and therto sobrely.
Ful thredbare was his overeste courtepy,
For he hadde geten hym yet no benefice,
New was so worldy for to have office.
For hym was levere have at his beddes heed
Twenty bookes, clad in blak or reed,
Or Aristotle and his philosophie
Than robes riche, or fithele, or gay sautrie.

There was a scholar from Oxford too,
Who was studying logic, but had not taken his degree.
His horse was as lean as a rake,
And the scholar himself was not fat either, let me tell you.
He looked hollow and, because of it, serious and sober.
His overcoat was threadbare
Because he had not yet gotten himself an income,
Being too devoted to study to find an office.
For he would much rather have at the head of his bed
Twenty books, bound in black or red leather,
By Aristotle and his philosophy
Than to have rich robes, or a fiddle, or even a beautiful psaltery.

(*Canterbury Tales*,
General Prologue, I (A), 285–97)

Education in the Middle Ages was both familiar and foreign to our structured system of today. The university is essentially a medieval invention, and the plan of study followed at one comprised what continues to be the liberal arts curriculum, with some minor alterations that have been adopted to fit the modern world.

Certainly, education today is far more egalitarian. In the Middle Ages, only the children of the elite—whether the aristocracy or, increasingly by Chaucer's day, the wealthy middle class—and essentially only the boys, received any substantive education. Girls typically learned some rudimentary lessons in Church doctrine, and then finished their studies with useful skills for taking on their adult roles as wives and managers of their husbands' homes.

For all children, both boys and girls, the first steps in education were basic prayers and doctrines. They were taught the Apostles' Creed, the Ten Commandments, the Two Laws of the Gospel, and the four sevens of the Church: Virtues, Deadly Sins, Sacraments, and Works of Bodily Mercy. Boys were taught to read initially, then perhaps how to write. Literacy was fairly rare in Chaucer's day, and, by the fifteenth century, a comfortable estimate of male literacy hovers around 10 percent. Some learned only to read haltingly, without comprehension, while some mastered reading, but

The four tenants of teaching young people: reading, drawing, combat, and song. © Bibliothèque nationale de France.

never writing. A few were able to tackle all aspects of literacy, which was required for entry into a university, where students would take a formal degree.

Boys entered the university at the age of 14. They would study the liberal arts, which were divided into the trivium and the quadrivium. The first comprised grammar, dialectic, and rhetoric—the speaking arts. The quadrivium included arithmetic, music, astronomy, and geometry.

Mastering this plan of education took approximately 8 years, 6 of which were devoted entirely to lectures, followed by 2 years of disputations and exams. The bachelor's degree would then be awarded around the age of 22. If the student wanted to continue, an additional year was required for a master's degree; for a professional degree such as law, theology, or medicine, an additional 12 years was required.

The first institutions of higher learning were colleges, which began as something roughly akin to boarding schools, providing students and lifelong scholars with a place to live and develop intellectually together. Funded by private individuals, they were designed to provide for informal sharing

The entrance to the Sorbonne. Courtesy of Lisa Kirchner.

of ideas. Eventually, many would develop a formal course of study, and they would coalesce into larger universities (which is why today universities like Oxford and Cambridge continue to be comprised of several smaller colleges).

The first real university appeared in Paris in the early twelfth century (although it would not be formally confirmed until the thirteenth). It was known initially as the University of Paris, but ultimately came to bear the name of its earliest benefactor, Robert de Sorbonne. It was soon followed by the University of Bologne, which would house the preeminent law school in Europe.

The Sorbonne followed the guild model in order to gain legal distinction for itself as an entity, which enabled it to be independent of other institutions, including the Church. The Church, however, could still place pressure on the university to try to control elements of its curriculum, creating a tense connection in which the Church could declare certain materials forbidden, but the university could not be disbanded for disobedience.

Oxford and Cambridge both trace their roots as formal universities to the early thirteenth century as well. Oxford, modeled after the University of Paris, has no clear date of formal founding, but it can claim to have its start in 1187, when Henry II banned English students from studying at Paris. Its masters, however, were not recognized as part of a corporation until 1231.

Throughout the thirteenth century, Oxford expanded to create the many colleges that are still in existence today, providing its students and scholars with residence halls. Balliol and Merton Colleges are its oldest. Almost from its inception, Oxford gained a reputation for academic excellence as well as controversy. Chaucer's age would encompass both of these, as during the fourteenth century, Oxford employed John Wycliffe as Master of Balliol while Edward III recognized the university for its contribution to learning.

Cambridge claims its earliest date as an institution of learning as 1209. The first college within Cambridge, Peterhouse, was founded by the Bishop of Ely in 1347, making it a relatively new institution formally during Chaucer's day. The tensions of town and gown are illustrated, in fact, in several of *The Canterbury Tales,* notably "The Miller's Tale" and "The Reeve's Tale," in which students outfox ordinary tradesmen.

The life of the university student in Chaucer's time was far less structured than it became in subsequent centuries. During these years, the liberal arts were studied without professors. Students who had passed the course of study themselves and were now known as masters were approved by their peers to teach. Education took the form of reading and explaining texts through lecture and disputation. All exams were conducted orally.

Those masters who passed through the entire curriculum and took advanced degrees in medicine, theology, or law became doctors. In order to differentiate themselves from the townsfolk and between their varying ranks of doctor, master, and student, varying styles and colors of the gown, hood, and cap became an instant indicator and have survived to this day.

Chaucer's Clerk is an example of the sober intellectual philosophical student who cares only for the life of the mind in many ways, preferring to spend his money on books rather than on clothing or other amenities. In contrast are the light-minded and randy students from "The Reeve's Tale," who use their intelligence to outsmart the miller economically while also seducing his wife and daughter under his own roof.

See also Childhood; Law; Lollardy

FURTHER READING

Astell, Ann W. *Chaucer and the Universe of Learning.* Ithaca, NY: Cornell University Press, 1996.

Brown, Peter, ed. *A Companion to Chaucer.* Malden, MA: Blackwell, 2002.

Gray, Douglas, ed. *The Oxford Companion to Chaucer.* New York: Oxford University Press, 2003.

Jeffery, Paul. *The Collegiate Churches of England and Wales.* London: Robert Hale, 2004.

King, Margot, H., and Wesley M. Stevens, eds. *Saints, Scholars, and Heroes: Studies in Medieval Culture in Honor of Charles W. Jones.* Collegeville, MN: Hill Monastic Manuscript Library, Saint John's Abbey and University, 1979.

Kircher, Timothy. *The Poet's Wisdom: The Humanists, the Church, and the Formation of Philosophy in the Early Renaissance*. Boston: Brill, 2006.

MacDonald, Alasdair A., and Michael W. Twonmey, eds. *Schooling and Society: The Ordering and Reordering of Knowledge in the Western Middle Ages*. Dudley, MA: Peeters, 2004.

Orme, Nicholas. *English Schools in the Middle Ages*. London: Methuen, 1973.

Edward III

Edward III (1312–77) was the first-born son of the ill-fated Edward II (1284–1327) and Isabella of France (1296–1358). Edward took the throne at the age of 14 after his father's forced abdication and probable murder at the hands of Isabella and her lover, Roger Mortimer, the Earl of March. In this capacity, young Edward would become the first king to rule by a parliamentary title. His kingdom, however, was in actuality ruled by his mother and Mortimer, who exploited the king's youth and inexperience to wield power for themselves.

As he reached maturity, Edward proved himself to be far more capable than his mother anticipated. In 1330, tired of being a mere puppet in the hands of a corrupt monarchy, Edward took the reins of power, imprisoned Isabella, and had Mortimer executed. Once he began to reign in his own right, Edward exhibited signs of being astute, capable, and charismatic, all very important characteristics in medieval rulers for whom the cult of personality held great influence.

Edward III would ultimately become one of England's most popular and successful kings, and he and his son, Edward, the Black Prince, were responsible for some of England's greatest victories in the Hundred Years War. Edward III had a knack for pacifying the contentious barons of his kingdom, whom he cannily manipulated to serve his own ends while simultaneously allowing them to increase their own power base. Edward in particular used the method of marital alliance to make strong connections at home rather than abroad, marrying his children by Philippa of Hainault (whom he married in 1329) into prominent baronial families.

He also provided the barons with the pomp they desired through his founding of the Round Table in 1344 and the Order of the Knights of the Garter in 1348. This reliance on the barons, and the consequent rise of the importance of Parliament, would have long-reaching and important implications for future monarchs. In addition, it was during Edward's reign that Parliament was divided into two houses, the Commons and the Lords.

And yet there are elements of Edward's reign that were less than successful. His questionable claim to the French throne in 1337 plunged England and France into the Hundred Years War, a protracted struggle that in retrospect seems to have cost England much in taxes while gaining nothing in the end. By the final defeat in 1453, England, which once controlled large and lucrative areas of France, was left with the port of Calais and little more.

The war caused severe economic strain on the country, and the resulting heavy taxation bred resentment. Edward's personal and mental weakness toward the end of his reign and increased dependence on his greedy mistress Alice Perrers led to a general uproar against the perceived mismanagement of the kingdom. The Commons rose up in 1376 in the "good" Parliament, the result of which brought the accusation of Perrers and the king's ministers of corruption and peculiations. Furthermore, Edward's courtship of the barons gave them an influence and measure of power that would return to haunt his grandson, Richard II, a far less capable king.

See also Edward, the Black Prince; Hundred Years War; John of Gaunt; Richard II

Edward III is pictured in his camp in this fifteenth-century illustration. © Bibliothèque nationale de France.

FURTHER READING

Bevan, Bryan. *Edward III: Monarch of Chivalry.* London: Rubicon Press, 1992.

Cantor, Norman. *The Encyclopedia of the Middle Ages.* New York: Viking Press, 1999.

Collins, Hugh E. L. *The Order of the Garter, 1348–1461: Chivalry and Politics in Late Medieval England.* New York: Oxford University Press, 2000.

Fraser, Antonia, ed. *The Lives of the Kings and Queens of England.* Rev. ed. Berkeley: University of California Press, 1998.

Edward, the Black Prince

Edward, Prince of Wales and Aquitaine, was born June 15, 1330, at Woodstock palace in Oxfordshire. As the eldest son of Edward III (1312–77) and Philippa of Hainault (1314?–69), he was the heir to both his father's throne and his legacy of military prowess. While he would predecease his father, and the crown would pass instead to his own son, Richard II, he would more than equal his father's accomplishments on the battlefield.

His fame rested not only on his battlefield prowess, but also upon his romantic life. In 1361, he made a famous love match to the twice-widowed Joan of Kent (1328–85), the legendary Fair Maid of Kent who secretly married the Black Prince a scant three months after the death of her second husband. All of these elements combined to make Edward a larger-than-life chivalric hero. During his life and afterward, the Black Prince rivaled England's most famous warrior kings in popularity and legendary status.

Edward became England's first Duke of Cornwall in 1337 and, at the age of eight, gained the title Guardian of England. In 1347, he became Prince of Wales and seven years later was titled the Earl of Chester. He entered military service in 1345 with the Crécy campaign, in which he distinguished himself through a decisive victory over the French army. In 1356, he managed to capture the French king at the battle of Poitiers. A subsequent treaty allowed for John II's safe return to France and his throne in exchange for a 3 million crown ransom and English control of vast territories in western France, including Guienne, Gascony, Poitou, and Calais. In 1367, Edward undertook a campaign to Castile to help Pedro the Cruel regain his throne.

Edward was also an enthusiastic participant in the tournaments that were popular in his day, using the opportunity to hone his battlefield skills and spread the fame of his name. He would also become one of the first Knights of Garter, the chivalric order founded by his father in 1348.

The tomb of Edward, the Black Prince. © Erich Lessing / Art Resource, NY.

Edward's final years were plagued by an illness that he contracted in Castile. Although generally accepted to have been dysentery, the true nature of Edward's illness remains a mystery. It would eventually incapacitate him during 1375. He died the following year and was buried at Canterbury Cathedral, where pieces of his armor still hang today.

It is this armor that has provided the most common theory on the nature of his nickname. There is no contemporary evidence, however, that he wore predominantly black armor. The nickname, in fact, is not even recorded until the sixteenth century. His own contemporaries most commonly referred to him as Edward of Woodstock.

See also Canterbury; Edward III; Hundred Years War; John of Gaunt; Richard II

FURTHER READING

Barber, Richard. *Edward Prince of Wales and Aquitaine.* Woodbridge, Suffolk, England: Boydell and Brewer, 1996.

Cantor, Norman. *The Encyclopedia of the Middle Ages.* New York: Viking Press, 1999.

Collins, Hugh E. L. *The Order of the Garter, 1348–1461: Chivalry and Politics in Late Medieval England.* New York: Oxford University Press, 2000.

Fraser, Antonia, ed. *The Lives of the Kings and Queens of England.* Rev. ed. Berkeley: University of California Press, 1998.

Sedgwick, Henry Dwight. *The Black Prince.* New York: Barnes and Noble, 1993.

Entertainment

Entertainment in Chaucer's day was a thriving world that encompassed a wide variety of activities to pass the time on holidays and such free time as people enjoyed. Public forms of entertainments included plays, musicians, jugglers, puppeteers, and acrobats, as well as the occasional animal act. These were performed usually at fairs and holiday celebrations by roving players. Like today, medieval people loved music, and, in the absence of wandering minstrels, many would perform for themselves. Certain instruments were inexpensive, and singing was always a free alternative. Additionally, as Chaucer's own works demonstrate, poetry and literature were also important forms of entertainment for those who could afford books, could borrow them, or could read.

There were not formal theaters in Chaucer's time, and so plays would be performed in the village square or the courtyard of the local church. Often plays were sponsored by the church, and one of the most popular forms was the "mystery play." These plays depicted events from the Bible, from the creation to the death and ascension of Jesus.

The plays were designed to be performed in cycles that told an ongoing story. They would be performed by actors belonging to a religious or trade guild, and each chapter in the cycle would be performed by a different

A fifteenth-century depiction of chanteurs, French-speaking singers. © Bibliothèque nationale de France.

guild. There is ample evidence that many of these cycles were performed in England; however, only four complete cycles survive to this day, each named for its region of origin: the Wakefield, Chester, and York cycles, and the *Ludus Coventriae,* of which the geographic origin is unknown.

Chaucer mentions the mystery play concerning Noah in "The Miller's Tale," as Nicholas explains his plan to save John and Alison from the flood: "'Hastou nat herd,' quod Nicholas, 'also / The sorwe of Noe with his felaweshipe, / Er that he myghte gete his wyf to shipe?'" (*"Haven't you heard," asked Nicholas "about / The sadness of Noah and his family / And his fear that he wouldn't get his wife on the ship?"* (*Canterbury Tales,* "The Miller's Tale," I (A), 3538–40). Earlier in the tale, the Miller's description of Absolom includes his role as Herod in a local production: "He pleyeth Herodes upon a scaffold hye" (*He played Herod up on a high scaffold*) (*Canterbury Tales,* "The Miller's Tale," I (A), 3384).

In the realm of literature, many stories and poems were devotional, reflecting the cultural importance of religion in the Middle Ages. However, there was also lighter fare. Romantic legends of such national heroes as Robin Hood, King Arthur, and Richard I as well as tales from Classical legends, of which *Troilus and Criseyde* is a prime example, were popular with a variety of audiences. Poetry was also a means to critique the government and society, and the Middle Ages, especially by Chaucer's time, produced a fair number of satires and allegories to this end. Finally, there were courtly love poems that promulgated the ideals of chivalry and love that pervaded the courts of Europe.

Music may have been the most widespread and readily available form of popular entertainment of the Middle Ages. While much of what remains preserved today is sacred music, secular music was an important part of daily life—it was just rarely written down. What survive today are the words to songs, but the tunes have been lost.

Secular music knew no class boundaries. The nobility employed court musicians who played and sang regularly at court functions such as banquets and dances. Wandering minstrels were also often welcome additions to court life as well as in the towns, through which they traveled and earned their living. These minstrels, also known as troubadours or jongleurs, were important also as sources of information. Through their travels and their connection with royal courts, they were remarkable repositories of gossip and news from far away. If they were headed in a convenient direction, they could also be relied on to carry messages to family in other towns.

Their habit of travel also resulted in the widespread dissemination of songs and tunes

A fourteenth-century Spanish depiction of three musicians. © Bibliothèque nationale de France.

throughout a region. After the minstrels left, peasants could continue to play these tunes for themselves. Songs were sung about every facet of life: love, sex, money, drinking, politics, and historical legends. Peasants often sang to accompany a dance or to pass the time at work. Instruments were also a popular part of musical entertainment, and nearly every village could boast of a piper, a drummer, or a fiddler. Instruments such as the bagpipes were excellent to use for outdoor dances, because their sound carried well.

Chaucer mentions such entertainments throughout his works. Not only are there the references in "The Miller's Tale" to mystery plays, but there is music in just about every one of his tales.

See also Allegory and Dream Visions; Music

FURTHER READING

Brown, Peter, ed. *A Companion to Chaucer.* Malden, MA: Blackwell, 2002.
Bumke, Joachim. *Courtly Culture.* New York: Overlook Press, 2000.
Childress, Diana. *Chaucer's England.* North Haven, CT: Linnet Books, 2000.
Holsinger, Bruce W. *Music, Body, and Desire in Medieval Culture: Hildegard of Bingen to Chaucer.* Stanford, CA: Stanford University Press, 2001.

Ogden, Dunbar H. *The Staging of Drama in the Medieval Church*. Newark: University of Delaware Press, 2002.

Porter, Pamela J. *Courtly Love in Medieval Manuscripts*. Toronto: University of Toronto Press, 2003.

Smoldon, William L. *The Music of the Medieval Church Dramas*. Edited by Cynthia Bourgeault. New York: Oxford University Press, 1980.

Wilkins, Nigel E. *Music in the Age of Chaucer*. Totowa, NJ: Rowman and Littlefield, 1979.

Estates

And whan this Walter saugh hire pacience,
Hir glade chiere, and no malice at al,
And he so ofte had doon to hire offence,
And she ay sad and constant as a wal,
Continuynge evere hire innocence overal,
This sturdy markys gan his herte dresse
To rewen upon hire wyfly stedfastnesse.

And when Walter saw her patience,
Her cheery attitude, and that she bore him no malice,
That even after he had treated her so badly,
She remained as constant and steadfast as a wall,
Continuing in innocence through everything
His stony heart began to take pity upon her
For all of her unfailing wifely loyalty.

(*Canterbury Tales,*
"The Clerk's Tale," IV (E), 1044–50)

The concept of the Three Estates (also termed the "Three Orders"), or the division of feudal society into separate and clearly defined social classes, is one of medieval Europe's most distinctive characteristics. In this system, each individual was defined by both the class into which one was born as well as what one did for a living. These definitions were rigid and, until the fourteenth century, largely unquestioned. By Chaucer's time, however, social mobility was beginning to occur on a small scale as the feudal system began to come into question and capitalism increasingly became the economic basis for European commerce.

Throughout most of the Middle Ages, the place of each estate was firmly based on a premonetary system in which land was the primary currency and wages were paid in kind or in housing. Peasants, for example, were given a cottage on a manor as well as a plot of land. They paid their rents in grain, chickens, or other produce, and earned their keep by working the overlord's land. There was not a lot of opportunity for social mobility in this system, because there was little chance for the average peasant to accumulate wealth through land or through cash, which was the primary means to buy land. Some enterprising peasants were able to produce sufficient excess in order to sell their goods at market, but, until Chaucer's day, this was the exception to the rule.

Once coinage began to predominate the economic system, however, through the growth of banking and mercantilism beginning in the thirteenth century, the hierarchical dominance of inherited titles and land began to weaken. Certainly the aristocracy would continue to rule Europe nearly exclusively for the next several centuries. However, the cash nexus allowed for the rise of a middle class that would gain power and prestige through accumulated wealth, not blood.

The First Estate was the clergy, whose function in its simplest definition was to pray. At the village level, the parish priest would administer sacraments, hear confession, perform mass, and generally oversee the spiritual health of his flock. During Chaucer's time, there were roughly 8,500 parishes in England, and priests at this level were rarely from the upper echelons of the aristocracy, although many were younger sons of impoverished noble families. Although a few of the parishes were rather wealthy for the times, the vast majority produced less than £10 in total annual revenues.

Being the most important and sometimes only contact peasants had with the Church, a local priest's position was one of great influence. In relatively isolated rural areas, the potential for abuse by priests was high. Many held several posts and collected the benefits while essentially neglecting the needs of the parishioners. While urban centers led to religious questioning based on greater exposure to intellectual issues, in the rural areas, the falling away from Catholic teachings was equally high and arose from the void left by bad clergymen.

In addition, after the Black Death, the vacuum left behind by the high mortality rates meant that less training was necessary to become a priest. Many of them knew little more than how to read. Their apparent lack of training and vocation left parishioners feeling their souls were not in accomplished and capable hands, resulting in an impulse to seek guidance elsewhere. This tendency gave rise to strengthened heretical movements and, eventually, to formally recognized Protestantism as disillusioned parishioners gained spiritual fulfillment via means other than the Catholic Church.

Higher positions in the Church establishment drew from the aristocracy almost exclusively, thereby providing overlap between the First Estate and the Second, the nobility. While the First Estate were known as the *oratores,* or "those who pray," the Second Estate were the *bellatores,* those who fight. Together these two groups comprised between 3 and 5 percent of the total population of England (the clergy alone made up roughly 1.5%) and controlled the land, politics, economics, social mores, and legal proceedings.

Until Chaucer's day, the most important function of the Second Estate, as a class of highly trained and specialized warriors, was to protect society. It is through this role, and the rights and responsibilities that came with it, that the knightly class rose to the position of pervasive secular power. Their essentially unquestioned role began to slip in the fourteenth century as the introduction of gunpowder as well as the changing economic structure made their role as highly trained protectors of society increasingly obsolete.

The rise of a mercantile middle class provided a means of challenging the unparalleled wealth in landholdings by the nobility as well as a new dominant economic system in capitalism. By the time of Chaucer's death, there were many middle-class merchants who had outstripped much of the nobility, who, as a class, had incomes that ranged from £20 per annum to as much as £12,000. The difference in rank, of course, arose from birth. No matter how wealthy a merchant became, he was not of gentle birth. It would take many centuries for this distinction to finally be essentially erased, through the rise of capitalism, the acquisition of land, and intermarriage into the aristocracy.

The middle class were members of what was known as the Third Estate—the *laboratores,* or "those who work." This third order comprised the bulk of society, their percentage of the total population within England lying somewhere between 95 and 97 percent. Throughout much of the Middle Ages, the Third Estate was chiefly made up of free-born peasants and serfs who worked the land. Increasingly, as urban culture developed during Chaucer's time, this class became quite diverse and consisted of greater numbers of artisans and merchants who were the leading edge of the middle class. The Third Estate was really the foundation on which the success of medieval society was built. They worked the land, providing the food and other means, such as wool production, for the maintenance of the rest of society.

Most peasants lived on manors, which incorporated the limits of a feudal lord's land, including farmland and one or more villages. Peasants worked the lord's land as well as their own plots. Land was divided into long strips, a design necessitated by the use of heavy ploughs that were difficult to turn in close spaces. Because of the costly nature of a plough and team of oxen or horses, peasants on a particular manor were forced to cooperate with one another, sharing resources and equipment.

In addition to the farmland, manors also contained open forest, uncultivated tracts for grazing sheep and cattle, and rivers and streams that could be fished to supplement the diet of all who lived on the manor. The position of a peasant varied greatly according to the definition of his or her tenure on a manor. Those who had "free holdings" had few duties to the overlord, including the payment of special taxes. They needed only to pay their rents and were free to come and go at will. Those who held "servile" positions were required to pay far more obeisance to the overlord, being legally required to obtain permission (and often paying a fee) before marrying outside the manor, moving, or entering holy orders.

Payment for labor for either free or servile holdings was generally made in kind—the use of land, a cottage, and the like. It was, thus, difficult to move up on the social ladder because wealth in the form of liquid assets or land could only be obtained and increased through real cash wages.

Around the time of the Black Death, peasants began to demand such real wages, instead of payment in kind, for their service to a landlord. In its wake, the Black Death left a shortage of able workers to accomplish the most necessary jobs of society, placing those left behind in a powerful bargaining position.

Peasants, unlike serfs, were freeborn and could potentially improve their social standing within the Third Estate by judicious management of funds earned selling surplus crops at local markets. With accumulated cash, peasants could purchase land or move to a city where they could take up a useful trade such as carpentry or baking. It is this introduction of a cash economy that fueled a kind of social mobility. Increasingly during Chaucer's time, there was a migration into the towns as more and more peasants sought their fortunes in urban settings, hoping for an increase in prestige and standard of living.

This social mobility, and the concomitant questions of inborn nobility and right to power in society, is central to most of Chaucer's works, most notably *The Canterbury Tales*. Perhaps the most striking handling of these themes occurs in "The Clerk's Tale," where the low-born Grisilde proves herself not only to be noble, pure, and faithful, but also morally superior to her higher-born husband, Walter. Time and again, throughout the course of their marriage, he tests her in increasingly questionable and punishing ways. While her quiet acquiescence to his domination might infuriate us, and probably many during Chaucer's time as well, there is no doubt that Grisilde possesses inborn gentilesse, a fact even Walter comes to appreciate and understand (*Canterbury Tales*, "The Clerk's Tale," IV (E), 1044–50).

See also Feudalism; Gentilesse; Knight; Merchant; Money; Monk; Nun; Peasant Revolt; Prioress

FURTHER READING

Bean, J.M.W. *From Lord to Patron: Lordship in Late Medieval England*. Manchester, England: Manchester University Press, 1989

Bellamy, John G. *Bastard Feudalism and the Law*. Portland, OR: Areopagitica Press, 1989.

Bisson, Lillian M. *Chaucer and the Late Medieval World*. New York: St. Martin's Press, 1998.

Bloch, Marc. *Feudal Society*. Translated by L. A. Manyon. New York: Routledge, 1961; 1989.

Cantor, Norman. *The Civilization of the Middle Ages*. Rev. ed. New York: Harper Collins, 1993.

DeWindt, Edwin Brezette, ed. *The Salt of Common Life: Individuality and Choice in the Medieval Town, Countryside, and Church: Essays Presented to J. Ambrose Raftis*. Kalamazoo: Medieval Institute Publications, Western Michigan University, 1995.

Duby, Georges. *The Three Orders: Feudal Society Imagined*. Translated by Arthur Goldhammer. Chicago: University of Chicago Press, 1980; reprinted 1982.

Dyer, Christopher. *Making a Living in the Middle Ages: The People of Britain 850–1520*. New Haven, CT: Yale University Press, 2002.

Farmer, Sharon, and Barbara H. Rosenwein, eds. *Monks and Nuns, Saints and Outcasts: Religion in Medieval Society: Essays in Honor of Lester K. Little*. Ithaca, NY: Cornell University Press, 2000.

French, Katherine L. *The People of the Parish: Community Life in a Late Medieval English Diocese*. Philadelphia: University of Pennsylvania Press, 2001.

Given-Wilson, Chris. *The English Nobility in the Late Middle Ages: The Fourteenth-Century Political Community*. New York: Routledge & Kegan Paul, 1987.

Goldberg, P.J.P. *Medieval England: A Social History, 1250–1550*. New York: Oxford University Press, 2004.

Hindley, Geoffrey. *The Medieval Establishment, 1200–1500*. New York: Putnam, 1970.

Knapp, Peggy. *Chaucer and the Social Contest*. New York: Routledge, 1990.

Lambdin, Laura C., and Robert T. Lambdin, eds. *Chaucer's Pilgrims*. Westport, CT: Praeger, 1999.

Mertes, Kate. *The English Noble Household, 1250–1600: Good Governance and Politic Rule*. New York: Blackwell, 1988.

Power, Eileen. *Medieval People*. New York: Barnes and Noble, 1924; reprinted 1968.

Strohm, Paul. *Social Chaucer*. Cambridge, MA: Harvard University Press, 1989.

Swabey, Ffiona. *Medieval Gentlewoman: Life in a Gentry Household in the Later Middle Ages*. New York: Routledge, 1999.

Esther

Esther (Old Testament) was the Jewish queen of the Persian King Ahasuerus. She was descended from a family that had been carried into captivity in 600 B.C. and had then decided to stay in Persia rather than returning home to Jerusalem when the captivity ended. Esther was chosen to replace Ahasuerus's first wife, Vashti, whom he banished from his kingdom after she refused his drunken request that she display herself naked to their guests. In her capacity as queen, she seems to have carried a fair amount of influence.

She was, in fact, the catalyst behind the feast of Purim. The king's advisor, Haman, acting out of revenge for a perceived slight, talked Ahasuerus into issuing an edict to kill all of the Jews and to seize their property. Fortunately, Esther found out about and exposed the plot. The king rescinded the edict upon her request, granting the Jews the right to defend themselves. The unsavory Haman was hanged on the same gallows prepared for Mordecai, the Jew he believed had disrespected him.

Like Abigail, Esther is used by Chaucer as example of the virtuous wife. As the Wife of Bath uses several old testament figures, January of "The Merchant's Tale" uses the example of Esther as a justification of his decision to marry: "and looke, Ester also / By good conseil delyvered out of wo /

The peple of God, and made hym Mardochee / Of Assuere enhaunced for to be" (*And look, Esther / by her good advice rescued from peril / God's chosen people and gave Mordecai an important position in her husband's court*) (*Canterbury Tales,* "The Merchant's Tale," IV (E), 1371–74).

In *The Legend of Good Women,* Esther is compared to Alsceste for her meekness, but comes up in second place: "Ester, ley thou thy meknesse al adown" (*Esther, lay your meekness down*) (*Legend of Good Women,* 250). Finally, Esther is compared to White by the Black Knight in *The Book of the Duchess:* "To speke of godnesse, trewly she / Had as moche debonairte / As ever had Hester in the Bible, / And more, yif more were possyble" (*Speaking of goodness, / She truly had as much of it / As ever did Esther in the Bible / More even if it is possible*) (*Book of the Duchess,* 985–88).

FURTHER READING

Brown, Peter, ed. *A Companion to Chaucer.* Malden, MA: Blackwell, 2002.

Frye, Northrop. *Biblical and Classical Myths: The Mythological Framework of Western Culture.* Buffalo, NY: University of Toronto Press, 2004.

Manser, Martin H. *The Facts On File Dictionary of Classical and Biblical Allusions.* New York: Facts On File, 2003.

Eve

Eve (Old Testament) was the first woman, created from Adam's rib to be his wife and to assuage his loneliness in Eden. It is through her temptation by Satan that just about every negative aspect of human life is unleashed upon humanity. She is also the archetype of the wicked woman, and it is in this capacity that she is most referenced in Chaucer's works. The entire story of the fall is, in fact, retold in "The Parson's Tale" (*Canterbury Tales,* "The Parson's Tale," X (I), 320–35).

In "The Man of Law's Tale," Eve's temptation is used as an example of how women can destroy:

O Sathan, envious syn thilke day
That thou were chaced from oure heritage,
Wel knowestow to wommen the olde way!
Thou madest Eva brynge us in servage;
Thou wolt fordoon this Cristen mariage.
Thyn instrument—so weylawey the while!—
Makestow of wommen, whan thou wolt bigile.

Oh Satan, envious since the day
That you were chased out of our world,
You well know the way to tempt women!
You made Eve deliver us into slavery;
And you plan to wreck this Christian marriage.

Your instrument of destruction—all the while—
You make women, when you plan to beguile.

(*Canterbury Tales,*
"The Man of Law's Tale," II (B¹), 365–71)

In an opposite perspective, January uses Eve as one of his justifications for marriage, claiming it is natural for a man to crave companionship: "The hye God, whan he hadde Adam maked, / And saugh him al allone, bely-naked, / God of his grete goodnesse seyde than, / 'Lat us now make an helpe unto this man / Lyk to himself'; and thanne he made him Eve" (*Then God, when he saw that he had made Adam / And saw him all alone, completely naked / in his great goodness, He said, / "Let me now make a helper for this man / Just like himself" and then he made for Adam Eve*) (*Canterbury Tales,* "The Merchant's Tale," IV (E), 1325–29).

FURTHER READING

Brown, Peter, ed. *A Companion to Chaucer.* Malden, MA: Blackwell, 2002.

Frye, Northrop. *Biblical and Classical Myths: The Mythological Framework of Western Culture.* Buffalo, NY: University of Toronto Press, 2004.

Manser, Martin H. *The Facts On File Dictionary of Classical and Biblical Allusions.* New York: Facts On File, 2003.

F

Falcon

The terslet seyde thanne in this manere:
"Ful hard were it to preve by resoun
Who loveth best this gentil formel heere;
For everych hath swich replicacioun
That non by skilles may be brought adoun.
I can not se that argumentes avayle:
Thanne semeth it there most be batayle."

The falcon spoke then, saying:
"It is so hard to prove by reason
Who loves this beautiful formel the most;
Because all three are so much alike in every way
That none might be chosen by their individual skills.
I can't see any other way around it.
There must be a battle to decide who wins her hand."

(*Parliament of Fowls*, 533–39)

The falcon was an important hunting bird, domesticated as far back as the Iron Age. Symbolically, the falcon as hunter was used in a Christian context during the Middle Ages, and the falcon attacking a rabbit came to stand for the victory of the righteous over sin.

In *The Parliament of Fowls,* the falcon is elected by the birds of prey to represent them, and he advises that the debate be resolved by battle, since it is impossible to determine by reason which tercel loves the formel the best (*Parliament of Fowls,* 533–39). Falcons also appear in *The Canterbury Tales.* "The Squire's Tale" recounts the sad tale of the broken-hearted falcon, deserted by her husband who cheated on her with a lowly kite. Yet, the Squire promises that the falcon returns, won back to the female falcon by her nobility and fidelity (*Canterbury Tales,* "The Squire's Tale," 439–670).

See also Animals; Birds

FURTHER READING

Rowland, Beryl. *Blind Beasts: Chaucer's Animal World.* Kent, OH: Kent State University Press, 1971.

Salisbury, Joyce E., ed. *The Medieval World of Nature: A Book of Essays.* New York: Garland, 1993.

Strickland, Debra Higgs. *Medieval Bestiaries: Text, Image, Ideology.* New York: Cambridge University Press, 1995.

Telesko, Werner. *The Wisdom of Nature: The Healing Powers and Symbolism of Plants and Animals in the Middle Ages.* New York: Prestel, 2001.

Fame

Y saugh, perpetually ystalled,
A femynyne creature,
That never formed by Nature
Nas such antoher thing yseye.
For alther-first, soth for to seye,
Me thoughte that she was so lyte
That the lengthe of a cubite
Was lengere than she semed be.
But thus sone in a whyle she
Hir tho so wonderliche streighte
That with hir fet she erthe reighte,
And with hir hed she touched hevene,
Ther as shynen sterres sevene,
And therto eke, as to my wit,
I saugh a gretter wonder yit,
Upon her eyen to beholde.

I saw, enthroned forever
A feminine creature
That the equal—formed by Nature—

Has never been seen.
For at first glance she was so light and tiny
That the length from my finger to my elbow
Seemed far longer than she was.
But shortly afterward, she seemed
To stretch so wonderfully straight
That with her feet she touched the earth
And with her head she grazed heaven,
Touching the seven planets,
Much to my awe
I saw an even greater wonder
When I looked into her eyes.

(*House of Fame,* Book III, 1364–79).

Fama (or Pheme in Greek mythology) was the Roman personification of fame and rumor. She is simultaneously hated and loved as, with her many eyes, ears, and tongues, she spreads what she hears to everyone, regardless of whether it is good or evil. However, despite the effects of her words, she is neither good nor evil herself. And, while she can just as easily spread falsehood, she also brings great renown to the names of some and thus she is eagerly sought by humanity.

Her size varies from the length of a cubit to the distance from Earth to heaven, an expansion and contraction that further demonstrates that her presence is devoid of logic or predictability. Fame never sleeps and is not allowed to enter heaven. Instead, she spends her days and nights hovering above the Earth, repeating what she hears first in a whisper, then growing increasingly louder until all hear her. She is usually represented as a winged creature holding a trumpet.

In *The House of Fame,* Chaucer gives us a humorous account of his own quest to find Fame, seeking her out in her whirling house of wicker, as flimsy and insubstantial as the wings of Icarus. He also names her as Fortune's sister.

See also Fortune

FURTHER READING

Brown, Peter, ed. *A Companion to Chaucer.* Malden, MA: Blackwell, 2002.

Frye, Northrop. *Biblical and Classical Myths: The Mythological Framework of Western Culture.* Buffalo, NY: University of Toronto Press, 2004.

Hansen, William F. *Classical Mythology: A Guide to the Mythical World of the Greeks and Romans.* New York: Oxford University Press, 2005.

Manser, Martin H. *The Facts On File Dictionary of Classical and Biblical Allusions.* New York: Facts On File, 2003.

Morford, Mark P. O. *Classical Mythology.* 7th ed. New York: Oxford University Press, 2003.

Nolan, Barbara. *Chaucer and the Tradition of the Roman Antique*. New York: Cambridge University Press, 1992.

Powell, Barry B. *Classical Myth*. Translated by Herbert M. Howe. 4th ed. Upper Saddle River, NJ: Pearson/Prentice Hall, 2004.

Price, Simon, and Emily Kearns, eds. *The Oxford Dictionary of Classical Myth and Religion*. New York: Oxford University Press, 2003.

Fashion

A FRANKELYN was in his compaignye.

…

An anlaas and a gipser al of silk
Heeng at his girdel, whit as morne milk.

…

And they were clothed alle in o lyveree
Of a solempne and greet fraternitee.
Ful fressh and newe hir geere apiked was;
Hir knyves were chaped noght with bras
But al with silver, wroght ful clene and weel,
Hire girdles and hir pouches everydeel.

A Franklin was in his company.

…

A broad dagger and a purse of pure white silk
Hung at his waist

…

And they were clothed all in the livery
Of their dignified and great fraternities.
Very new and fresh were their clothes
Their knives were not topped with cheap brass,
But instead with silver, wrought masterfully,
And their belts and purses were expertly stitched as well.

(*Canterbury Tales*,
General Prologue, I (A), 331, 357–58, 363–68)

Medieval fashion was far more complex than costume dramas would generally indicate. Not only was the layering and design of clothing quite intricate, but also the symbolism of the type and style of dress provided important social clues. One's clothing indicated one's place in society.

In Chaucer's day, when increasing numbers of middle-class commoners were able to afford the same fine fabrics and styles of the nobility, lines were blurring and it became difficult to determine someone's status simply by his or her clothing. These visible signs were important in maintaining the status quo. Therefore, to combat the conspicuous consumption of the middle-class upstart, legislation was passed to provide clear-cut boundaries for appropriate dress.

The sumptuary laws of the 1330s and 1363 attempted to limit certain styles and fabrics to appropriate social strata as well as controlling styles that were simply deemed to be morally offensive by their sheer outlandishness. For instance, craftsmen could not wear silk, silver, or gold cloth, or any that cost more than four shillings. Their wives could not have any embroidered clothes, and their veils had to be made of English cloth.

Poorer squires were limited essentially to the same clothing as craftsmen. However, squires whose land and rents were valued at 200 marks or more and merchants whose goods were worth 1,000 pounds or more could wear silver, gems on their headdresses, and any fur except ermine.

Shoes, which were known during this period for their extravagantly pointy toes were limited to 24-inch extensions for the nobility, 12-inch for gentlemen, and 6.5-

A woman gazes into a mirror her servant holds for her. © Bibliothèque nationale de France.

inch for merchants. Prostitutes were required to wear special hats, bells, and colored patches, while Jews wore small yellow symbols and the pointed caps known as the Judenhut.

In the early Middle Ages, styles were adapted from the Roman Empire and were made from simple, straight lines. Garments were loose to slip over the head, or were fastened with buckles or laces. Materials, while sometimes expensive, reflected the degree to which trade was conducted.

After the Crusades, knights brought back sumptuous fabrics such as damask, velvet, and baldachin, which combined silk and gold thread. The more common fabrics by Chaucer's day were wool and linen. The former was very versatile and long-lasting. It could be used for outergarments because it is naturally water-resistant and insulates well. Wool could also be used for kirtles and coathardies because it could be woven into soft, lightweight yet warm cloth that dyes nicely.

People of the Middle Ages preferred bright vibrant colors, and so it was important for those who could afford it to have eye-catchingly bright clothing. Dyes all came from natural sources, mostly plants and insects. Scarlet, for instance, was highly favored and was only obtainable from a Mediterranean insect, making it extremely expensive. A deeper brick red was derived from the madder plant, while woad and indigo produced shades of

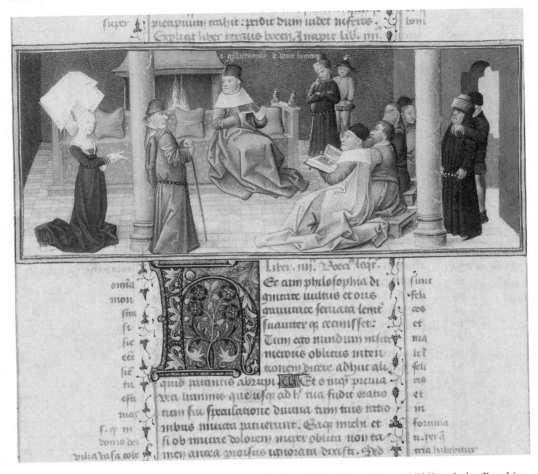

Illustration from *Boece*, Geoffrey Chaucer's translation of *The Consolation of Philosophy* by Boethius. © Bibliothèque nationale de France.

blue. Black was very difficult to achieve, and thus was the most expensive and rare of all colors.

Linen, which is difficult to dye, was worn closest to the skin as undergarments and lining of woolens and other fabrics requiring inner softness or reinforcement. Often a thin strip of linen would be sewn around the inside of neck and wrist holes and the outer edges would be finished with decorative braid or ribbon. Some of these edgings were quite fashionable and decorative. Dagging—produced by notching the edges of a garment such as a hood or coatbottom—became increasingly fanciful and creative.

Silk was common for finer fabrics worn by the nobility and wealthy merchants. It was always imported, making it expensive and, thus, highly coveted. Silk was used to make a variety of other luxury fabrics such as velvet, satin, and taffeta. Outerwear was often lined with fur to make it warmer and as a show of wealth. Popular furs included squirrel, marten, sable, and ermine.

Crusaders also brought back ideas for style innovations, some of them based on practical needs. The surcoat, for instance, developed from the need to protect armored knights from the blazing heat of the sun. This distinctive long garment, resembling a priest's vestment, has become one of the more recognizable fashions of the Middle Ages, and came to be an essential element of the knightly costume. Like standards and other shows of arms, the surcoat was decorated with heraldic symbols, identifying a knight's familial allegiances.

The surcoat was not the only style innovation to come out of the Middle Ages, and by Chaucer's day, the cut of garments and new devices such as buttons allowed styles to become much more formfitting and shapely. So much so, in fact, that churchmen became concerned about the moral implications of sexy fashions as well as the display of vanity they represented.

Allas, may man nat seen, as in oure dayes, the synful costlewe array of clothynge, and namely in to muche superfluite, or elles in to desordinat scantnesse?

As to the first synne, that is in superfluitee of clothynge, which that maketh it so deere, to harm of the peple; / nat oonly the cost of embrowdynge, the degise endentynge or barrynge, owndynge, palynge, wyndynge or bendynge, and semblable wast of clooth in vanitee, / but ther is also constlewe furrynge in hir gownes, so muche pownsonynge of chisels to maken holes, so muche daggynge of sheres; / forthwith the superfluitee in lengthe of the forseide gownes, trailynge in the dong and in the mire, on horse and eek on foote, as wel of man as of womman, that al thilke trailyng is verraily as in effect wasted, consumed, thredbare, and roten with donge, rather than it is yeven to the povre, to greet damage of the forseyde povre folk. / …. Upon that oother side, to speken of the horrible disordenat scantnesse of clothing, as been thise kutted slopes, or haynselyns, that thurgh hire shortnesse ne covere nat the shameful members of man, to wikked entente. / Allas, somme of hem shewen the boce of hir shap, and the horrible swollen membres, that semeth like the maladie of hirnia, in the wrappynge of hir hoses; / and eek the buttokes of hem faren as it were the hyndre part of a she-ape in the fulle of the moone. / And mooreover, the wrecched swollen membres that they shewe thurgh disgisynge, in departynge of hire hoses in whit and reed, semeth that half hir shameful privee membrews weren flayne.

Alas, do men not see in our time the sinful way that they wear expensive and elaborate clothing, which is wasteful in its extravagance, or is shamefully scanty?

As for the first sin, which is the wastefulness of fashions, which make it so expensive that it actually harms people / because of the cost of embroidering, the designs that ostentatiously notch the borders of the fabric, the ornamental strips, the alternating stripes, the folding, the decorative borders, the vertical striping, and the general waste of cloth in vanity / but there is also the costly furring of gowns, and so much punching with ornamental holes, so much dagging of borders / as well as the superfluity of length of the gowns themselves, trailing along the ground in the dung and the mire, whether they are on horseback or on foot, for men or for women, that all that trailing is actually wasted because the material is ruined, made threadbare, or rotten with dung, when it should be given to the poor, and thus it damages the aforesaid poor folk. / ... Upon the other side, to mention the horrible scantiness of clothing, these loose coats cut so short that they do not even cover the private parts of men, all to wicked intent. / Alas, some of them show the bulge of their shape, and the horrible swollen members, that seem to be some malady like a hernia, within the wrappings of their hose / and then there are the buttocks of men looking like the rear-end of a she ape in the full moon. / And moreover, the wretched swollen members that these men show to their shame, when displayed in hose of alternating white and red stripes, make them look like their private parts are on fire.

(*Canterbury Tales,*
"The Parson's Tale," X (I), 415–25)

Underwear

The notion of what it meant to be properly and appropriately dressed differed from how we define it today. Uncovered arms were far more risqué than a man's underwear, which was fairly common to see in public. Known as breeches and usually made of linen, men's underwear loosely covered their private areas and with the aid of a belt, supported the leggings or hose. As the fourteenth century progressed, as the Parson notes, leggings became a little tighter as it was discovered that cutting wool fabric on a bias created a certain degree of elasticity.

Leggings were attached to the breeches by the aid of laces (points) that fitted through the belt or holes cut into the breeches for that purpose. More fashionable men skipped the breeches altogether and had leggings that laced directly to their shirts, a practice that, as the Parson complains, accentuates their "shameful members ... to wikked entente." Some leggings had leather soles on the feet so that the wearer did not need separate shoes or boots. For women, leggings came up to the knee and were tied to garters. There were no breeches or shorts, but women did wear breast bands.

The final element of undergarments was the shirt for men and the smock for women, both typically made of white linen, cut with straight lines, and pulled straight over the head with no lacing or openings beyond the head and wrists. This was an essential part of every outfit and to be seen in public with nothing worn over it was to be considered naked.

Outerwear

Medieval fashions typically were comprised of many layers, enabling the wearer to warm or cool him- or herself without risk of exposing too much skin. Over the shirt was worn a kirtle of either linen or wool. Although the kirtle originally maintained a shape very similar to the shirt below it, from the fourteenth century forward, it began to take on a shape more close to the human body. Seams were angled to accentuate the waist and sometimes there were side gores and buttons that allowed for a much tighter, figure-enhancing fit, in women's fashions in particular.

Over the kirtle was worn the coathardie or doublet, which were longer formfitting garments, cut to hug the waist and sometimes the hips for women. Men's coathardies were shorter than a kirtle, stopping generally at the upper thighs. As the century progressed, they became increasingly short. Women's coathardies usually grazed the floor or at least reached to the ankles.

Throughout the fourteenth century, waists became increasingly tight and the effect was further enhanced by shoulder padding. Sleeves also were decorated with slashing and long strips of cloth that were sewn to the upper arms.

Over the coathardie or doublet was worn the houppelande, a very loose gown that was designed to fit the shoulders and drape straight to the floor (although the men's houppelande was sometimes cut short to reflect trends of accentuating the legs). It had a hood or extended collar and could be belted at the waist, creating an effect similar to a hooded bathrobe. The sleeves of the houppelande were its most distinctive feature, long and flowing, sometimes reaching the floor and decorated with elaborate dagging. Some were lined with fur or silk in contrasting colors. The collar could be worn up, extending to the middle of the back of the head and buttoning to the chin in front, or could be turned down to allow the often contrasting color to accentuate the face. Finally for outerwear, or especially cold winters indoors, both men and women wore a mantle—a kind of large hooded cape, over their entire ensemble.

Hats, Hoods, Hair, and Shoes

Some form of headcovering was common during the Middle Ages, as it provided warmth and an additional outlet for stylistic expression. The hood was the most common form of headgear for men. Many hoods had a long tail in which one could carry small items. Hoods often had fashionable dagging and short shoulder capes that helped to keep them in place and provided an additional layer of insulation around the neck, in much the same way as a scarf functions.

While women also wore hoods, the most characteristic headgear was the veil and wimple. The veil was a simple rectangular piece of white linen (or sometimes silk), that draped over the head and down the back. The wimple went over the veil and draped around the chin and neck, where it was fastened with pins. Across the top of the head, both pieces were secured with a headband.

Later in Chaucer's time, the wimple fell out of fashion and women began to prefer simple veils that narrowed around the brow. This allowed for increasingly elaborate hairstyles, such as large braids that were bundled or wound into buns at the sides of the face. Eventually veils would be supplanted by the very fashionable with chaplets and wreathes of flowers or jewelry and padded rolls of fabric. Hair for men was typically at least to the collar if not past it. Facial hair also went through fashion trends, with mustaches very rare but beards quite common.

Shoes were made almost entirely of leather, although fancy court shoes were often embellished with silk and embroidery. The soles were made from very heavy leather that could be replaced if it wore out. In a time when items were not mass marketed, even for peasants shoes were made specifically for the individual, with a form for each customer kept at the cobbler's shop. Shoes were cut below the ankle and were secured with buckles or laces.

Ankle shoes were far more common than boots, which extended up the calf and were secured in the front with laces. For the very fashionable, as alluded to above, the rounded toe of the early fourteenth century was replaced by increasingly lengthy pointed toes. Toes sometimes curled upward and were held in place with laces that tied to the ankle. The inside of the extended toe was often stuffed with moss or linen to help it retain its distinctive shape.

Fashion trends in general helped to characterize people socially, and Chaucer certainly provides his readers with a physical description of each pilgrim, complete with details of their dress. The Knight has travel-stained, low-quality garb, while the Squire is attired at the height of male court fashion: "Embrouded was he, as it were a meede / Al ful of fresshe floures, whyte and reede. / ... / Short was his gowne, with sleves longe and wyde" (*His clothes were embroidered, like a maid's / All full of flowers of white and red. / ... / His gown was short, with sleeves that were long and wide*) (*Canterbury Tales*, General Prologue, I (A), 73–78, 89–93). The Merchant is clad in fine fabrics that indicate his success, while the Clerk is in old clothes that demonstrate his mind is on other things:

Upon his heed a Flaundryssh bever hat,
His bootes clasped faire and festisly

...

A Clerk ther was of Oxenford also

...

Ful thredbare was his overeste courtepy,
For he hadde geten hym yet no benefice,

...

For hym was levere have at his beddes heed
Twenty bookes, clad in blak or reed,
Of Aristotle and his philosophie
Than robes riche, or fithele, or gay sautrie.

He wore on his head a beaver hat made in Flanders,
And his boots were of the highest fashion.

...
His overcoat was threadbare
Because he had not yet gotten himself an income,
Being too devoted to study to find an office.
For he would much rather have at the head of his bed
Twenty books, bound in black or red leather,
By Aristotle and his philosophy
Than to have rich robes, or a fiddle, or even a beautiful psaltery.

(*Canterbury Tales,*
General Prologue, I (A), 272–73, 285–96)

The Franklin and the group of London guildsmen—the Haberdasher, Carpenter, Weaver, Tapestry Weaver, and Dyer—all reflect prosperity through their attire (*Canterbury Tales*, General Prologue, I (A), 331, 357–58, 363–68).

See also Business and Commerce; Merchant

FURTHER READING

Burns, E. Jane, ed. *Medieval Fabrications: Dress, Textiles, Clothwork, and Other Cultural Imaginings.* New York: Palgrave Macmillan, 2004.
Hodges, Laura F. *Chaucer and Clothing: Clerical and Academic Costume in the Prologue to the "Canterbury Tales."* Rochester, NY: D. S. Brewer, 2005.
———. *Chaucer and Costume.* Cambridge, England: D. S. Brewer, 2005.
Koslin, Désirée G., and Janet E. Snyder. *Encountering Medieval Textiles and Dress: Objects, Texts, Images.* New York: Palgrave Macmillan, 2002.
Netherton, Robin, and Gale R. Owen-Crocker, eds. *Medieval Clothing and Textiles.* Woodbridge, Suffolk, England: Boydell Press, 2005.
Richardson, Catherine, ed. *Clothing Culture, 1350–1650.* Burlington, VT: Ashgate, 2004.
Scott, Margaret. *Medieval Clothing and Costumes: Displaying Wealth and Class in Medieval Times.* New York: Rosen, 2004.

Feudalism

The system that we call feudalism first appeared in rudimentary form during the eighth century in France. It eventually spread to most of Europe during the Middle Ages. During the early medieval period, governments were diffused and incapable of providing real protection to citizens. At the same time, kings needed fighting men to defend their kingdoms but were unable to support standing armies. A system that created armies on call was instrumental in fulfilling both of these needs.

This was accomplished by a contract, sworn between a lord and a subordinate that paid in land and committed the subordinate to fight in payment when called upon to do so. Feudalism in essence decentralizes power, because, while there is a pyramidal structure in theory, with a king at the top and the simple knight at the bottom, power is diffused between each level of the pyramid and even within levels.

The name seems to derive from *fehu,* the Old High German word for cattle, property, or money, underlining the emphasis on a property rather than a monetary exchange. At its simplest, feudalism consists of two parts reflecting early Europe's joint heritage from the Germanic tribes and the Roman Empire. The first part, the *vassalage,* is a personal promise that has its roots in the Germanic *comitatus*—the warrior bands who were attracted to charismatic and physically powerful leaders, much like we see in *Beowulf.* The second part is the *benefice,* which derives from the late Empire when it became customary for landowners to hire retainers to manage their lands for them. The lord granted his retainer a parcel of land, known as a *benefice,* in repayment for managing the rest. Under the Carolingian rulers of Europe, these two parts merged into one, with the lord's military vassals holding benefices for their personal maintenance.

The cost of maintaining a noble soldier became increasingly expensive as warriors became a social elite, evolving from armored foot soldiers to the mounted knight of the high Middle Ages. In order to fight with a sword or lance on horseback, a man had to complete many years of specialized training, beginning at about the age of seven.

The upkeep of armor, weaponry, and the horse also required vast resources. Therefore, the aspiring knight required financial support—by providing a benefice, the lord was providing the vassal with the means, through the collection of rents, to support himself comfortably. The knight received an agrarian estate, usually with an attached village, and the peasants or serfs to work the land. In return for their work, the knight (now an overlord in his own right) protected his peasants.

The primary purpose from the lord's point of view was military service. Great lords were responsible not only for personal service to the king, but also for providing knights for his army. They also had to offer hospitality for itinerant kings, sit in judgment on legal cases when required, and pay the lord when his eldest son was knighted or his eldest daughter married. In return, the lord promised to protect the vassal if he was attacked.

While the relationship between lord and vassal began informally, over time it evolved into a ceremony at which the vassal performed homage to the overlord. In a public ceremony that echoes marital vows, they promised to fulfill their duties and responsibilities to one another, clasp hands, and exchange the kiss of peace to seal the deal. As time went on, the vassal developed increasing political power over his own fief, with full legal authority and jurisdiction. This aided the king on the one hand, because he did not have to administer the law to every far-flung corner of the realm. On the other hand, it weakened the king's position as the central authority. Unscrupulous vassals did not always take their vows seriously and sought to exert full power within their petty fiefdoms.

By Chaucer's day, written charters had taken the place of verbal promises, sweeping away some of the romantic associations of the days when men lived by their word. Feudalism had run its course, from widespread acceptance in the eleventh century, to abuse by monarchs in the thirteenth, and declining into what is known as "bastard feudalism" by the fourteenth. Capitalism and the cash nexus, rather than simple gifts of land, were the new modes of exchange. The feudal system was all but vanished, with the role of the knight rapidly diminishing with the introduction of gunpowder and the increasing use of common foot soldiers on the battlefield.

See also Estates; Knight

FURTHER READING

Arnold, Morris, et al. *On the Laws and Customs of England: Essays in Honor of Samuel E. Thorne*. Chapel Hill: University of North Carolina Press, 1981.

Bean, J.M.W. *From Lord to Patron: Lordship in Late Medieval England*. Manchester, England: Manchester University Press, 1989.

Bellamy, John G. *Bastard Feudalism and the Law*. Portland, OR: Areopagitica Press, 1989.

Bloch, Marc. *Feudal Society*. Translated by L. A. Manyon. New York: Routledge, 1961; 1989.

Cantor, Norman. *The Civilization of the Middle Ages*. Rev. ed. New York: Harper Collins, 1993.

Collins, Hugh E. L. *The Order of the Garter, 1348–1461: Chivalry and Politics in Late Medieval England*. New York: Oxford University Press, 2000.

Curry, Anne, and Elizabeth Matthew, eds. *Concepts and Patterns of Service in the Later Middle Ages*. Rochester, NY: Boydell Press, 2000.

Duby, Georges. *The Three Orders: Feudal Society Imagined*. Translated by Arthur Goldhammer. Chicago: University of Chicago Press, 1980; reprinted 1982.

Hicks, M. A. *Bastard Feudalism*. New York: Longman, 1995.

Jones, Terry. *Chaucer's Knight: The Portrait of a Medieval Mercenary*. Baton Rouge: Louisiana State University Press, 1980.

Reynolds, Susan. *Fiefs and Vassals: The Medieval Evidence Reinterpreted*. New York: Oxford University Press, 1994.

Food

To boille the chiknes with the marybones,
And poudre-marchant tart and galyngale.
Wel koude he knowe a draughte of Londoun ale.
He koude rooste, and sethe, and broille, and frye,
Maken mortreux, and wel bake a pye.
...
For blankmanger, that made he with the beste.

To boil a chicken with marrow bones,
With a tart powdered spice and some galengal.
He could judge well the quality of a London ale.
And he could roast, and seethe, and boil, and fry,
Make a hearty soup, and well bake a pie.
...
As for blancmange, he made it to rival the best.

(*Canterbury Tales,*
General Prologue, I (A), 380–87)

The preparation of daily meals and fancy banquets in the Middle Ages, while far more labor intensive without our modern conveniences, was not as different as one might assume. Certainly, there were more "exotic" dishes served, such as boar's head or peacocks re-feathered. Additionally, nearly every part of a particular animal was consumed—parts such as the genitalia, swim bladder, and stomach that we, for the most part, would consider inedible offal today.

The exigencies of cooking over an open fire and of keeping a kitchen clean without the use of running water or an arsenal of cleaning products

Illustration from *Boece*, Geoffrey Chaucer's translation of *The Consolation of Philosophy* by Boethius. © Bibliothèque nationale de France.

also led to practices we might find strange today, such as the use of ashes or sand to scrub pots and surfaces clean. And yet, today's cook would not be at a loss in the medieval kitchen, whether it belonged to the greatest lord or the lowliest peasant.

Medieval kitchens had saucepans, frying pans, deep pans resembling Dutch ovens, and a variety of knives and cooking utensils, including feathers that were used to baste food and to kill fowl. The foods prepared on a daily basis featured familiar ingredients—chicken, fish, beef, cabbage, peas, artichokes, cucumbers, greens, root vegetables—and the methods of preparation—boiling, frying, roasting—are equally familiar. In fact, many dishes that we enjoy today (ravioli, for instance) were first created during the Middle Ages. In addition, many of the governmentally controlled food regulations of today have their roots in the Middle Ages.

Pottery found in Canterbury, ca. 1200. Courtesy of Lisa Kirchner.

The Medieval Kitchen

There are significant differences, however, that make the medieval table a unique place. The first obvious difference is in the layout of kitchens. The typical one-room peasant home included a hearth in the center of the dirt floor that would provide heat, light, and a fire for cooking. A hole in the straw-thatched roof, bordered by tiles to prevent the roof catching fire, allowed much of the smoke to escape, although some inevitably remained within the living quarters.

The kitchens of the wealthy were far more elaborate. The walls and floor were usually made of stone—which improved hygiene and lessened fire hazard—with more than one oven built into the walls. The Duke of Burgundy's kitchen, for instance, had six hearths that occupied three walls with the fourth wall taken up by windows and sinks.

Even with such generous amenities at their disposal, which allowed for multiple dishes to be simultaneously prepared, the cooks still had to command a great deal of skill to manage the fire. Cooking pots were hung on adjustable hooks that were often attached to swinging cranes. This combination allowed the cook to regulate the heat source by moving the pot vertically as well as horizontally.

For kitchens less well-equipped than the Duke's, small baskets of hot coals could be attached to vertical poles to provide additional heat sources. The fuel necessary to keep such kitchens functioning could be enormous.

A medieval chalace. Courtesy of Lisa Kirchner.

One medieval advice book estimates that for a two-day banquet—four meals in all—the ovens would require upwards of 1,000 cartloads of wood as well as one large barnful of coal.

Food Preparation

The actual preparation of dishes, especially for banquets, was often quite elaborate and surprisingly dependent upon sophisticated methods of food styling. Everyday cooking required a degree of resourcefulness in order to utilize fresh ingredients, preserve surplus without refrigeration, and create nutritious and palatable meals.

For the peasant cook, the primary concern was to prepare food that was satisfying and frugal. Peasants mostly prepared potages of oatmeal and peas, stews, and soups because they could incorporate a variety of ingredients while preserving nourishing juices. Bread was sometimes difficult to bake due to the lack of ovens in peasant homes, but flat brown or rye bread was easily prepared in a pan or on a flat stone over the fire. Most peasants kept chickens and, if space allowed, a pig for meat, and a cow or sheep for milk. Therefore, dietary protein came from the pig, the occasional rabbit, cheese and butter made from the milk, and plentiful eggs. An herb garden provided gustatory interest as well as medicinal plants.

With wealth came greater access to a variety of ingredients and spices. While it is difficult to determine amounts used from medieval recipes that are often quite vague, it is clear that spices were extremely important elements in medieval cookery. Not only did they add flavor and interest to a meal, they were believed to have health benefits and were a sign of conspicuous wealth. In "The Miller's Tale," Absolon chews cardamom seed, also known as grain of paradise, and licorice to sweeten his breath (*Canterbury Tales,* "The Miller's Tale," I (A), 3690–91). Cinnamon and ginger were believed to aid digestion and were incorporated into a variety of dishes that might strike us as odd pairings of flavors. One popular recipe, for example, pairs cinnamon and eggs.

One knight's unpaid grocer's bill that found its way into the common pleas court in 1380 gives us an indication of the variety and expense of spices purchased at the time. Robert Passelewe was ordered to pay £6 for "pepper, saffron, ginger, cloves, dates, almonds, rice, saunders (Alexander or horse parsley), powdered ginger, 'powderlumbard,' powdered cinnamon, figs, raisins, and myrrh."

Salt was used as a staple flavoring agent—probably the most popular—as well as a preservative for meats and some vegetables over the winter months. While medieval people did not understand the science behind putrefaction and its prevention, salt was understood to preserve because it was warm and dry while decomposition was moist. Therefore salt's nature worked to balance the "humors" of the food. Surplus food could also be preserved in gelatin (made from hooves), honey, sweet wine, and sugar.

Menu planning often took health considerations into account. If advice books are to be believed, choosing items that kept the humors in balance was as important to the medieval cook as were taste and availability considerations. Sometimes these choices involved avoiding foods that heightened the negative seasonal effects on the four humors. For instance, in February, chard should be avoided, while in March, no lentils or sweets

---

The following menu from a feast given by Richard II and John of Gaunt on September 23, 1387 gives an idea of the number and variety of dishes served.

First Course

Venison and frumenty
Viaundbruse (meat potage)
Boar's heads
Roasted haunches of meat, swans, and pigs (served with appropriate sauces)
Lombardy custard
Sotelty

Second Course

Gele (jellied soup)
White dish from Syria
Roasted pigs, cranes, pheasants, herons, chickens, and bream
Tarts
Carved meat
Roasted conies (two-year-old rabbits)
Sotelty

Third Course

Almond potage
Stew in the style of Lombardy
Roasted venison, chickens, rabbits, partridge, quails, and larks
Payne puff (bread puff, like a fritter)
Jelly dish
Sweet curd
Longe Fritours (egg fritters)
Sotelty

---

should be served. In August, any food that could "'engender black bile'—that is, whatever might be cold and dry" should be stricken from the menu. In addition, certain foods were thought to have a direct effect on moods. Much like our belief today in oysters as an aphrodisiac, pomegranates, pears, and sparrow eggs were all thought to encourage amorous activity.

For elegant banquets, these everyday methods and strategies had to be called upon and enhanced in order to make a lasting impression. Multiple cooking was a popular means of impressing dinner guests. A whole fish, for example, could be prepared three different ways: the tail boiled, the middle roasted, and the head fried. The parts would not be separated until the fish came to the table, making for what must have been an impressive display of culinary skill. Imitation foods, such as ham and bacon made from salmon and pike meat, were popular during Lent when meat was forbidden. Cooks (and the Church) became quite adept at finding meat substitutes, in fact. Fetal rabbits were considered non-meat, and beaver tail was regarded as fish.

One of the most famous dishes of the Middle Ages, which could be made with chicken or other non-meats such as fish, was the *blancmangere* (white dish) (*Canterbury Tales,* General Prologue, I (A), 387). As with any recipe, the specifics varied, but the basics of the dish remained relatively constant and the basic white sauce is still used today.

Special effects, particularly for the *sotelties* (subtleties) or *entremets* that concluded each course were breathtakingly elaborate. The simplest consisted of food painted to look like something it was not, such as gold or flowers, or a more intense version of itself. Gold was taken from dandelions and egg yolk, green from parsley, red from sandalwood, and amber from saffron.

More elaborate effects must have created quite a stir tableside and, as the Middle Ages progressed, became less about edibility and more about illusion. English cooks enjoyed making castles from dough, so that the bread at table might resemble the castle in which the banquet was being held. Dough castles were positively sedate, however, when compared to the marvels fashioned by creative medieval cooks. Perhaps the most famous is the cockantrice, a curiosity made by roasting a suckling pig and a cock, splitting each in half and sewing the head of the cock to the body of the pig or vice versa. A whimsical variation of this theme was a cock, complete with a paper lance and helmet, mounted astride a piglet.

Pies were baked, the tops carefully separated from the bottoms, and live animals such as blackbirds or frogs were placed inside to be set free when the pie was sliced open. Boar's heads or swans were made to breath fire by filling the mouth with alcohol-soaked cotton and lighting it. There were even more pedestrian methods of creating illusions to save the host who was caught without the appropriate wine to serve. "Take in spring the flowers that grow in wheat which are called darnel or passerose, and dry

Canel Eyroun (Figs Stuffed with Cinnamoned Eggs)
Ingredients

12 large fresh figs
4 large hard-boiled eggs
1 tablespoon cinnamon
¼ teaspoon salt
½ teaspoon crushed fresh basil
? cup flour
½ cup oil for sautéing

Directions

With a spoon or with fingers, make a crater in the side of each fig.
Chop the eggs finely. Blend cinnamon, salt, and basil, and add to the eggs.
Stuff each fig with the spiced egg mixture.
Lightly dredge each stuffed fig in the flour. Sauté in a heavy skillet with hot
oil for 4 to 6 minutes, until golden brown.
Drain. Serve warm.

Blancmangere (Chicken with Cumin and Cream)
Ingredients

20 small individual pastry shells
4 chicken breasts, skinned and boned
4 tablespoons oil for sautéing
1 cup chicken broth
1 cup ale
½ teaspoon salt
1 cup slivered almonds
1 cup heavy cream
1 teaspoon cumin seeds
1 teaspoon rosemary, finely ground

Directions

Bake pastry shells at 425° so that they are crisp for serving.
In heavy skillet, sauté chicken in butter until white on all sides. Cut chicken
into small cubes and return to pan.
Add broth and simmer with chicken on low flame for 20 minutes or until
tender.
Drain broth; pour hot ale over chicken. Let steep 20 minutes; drain off ale.
Roast almonds for 5 minutes at 400° on well-greased cookie sheet.
Add cream, almonds, rosemary, and cumin to chicken. Stir thoroughly. Gen-
tly heat, but do not boil, for 7 minutes.
Spoon into crisp, warm pastry shells, or reheat for 5 minutes in warm oven
before serving.

them until they can be powdered. Put some of this, without being observed, into the wine glass, and the wine will turn red" (Rickert, 84).

Beverages

Wine was the most popular beverage in the Middle Ages for those who could afford it. For the rest, ale and beer had to suffice. Water, because of pollutants that came from medieval industry and the habit of channeling kitchen and human waste into waterways, was generally unsafe to drink unless it came from a clear spring. In London during the fourteenth century, regulations were passed to protect the populace and limit the amount of dumping. In 1345, for instance, the mayor of London found the Thames to be so polluted at Douegate that he forbade water fetchers from using it. Furthermore, a group of five carters was appointed, at the expense of taxpayers, to keep the dock and water clean. Imprisonment was threatened should either side fail to keep up the bargain.

Alcoholic beverages were free from bacteria, as the process of fermentation killed any unwanted microbes. Although many doctors cautioned against overindulgence, and generally maintained a low opinion of beer, everyone—including children—drank it at all meals. The alcohol content of medieval beer was on a par with Belgian ales and tripple bocks, which made it much higher than the ubiquitous lagers consumed today. "Small beer," brewed from a second or third running from a brewer's mash (a process akin to using a teabag twice), had an alcohol level of about 2.5 percent, making it much weaker than ordinary beer, and thus suitable for children. Mead, a drink made from fermented honey and enjoyed by Beowulf and his *comitatus*, fell somewhere in between wine and beer in mouth feel and flavor. Its popularity rose and fell with Anglo-Saxon pride.

For the wealthy middle class and nobility, however, wine was the favorite drink. It offered status and variety with nearly sixty types of French wine and thirty of Italian and Spanish available in London in Chaucer's time. The stock of La Galeye Tavern on London's Lombard Street reveals an array of varietals including red Gascon, Rhenish, vernage, Romney, malmsey, Rhone, and vordor. Claret from Bordeaux (Eleanor of Aquitaine's lands) and *Romeney* were particularly expensive and well-loved choices.

With such popularity came dishonesty and devious wine dealers sought to boost profits by creating fake *Romeney*, a process that involved reboiling old wine and adding resin, pitch, and other inedible and potentially dangerous substances. Other kinds of popular mulled wines were made more safely with the addition of spices. Hippocras was the most popular of these and, while recipes vary, the consensus indicates the heating of red wine with ginger, cinnamon, galangal, and sugar with nutmeg, cloves or grain of paradise often thrown in.

At the Table

People in the Middle Ages generally ate two meals per day. Dinner was the main meal, served around mid-morning to early afternoon and supper around sunset. Breakfast was only considered appropriate for very early risers and agricultural laborers who had to keep their strength up. For anyone else, an early morning wine-sop—bread soaked in wine—was sheer hedonism. There were instances in which extra meals were allowed. Workers were sometimes rewarded for hard labor with *nuncheon,* a mid-day meal that seems to be the ancestor of our own word luncheon. For those burning the midnight oil, a midnight snack of wafers and wine, known as *re-resoper,* was an occasionally acceptable indulgence.

While everyday meals offered a relatively simple menu with limited choices, banquets were a time for overindulgence and variety. A typical banquet featured two courses plus dessert, but within those courses the variety of dishes was staggering. One serving (known as a *messe*) brought from the kitchen on a platter known as a charger, was shared between two, four, or six people with higher ranked guests sharing with fewer other diners.

Within each group sharing a platter, a diner of lower rank served one of higher, men served the women, and younger guests served their elders. The beverage was usually shared as well, served in goblets and tankards of glass or metal. An unusual vessel of the Middle Ages was the *hanap,* a double cup, the upper part of which was another cup. *Mazers* served a dual role as bowls and drinking vessels.

Food was served on trenchers, stale sturdy bread cut into edible plates that soaked up the juices while keeping food off of the table. Forks were a rarity, considered by the English during Chaucer's time to be an Italian affectation. Spoons, however, and sometimes knives were set at each place, although diners often brought their own knives to the table. Knives were used to spear food, lift meat into the trencher, or carry food to the mouth. Most food, however, was eaten with the fingers, making proper hygiene an important element of table manners. One of the distinguishing characteristics of Chaucer's well-bred Prioress is her immaculate table manners. He writes:

At mete wel ytaught was she with alle;
She leet no morsel from hir lippes falle,
Ne wette hir fyngres in hir sauce depe;
Wel koude she carie a morsel and wel kepe
That no drope ne fille upon hire brest.

At the table she was well-taught to behave
She let no morsel fall from her lips,
And she never dipped her fingers in the sauce

She carried each morsel daintily up to her mouth
So that no drop of sauce fell upon her breast.

(*Canterbury Tales,*
General Prologue, I (A), 127–31)

Hands were washed before the meal, between each course, and afterward. Special servants known as ewerers brought the water, usually scented with herbs, to the table.

In addition, a familiar litany of proper table manners governed proper behavior for diners. People were cautioned to break shared bread, not bite it, to wipe their mouths before drinking, and then to be careful neither to slurp nor dunk their beards. Elbows were to be kept from the tabletop, and scratching one's head (probably for fear of dropping lice or fleas), blowing one's nose, or burping were all considered objectionable behavior. Because of the practice of sharing dishes, dunking a bit of food twice in its appropriate sauce was considered to be quite rude and unhygienic. Finally, care was to be taken when dipping from the salt cellar. The salt was placed in an open container, in front of the most honored guest—hence the term "below the salt" for those of lesser rank.

Besides the placement of the salt, the proper seating of guests was a matter of great import. The hosts and their most honored guests sat at the high table that was set above and perpendicular to the rest of the tables. The guest of honor sat in the middle rather than at the head of the table. The rest of the guests were seated in descending order of rank at an assortment of tables set parallel to one another. The stable table or table dormant was made of heavy oak and held a permanent spot in the hall, usually laden with food. Trestle tables were temporary tables with detachable tops set atop sawhorses for easy placement and removal. The great number of dishes piled on the table dormant led to the phrase "groaning board."

Provisioning the Medieval Kitchen

Although most medieval homes, even those in cities, kept at least a small garden, there remained many items that needed to be purchased from markets and shops. In London, where Chaucer lived, shops of a similar type were clustered together giving streets and sections their names. The Shambles, for instance, housed the butchers. Bread Street and Milk Street contained the bakeries and cheese shops. The Chepes were the markets, a name taken from the Anglo-Saxon *ceap,* meaning "to buy." The Chepe was divided into Eastchepe and Westchepe (names that survive to this day, but modernized to Eastcheap and Westcheap).

Local authorities strictly regulated the hours markets were allowed to operate. Any goods sold after-hours were subject to fine or forfeiture. An indication of the secularization of later medieval society as well as an increasingly modern perception of time is apparent in the movement away from the use of church hours such as prime, vespers, and nones to specific times, such as 11:00.

Besides the rules regulating the markets themselves, each type of food sold carried its own set of restrictions. One of the most basic regulatory functions was the conforming of weights and measures to a local or national standard (known as the king's weight). Weights were stamped with a town's insignia and only official weights were legal to use. Two "beams" existed—the small beam that weighed lighter goods by pounds, and the great beam that measured by the hundredweight. The Keeper of the Beam handled calibration and was an important elected position because anyone caught shorting goods was subject to punishment in the pillory with their goods burned beneath them. Wet measure in its simplest form conformed to the following scale: 1 barrel = 30 gallons; 1 ferdkyn = 7 ½ gallons; 1 tun = 252 gallons; 1 potell = 2 quarts; 1 gyll = ½ pint.

The Miller is known for stealing grain and taking payment three times, and Chaucer's reference to his "thombe of gold" reminds us of the need for strict weighing regulations (*Canterbury Tales*, General Prologue, I (A), 563).

Because bread formed a fundamental portion of the medieval diet, and many depended on bakers for this staple food, very strict regulations governed the actions of bakers, including ingredients, preparation, and measurements. In 1378 London, the following regulations were set:

First that every baker swear to charge his servants to bolt their meal twice, that is to say with a large bolter and a smaller one, and that he will use diligence to make his servants work well in kneading, as well as to keep the proper time for so doing....

Also that they buy not bad meal to mix with good....

Also that no brown-bread baker handle a bolter or make white bread....

Also that no horse bread be made except of pure beans and peas without mixture of other grain or other bran, under heavy penalty. (Rickert, 196–197)

The practice of including "garbage" (i.e., entrails and questionably fresh meat) into pies prompted the following:

Because the pastelers of the city of London have heretofore baked in pasties rabbits, geese, and garbage not befitting and sometimes stinking, in deceit of the people, and have also baked beef in pasties and sold the same for venison, in deceit of the people; therefore by the assent of the four master pastelers and at their prayer, it is ordered and assented to:

....That nobody of the said trade shall bake rabbits in pasties for sale, on pain of paying, the first time, if found guilty thereof, 6s. 8d. to the use of the Chamber and of going bodily to prison, at the will of the mayor....

Also that no one of the said trade shall buy of any cook of Bread Street or at the hostels of the great lords, of the cooks of such lords, any garbage from capons, hens, or geese to bake in a pasty and sell, under the same penalty. (Rickert, 21–22)

Furthermore, all bakers and pastelers had to put their official stamp on every product so that their good could be traced back to them in the event of a legal issue or customer dissatisfaction. Bakers and brewers were required to bake and brew one-farthing measures for the poor "as ale is as necessary as bread." Finally, because rotten meat was a serious health hazard, poulterers and fishmongers faced strict punishments if they knowingly sold food that was "rotten or stinking or not proper for man's body."

There is a lot of food and references to food in a social context in Chaucer's *The Canterbury Tales,* and it is this gustatory aspect of his writing that helps to provide the details from life for which he is famous. The reader is provided with a clue to the character of the Prioress when Chaucer tells us that she feeds her little dogs on milk, very expensive white bread, and roasted meat (*Canterbury Tales,* General Prologue, I (A), 146–47). Her religious colleague, the Monk—even more flagrantly worldly than Madame Eglantine—not only enjoys hunting but has a taste for good food: "A fat swan loved he best of any roost" (*Canterbury Tales,* General Prologue, I (A), 191–92, 206). Similarly, the Friar "knew the taverns wel in every toun" (*Canterbury Tales,* General Prologue, I (A), 240). Better, in fact, than he does the beggars and lepers whom he considers below his station, although he is of a mendicant order himself.

Chaucer's secular characters are likewise characterized by their gourmet tastes. The red-faced Franklin demonstrates overweening love of pleasure in his taste for wine-soaked bread and the sheer opulence of his table, which changed its menu according to the seasonal shortage of certain ingredients as well as the needs to balance the humors seasonally:

His breed, his ale, was alweys after oon;
A bettre envyned man was nowher noon.
Withoute bake mete was nevere his house,
Of fissh and flessh, and that so plentevous
It snewed in his house of mete and drynke;
Of alle deyntees that men koude thynke,
After the sondry sesons of the yeer,
So chaunged he his mete and his soper.
Ful many a fat partrich hadde he in muwe,
And many a breem and many a luce in stuwe.

His bread and his ale were always of top quality
There was not a better wine cellar known.
His house was never without roasted meat and fish
And it was so plenteous there that it

Seemed that it snowed meat and drink in his home,
As well as any delicacies that a man could imagine.
During each season of the year
He changed his supper menu to reflect what was in season.
He had many fat partridges in a coop,
And his fishpond was stocked with pike and carp.

(*Canterbury Tales,*
General Prologue, I (A), 334, 341–49)

The Cook is brought along by the gluttonous Franklin to make sure that he eats well. The ulcer on his shin undercuts his reputation as a skilled chef, as cleanliness and hygienic conditions in the kitchen were of great importance. However, his skill with ingredients opens a window into the type of dishes served in Chaucer's time. Finally, the Shipman is fond of Bordeaux wine, a taste that elevates him socially in some ways above the Monk (*Canterbury Tales,* General Prologue, I (A), 396–97).

See also Daily Life; Private Houses

FURTHER READING

Adamson, Melitta Weiss. *Food in Medieval Times.* Westport, CT: Greenwood Press, 2004.

Cosman, Madeleine Pelner. *Fabulous Feasts: Medieval Cookery and Ceremony.* New York: George Braziller, 1976.

Mennell, Stephen. *All Manners of Food: Eating and Taste in England and France from the Middle Ages to the Present.* 2nd ed. Urbana: University of Illinois Press, 1996.

Rickert, Edith. *Chaucer's World,* ed. Clair C. Olson and Martin M. Crow. New York: Columbia University Press, 1948; reprint 1968.

Scully, Terence. *The Art of Cookery in the Middle Ages.* Woodbridge, Suffolk, England: Boydell Press, 1995.

Stannard, Jerry. *Herbs and Herbalism in the Middle Ages and Renaissance.* Edited by Katherine E. Stannard and Richard Kay. Aldershot, England: Ashgate, 1999.

Unger, Richard W. *Beer in the Middle Ages and the Renaissance.* Philadelphia: University of Pennsylvania Press, 2004.

Fortune

Allas, why pleynen folk so in commune
On purveiaunce of God, or of Fortune,
That yeveth hem ful ofte in many a gyse
Wel bettre than they kan hemself devyse?
Som man desireth for to han richesse,

That cause is of his mordre or greet siknesse;
And som man wolde out of his prisoun fayn,
That in his hous is of his meynee slayn.
Infinite harmes been in this mateere.

Alas, why do so many people complain
About God's providence, or of Fortune
When they often give them so much more
Than they could think of on their own?
One man wants vast riches
But it becomes the cause of his murder or bad health;
Another man wants to be free of his prison
But once he is back in his house, his servants kill him.
Much harm has been accomplished in this manner.

(*Canterbury Tales*,
"The Knight's Tale," I (A), 1251–74)

Dame Fortuna and her wheel were two of the most pervasive symbols of the Middle Ages and, in particular, of Chaucer's poetry. The idea of a personified Fortune is quite old, dating back at least to Cicero's writings. In the Roman pantheon, Fortuna (or the Greek Tyche) was depicted as blindfolded, like Justice, and symbolized luck. While good luck was the hope, her blindness denoted a certain unpredictable and even fickle nature. Thus, bad luck might just as easily befall one at her hands (*Canterbury Tales*, "The Knight's Tale," I (A), 1251–74; see also *Canterbury Tales*, "The Monk's Tale," VII, 2135–42, 2239–46; *Troilus and Criseyde*, Book III, 317–23, 1623–31).

Fortune was even known to play games, such as chess (*Book of the Duchess*, 618–82). Blindly capricious, she might easily favor a good man as a bad one, and, like her sister Fame, Fortune is cursed as often as she is praised:

Thanne shal I yeve Emelya to wyve
To whom that Fortune yeveth so fair a grace.

Then I shall have Emily as my wife,
She to whom Fortune has given so much beauty.

(*Canterbury Tales*,
"The Knight's Tale," I (A), 1860–61)

And Fortune ay they cursen as they goon;

And Fortune who they curse as they go.

(*Canterbury Tales*,
"The Clerk's Tale," IV (E), 898)

O sodeyn hap! O thou Fortune unstable!
Lyk to the scorpion so deceyvable,
That flaterest with thyn heed whan thou wolt stynge;
Thy tayl is deeth, thurgh theyn envenymynge.
O brotil joye! O sweete venym queynte!
On monstre, that so subtilly kanst peynte
Thy yiftes under hewe of stidefastnesse,
That thou deceyvest bothe moore and lesse!

Oh sudden misfortune! O you Fortune unstable!
Just like the scorpion that deceives,
Who flatters with the head while the tail would give a deadly sting;
Your tail is death, through your venom.
Oh brutal joy! O sweet and cunning venom!
You monster, who can subtly paint a picture
Of steadfastness and loyal,
While you deceive utterly underneath!

(*Canterbury Tales,*
"The Merchant's Tale," IV (E), 2057–64)

"Allas," quod she, "on thee, Fortune, I pleyne,
That unwar wrapped hast me in thy cheyne,
Fro which t'escape woot I no socour,
Save oonly deeth or elles dishonour."

"Alas," she said, "to you, Fortune, I complain
Who has wrapped me in your chains all unaware
And from which I can have no hope to escape
Except either through death or dishonor."

(*Canterbury Tales,*
"The Franklin's Tale," V (F), 1355–59)

Than seyde he thus: "Fortune, allas the while!
What have I don? What have I thus agylt?
How myghtestow for rowthe me bygile?
Is there no grace, and shal I thus be split?
Shal thus Creiseyde awey, for that thow wilt?
Allas, how maistow in thyn herte fynde
To ben to me thus cruwel and unkynde?"

Then he said: "Fortune, alas all the while!
What have I done? Why has this happened to me?

How might you try to trick me?
Is there no hope and will I be forced to be split in two?
Does Criseyde have to go away, is that what you want?"

Have I the nought honoured al my lyve,
As thow wel woost, above the goddes alle?
Whi wiltow me from joie thus deprive?
O Troilus, what may men now the calle
But wrecche of wrecches, out of honour falle
Into miserie, in which I wol bewaille
Criseyde—allas!—hi that the breth me faille?

Have I not honored all of my life,
As you well know, the goddess Venus above all others?
Then why will you deprive me of my joy?
Poor Troilus, who men will now call
The wretch of all wretches, will fall out of honor
And into misery, in the depths of which I will cry
Criseyde's name. Will the breath in my body fail?

Allas, Fortune, if that my lif in joie
Displesed hadde unto thi foule envye,
Why ne haddestow my fader, kyng of Troye,
Byraft the lif, or don my bretheren dye,
Or slayn myself, that thus compleyne and crye—
I, combre-world, that may of nothyng serve,
But evere dye and nevere fulli sterve.

Alas, Fortune, if my happiness in life
Has displeased you into such wretched envy,
Why did you not let my father, the King of Troy,
Die, and why don't my brothers die,
Or why don't you slay me, since I so complain and cry to you—
I, broken-hearted, who can serve nothing and no-one
But instead die every day, and never fully live.

(*Troilus and Criseyde*, Book IV, 260–80)

See also *Troilus and Criseyde*, Book IV, 386–92, 515–18, 600–02, 1189–92; *Troilus and Criseyde*, Book V, 468–69, 1133–34, 1461–62, 1745, 1763–64; *Legend of Good Women*, 589; *Book of the Duchess*, 811–16; *House of Fame*, 1544–48, 2016–25; "A Complaint to His Lady," 35; "Truth," 9.

The chief influence on the medieval notion of Fortune is Boethius's *Consolation of Philosophy*, which served to fully integrate the idea of Fortune and her wheel into the medieval consciousness. She is often depicted in medieval art standing beside a large wheel that she spins with a lever.

There are figures attached to the wheel, usually representing kings. As her wheel turns, the kings rise and fall.

In "The Monk's Tale," Pedro of Castile and Holofernes are particular victims of Fortune and her wheel (*Canterbury Tales,* "The Monk's Tale," VII, 2347–76, 2397–98, 2445–46, 2556–58). She also plays tricks, acting as Nero's friend, then ultimately bringing him to grief (*Canterbury Tales,* "The Monk's Tale," VII, 2457–59, 2478, 2519–50). *Troilus and Criseyde,* in particular, contains the most extended images of Fortune and her wheel. She spins it during the Trojan War, bringing victory and defeat for each side with no rhyme or reason:

Fortune and her wheel; from Boccaccio De Casibus's *Virorum Illustrium,* 1467. Courtesy of the Glasgow University Library.

> The thynges fellen, as they don of werre,
> Bitwixen hem of Troie and Grekes, ofte;
> For som day boughten they of Troie it derre,
> And eft the Grekes founden nothing softe
> The folk of Troie, and thus Fortune on lofte
> And under eft gan hem to whielen bothe
> Aftir hir course, ay whil that thei were wrothe.

> *Things fell out, as they will in a war,*
> *Between the men of Troy and the Greeks, quite often;*
> *For many days those of Troy bought their lives dearly*
> *And on others the Greeks found nothing weak about them,*
> *And in this way Fortune lifted them up*
> *And then again dropped them down around her wheel,*
> *Until their anger was spent.*

(*Troilus and Criseyde*, Book I, 134–40)

She spins her wheel and Troilus loses Criseyde:

> But al to litel, weylaway the whyle,
> Lasteth swich joie, ythonked be Fortune,
> That semeth trewest whan she wol bygyle
> And kan to fooles so hire song entune
> That she hem hent and blent, traitour commune!
> And whan a wight is from hire whiel ythrowe,
> Than laugheth she, and maketh hym the mowe.

But all too short the while
When joy will last, before Fortune
Who seems to be the truest when she seeks to beguile
And makes of fools those who listen to her song
By blinding and binding them, the traitoress!
And when a man is thrown down on her wheel
Then she laughs at him, and makes of him a mockery.

From Troilus she gan hire brighte face
Awey to writhe, and tok of hym non heede,
But caste hym clene out of his lady grace,
And on hire whiel she sette up Diomede;
For which myn herte right now gynneth blede,
And now my penne, allas with which I write,
Quaketh for drede of that I moste endite.

From Troilus, she turned away her bright face
While he writhed in pain, and took of him no notice,
But threw him clean out of his lady's grace.
And upon her wheel she instead set up Diomede;
And for this my heart now begins to bleed
And now my pen, with which I write,
Shakes for the dread of what I must recount.

For how Criseyde Troilus forsook—
Or at the leeste, how that she was unkynde—
Moot hennesforth ben matere of my book,
As written folk thorugh which it is in mynde.
Allas, that they sholde evere cause fynde
To speke hire harm! And if they on hire lye,
Iwis, hemself sholde han the vilanye.

For the way that Criseyde forsook her Troilus—
Or, at the very least, of how she was untrue—
Must from here onwards be the subject of my book,
As it is written by folk who keep the tale in mind.
Alas that they should ever be in a position
To speak to her harm! And if they should lie,
Then upon them should fall all the villainy!

(*Troilus and Criseyde*, Book IV, 1–21)

The metaphor of the wheel was meant to remind people—especially those in a position of power, wealth, or influence—that worldly good fortune was fleeting and capricious:

She seyde, "Lord, to whom Fortune hath yiven
Victorie, and as a conqueror to liven,
Nat greveth us youre glorie and youre honour,
But we biseken mercy and socour.
Have mercy on oure wo and oure distresse!
Som drope of pitee, thurgh thy gentillesse,
Upon us wreched wommen lat thou falle,
For, certes, lord ther is noon of us alle
That she ne hath ben a duchesse or a queene.
Now be we caytyves, as it is wel seene,
Thanked be Fortune and hire false wheel."

…

syn Fortune is chaungeable,
Thow maist to thy desir somtyme atteyne.

She said, "Lord, to whom Fortune has given the
Victory, and as conqueror the glory,
We don't begrudge you your glory and honor,
But we do crave from you mercy and pity.
Have mercy on our woe and our distress!
Some drop of pity, through your gentleness,
Please let drop upon us wretched women,
For certainly, there are none of us here
Who was not a duchess or a queen.
Now we are all destitute as you can see,
Thanks to Fortune and her false wheel."

…

Since Fortune is so changeable,
You may sometime achieve your desire.

(*Canterbury Tales,*
"The Knight's Tale," I (A), 915–26, 1242–43)

See also Canterbury Tales, "The Monk's Tale," VII, 2457–59, 2661–70, 2734, 2763–66; *Canterbury Tales,* "The Nun's Priest's Tale," VII, 3403–4; *Troilus and Criseyde,* Book I, 211–17, 837–54.

It was better to put one's faith and hope in God and his heavenly reward than material things of the secular world. Chaucer gives Fortune a chance to defend herself in the short poem "Fortune," in which she maintains that her very mutability teaches men to see reality:

I have thee taught divisioun bitwene
Frend of effect and frend of countenaunce;
Thee nedeth nat the galle of noon hyene,

That cureth eyen derked for penaunce;
Now seestow cleer that were in ignoraunce.

I have taught you the difference between
A friend in actuality and a friend in appearance,
You do not need the gall of the noon hyena
That unclouds the eyes that were blinded for penance
And in ignorance, but now see clearly.

("Fortune," 33–37)

See also Fame

FURTHER READING

Brown, Peter, ed. *A Companion to Chaucer.* Malden, MA: Blackwell, 2002.

Frye, Northrop. *Biblical and Classical Myths: The Mythological Framework of Western Culture.* Buffalo, NY: University of Toronto Press, 2004.

Hansen, William F. *Classical Mythology: A Guide to the Mythical World of the Greeks and Romans.* New York: Oxford University Press, 2005.

Manser, Martin H. *The Facts On File Dictionary of Classical and Biblical Allusions.* New York: Facts On File, 2003.

Morford, Mark P. O. *Classical Mythology.* 7th ed. New York: Oxford University Press, 2003.

Nolan, Barbara. *Chaucer and the Tradition of the Roman Antique.* New York: Cambridge University Press, 1992.

Powell, Barry B. *Classical Myth.* Translated by Herbert M. Howe. 4th ed. Upper Saddle River, NJ: Pearson/Prentice Hall, 2004.

Price, Simon, and Emily Kearns, eds. *The Oxford Dictionary of Classical Myth and Religion.* New York: Oxford University Press, 2003.

Four Humors

His slep, his mete, his drynke, is hym biraft,
That lene he wex and drye as is a shaft;
His eyen holwe and grisly to biholde,
His hewe falow and pale as asshen colde,
And solitarie he was and evere allone,
And waillynge al the nyght, makynge his mone;
And if he herde song or instrument,
Thanne wolde he wepe, he myghte nat be stent.
So feble eek were his spiritz, and so lowe,
And chaunged so, that no man koude knowe
His speche nor his voys, though men it herde.
And in his geere for al the world he ferde
Nat oonly lik the loveris maladye

Of Hereos, but rather lyk manye,
Engendred of humour malencolik
Biforen, in his celle fantastic.

His sleep, his meat, his drink, is all to him bereft,
So that he became lean and dry as a stick,
His eyes hollow and grisly to behold
His skin sallow and pale as ashes cold,
And he was solitary and ever always alone,
Wailing in the night and always moaning.
And if he heard a song or an instrument
Then he would cry and could not stop.
His spirits were so feeble and so low,
And so changed was he that no man would know
His voice or his speech, though men heard him.
And in his behavior for all the world he acted like
Not just one who was lovesick,
But like one who is manic,
Afflicted with a melancholy humor
In his forehead, the seat of all imagination.

(*Canterbury Tales,*
"The Knight's Tale," I (A), 1361–76)

The balance of the humors in the human body was the foundational principle of medieval medicine. Dating their understanding of the humors to Hippocrates, physicians of the Middle Ages believed that all of the body's ailments—physiological and mental—could be explained by an imbalance in the humors, which could be brought back into equilibrium through diet, herbal purgatives, and bloodletting (*Canterbury Tales,* General Prologue, I (A), 421). The four humors represented the four elements, embodying combinations of temperature and humidity. Blood represented air, was hot and moist, and was associated with the heart. An overabundance of blood led to a sanguine temperament that was happy and passionate. Blood was believed by some to dominate at night:

The norice of digestioun, the sleep,
Gan on hem wynke and bad hem taken keep
That muchel drynke and labour wolde han reste;
And with a galpyng mouth hem alle he keste,
And seyde that it was tyme to lye adoun,
For blood was in his domynacoiun.
"Cherisseth bood, natures freend," quod he.
They thanken hym galpynge, by two, by thre,
And every wight gan drawe hym to his reste,
As sleep hem bad; they tooke it for the beste.

> *The nurse of digestion, sleep,*
> *Came over him with a wink and a warning*
> *As much drink and hard labor demands rest;*
> *And with a yawning mouth he kissed them all*
> *And said it was time to lie down and sleep*
> *Because blood dominates from midnight to dawn.*
> *"Cherish blood, nature's friend," he said.*
> *They thanked him yawning and by twos and threes*
> *They all began to head toward bed.*
> *As he had asked them to sleep, they took it to be good advice.*

(*Canterbury Tales*,
"The Squire's Tale," V (F), 347–56)

Yellow bile, the fire humor, was hot and dry and associated with the gall bladder. Too much yellow bile made one choleric, or violent and aggressive. Phlegm, the cold, moist humor, represented water and was associated with the liver. Phlegmatic people were pale and sickly, passive and cowardly. Finally, black bile—the cold, dry earth humor—was associated with the spleen and was the mark of a melancholic or depressive.

Chaucer mentions the humors throughout his works, particularly in relation to emotional distress. The mortally lovesick Arcite has a melancholic humor in his forebrain. In "The Nun's Priest's Tale," stomach vapors upset the humors and inspire bad dreams. Herbal remedies help to bring the humors back into balance (*Canterbury Tales*, "The Nun's Priest's Tale," VII, 2923–38, 2955–68). *The Book of the Duchess* makes clear the seriousness of humoral imbalance, as melancholy is said to be potentially fatal:

And wel ye woot, agaynes kynde
Hyt were to lyven in thys wyse,
For nature wolde nat suffyse
To noon erthly creature
Nat longe tyme to endure
Withoute slep and be in sorwe.
And I ne may, ne nyght ne morwe,
Slepe; and thus melancolye
And drede I have for to dye.
Defaute of slep and hevynesse
Hath sleyn my spirit of quyknesse
That I have lost al lustyhede.
Such fantasies ben in my hede
So I not what is best to doo.

And well you know, it is against nature
To live here in this way
For nature will not allow

Any earthly creature
For very long to live
Without sleep and be in sorrow.
And I may not, not tonight or tomorrow,
Sleep; and thus because of melancholy
And sadness I will die.
Lack of sleep and sadness
Have taken away all of my liveliness
So that I have lost my desire to live
Such ideas have been in my head
So that I no longer know what is best to do.

(*Book of the Duchess*, 16–29)

See also Black Death; Medicine; Physician

FURTHER READING

French, Roger. *Canonical Medicine: Gentile da Foligno and Scholasticism.* Boston: Brill, 2001.

French, Roger, Jon Arrizabalaga, Andrew Cunningham, and Luis García-Ballester, eds. *Medicine from the Black Death to the French Disease.* Aldershot, England: Ashgate, 1998.

Gottfried, Robert S. *Doctors and Medicine in Medieval England, 1340–1530.* Princeton, NJ: Princeton University Press, 1986.

Hildegard of Bingen. *On Natural Philosophy and Medicine: Selections from "Case et Cure."* Translation and introduction by Margret Berger. Cambridge, England: D. S. Brewer, 1999.

Kibre, Pearl. *Studies in Medieval Science: Alchemy, Astrology, Mathematics, and Medicine.* London: Hambledon Press, 1984.

Fox

The fox was not considered during the Middle Ages to be a morally upright creature. Yet he nearly always was successful in his schemes, thereby clouding the waters of medieval moral lessons. The fox lives by its wits, is a survivor, and nobody is safe from its machinations. The ultimate trickster, it was believed that the fox hunted by deception, not skill, although the fox's swiftness and stealth made it an ideal hunter even without the use of foul play. It was believed that, in order to catch birds, the fox would first roll in red clay mud to counterfeit blood, and then play dead. As hungry birds approached to peck at the "corpse," the fox would suddenly come to life and devour the unsuspecting prey.

In a world dominated by courtly notions of fair play and proper warfare, such behavior appeared cowardly. Yet it was impossible to deny that there was a certain power in the fox's cunning. The fox uses its wits—a more cerebral and subtle (and thus perhaps more dangerous) type of skill—rather than physical strength to accomplish its goals. It was only natural, then, that the fox would eventually come to represent the devil. Although possessed of potentially great physical power, the devil prefers to trick the faithful into straying into sin, presenting temptation as opportunity, then finally revealing the truth when it is too late. After all, the road to hell is paved with good intentions, a proverb illustrating that those who mean well can fall into sin without even realizing their mistake.

In *The Canterbury Tales*, the fox symbolizes this very negative aspect. Chaucer helps to characterize the offensive Miller by comparing him to a fox and a sow, a most unusual and unflattering combination:

His berd as any sowe or fox was reed,
And therto brood, as though it were a spade.
Upon the cop right of his nose he hade
A werte, and theron stood a toft of herys,
Reed as the brustels of a sowes erys;

...

Wel koude he stelen corn and tollen thries;
And yet he hadde a thombe of gold, pardee.

His beard was as red as any sow or fox,
And very broad, like a spade.
On the end of his nose on the right he had
A wart which was topped by a tuft of hair,
Which was as red as the bristles in a sow's ears.

...

He was very good at stealing corn and tripling prices,
Oh, yes, he certainly did have a thumb of gold!

(*Canterbury Tales,*
General Prologue, I (A), 552–56, 562–63)

This particular description not only evokes the physicality of a fox in a negative way, but also uses the reputation of the animal to emphasize the Miller's dishonesty. Like the fox, he steals and cheats. Before he even tells his tale, we know that the Miller is not a nice man.

Later, in "The Nun's Priest's Tale," which features the character of Reynard, Chaucer offers a fable in which a rooster succeeds in outwitting the wily fox. The noble rooster Chaunticleer initially falls prey to his pride and is captured by a fox that has been lurking around the barnyard. Trapped in the fox's jaws as they are pursued by all of the farm's animals, Chaunticleer convinces the fox to turn around and shout insults at his enemies. Foolishly, and perhaps out of keeping with his character, the fox acquiesces and Chaunticleer seizes the moment to escape. Not one to give up so easily, the fox attempts flattery again to regain his prey, but Chaunticleer has learned his lesson and will not fall to the trickster a second time. The fox is eventually captured.

In the course of the tale, Chaucer provides a parody of notable traitors: "Oh newe Scariot, newe Genylon, / False dissymulour, o Greek Synon, / That broughtest Troye al outrely to sorwe!" (*"Oh new Iscariot, new Ganelon / Oh false dissembler, like the Greek Sinon / who brought such devastation to Troy!"* (*Canterbury Tales*, "The Nun's Priest's Tale," VIII, 3227–29). Judas Iscariot, of course, was also notably a redhead, further connecting foxes and those who do the devil's work. And yet the corollary is even more complicated than it seems. Judas may have betrayed Christ, but it is all part of God's larger plan. The fox might trick birds and seem immoral, but it is created by God and also plays its part in the larger plan and teaches its lessons in the book of nature.

FURTHER READING

Rowland, Beryl. *Blind Beasts: Chaucer's Animal World*. Kent, OH: Kent State University Press, 1971.

Salisbury, Joyce E., ed. *The Medieval World of Nature: A Book of Essays*. New York: Garland, 1993.

Strickland, Debra Higgs. *Medieval Bestiaries: Text, Image, Ideology*. New York: Cambridge University Press, 1995.

Telesko, Werner. *The Wisdom of Nature: The Healing Powers and Symbolism of Plants and Animals in the Middle Ages*. New York: Prestel, 2001.

Franklin

A FRANKELEYN was in his compaignye;
Whit was his berd as is the dayesye;
Of his complexioun he was sangwyn.
Wel loved he by the morwe a sop in wyn;
To lyven in delit was evere his wone,
For he was Epicurus owene sone,
That heeld opinioun that pleyn delit
Was verray felicitee parfit
An housholdere, and that a greet, was he;
Seint Julian he was in his contree.
His breed, his ale, was always after oon;
A bettre envyned man was nowher noon.
Withoute bake mete was nevere his hous,
Of fissh and flessh, and that so plentevous
It snewed in his hous of mete and drynke;
Of alle deyntees that men koude thynke,
After the sondry sesons of the yeer,

So chaunged he his mete and his soper.
Ful many a fat partrich hadde he in muwe,
And many a breem and many a luce in stuwe.
Wo was his cook but if his sauce were
Poynaunt and sharp, and redy al his geere.
His table dormant in his halle alway
Stood redy covered al the longe day.

A Franklin was in the company;
His beard was as white as a daisy
And his complexion was sanguine.
He loved a sop of bread in wine in the morning;
And to live the good life was forever his goal,
For he was Epicurus's own son,
Who help the opinion that plain delight
Was the epitome of perfection
His house was always open and lavishly provisioned;
A veritable Saint Julian was he in his county.
His bread and his ale were always of top quality
There was not a better wine cellar known.
His house was never without roasted meat and fish
And it was so plenteous there that it
Seemed that it snowed meat and drink in his home,
As well as any delicacies that a man could imagine.
During each season of the year
He changed his supper menu to reflect what was in season.
He had many fat partridges in a coop,
And his fishpond was stocked with pike and carp.
Woe to his cook if his sauces were not piquant and sharp
And his equipment not always at the ready
His table dormant always stood in the great hall
Covered and ready all day long.

(*Canterbury Tales,*
General Prologue, I (A), 331–54)

A franklin was a landowner, usually of substantial tracts of land, who was not of noble birth. He was part of the emerging middle class of the fourteenth and fifteenth centuries, descended from the peasant class who had benefited from the rise of capitalism to accumulate funds, buy land, and increase its wealth in both of the chief assets of the time: cash and land.

As Chaucer's Franklin demonstrates, socially this position might carry a certain degree of insecurity, the prejudice that comes with new money. The Franklin is extravagant in his approach to fine living. An epicurean known for the quality of his wine cellar and his table is always groaning with good food, his cook in a constant state of activity to keep the table stocked with gourmet dishes and their accompanying sauces.

Yet Chaucer's description of him seems to indicate that, despite any sort of insecurity, the Franklin is an exemplary host and a jovial fellow who was liked by many as well as trusted as a fixture in the community. He notes that the Franklin served in various legal and governmental capacities within his shire. He would not have gotten to that position without some trust on the part of his peers. Certainly he could not have achieved it by hospitality and good wine alone, although they probably did him no harm among his neighbors.

See also Estates; Food

FURTHER READING

Bean, J.M.W. *From Lord to Patron: Lordship in Late Medieval England*. Manchester, England: Manchester University Press, 1989.

Boitani, Piero, and Jill Mann. *The Cambridge Chaucer Companion*. New York: Cambridge University Press, 1986.

Britnell, Richard, ed. *Daily Life in the Late Middle Ages*. Stroud, England: Sutton, 1998.

Lambdin, Laura C., and Robert T. Lambdin, eds. *Chaucer's Pilgrims*. Westport, CT: Praeger, 1999.

Friar

A FRERE ther was, a wantowne and a merye,
A lymytour, a ful solempne man.
In alle the ordres foure is noon that kan
So muchel of daliaunce and fair langage,
He hadde maad ful many a mariage
Of yonge wommen at his owene cost.
Unto his ordre he was a noble post.
...
He knew the tavernes wel in every toun
And everich hostiler and tappestere
Bet than a lazar or a beggestere,
For unto swich a worthy man as he
Accorded nat, as by his facultee,
To have with sike lazars aqueyntaunce.

There was a Friar, a wanton and merry man
A Limiter, and an important personage.
In all of the four Orders there was no one
Else who was so good at glib speech and flattery.
He had performed a great many marriages
In a hurry for young women, and some at his own cost.
He was a true asset to his order.
...

He knew the taverns well in every town
And every hosteler and tapster,
Better than he did any lazar or beggar
For being such a worthy man as he was
He did not think that he should spend his time
With lowly sorts like lepers.

(*Canterbury Tales,*
General Prologue, I (A), 208–45)

The Friar is one of Chaucer's most pointed examples of churchmen behaving badly. He is extremely worldly, spends much of his time in taverns, flirts (and perhaps worse) with women, takes bribes, and ignores the needs of the sick (*Canterbury Tales,* General Prologue, I (A), 208–69). Hubard the Friar makes his living through begging, but despises beggars and other unfortunates with whom he should feel some affinity. Even worse, he grants easy penances to those who will give him gifts, enabling him to make a profit at the expense of local priests with whom he shares the duties of hearing confession.

While he is most likely an extreme caricature, as are several of Chaucer's characters, Hubard demonstrates the broader concerns society had with his profession. Friars were by their very nature open to a great deal of criticism. These mendicant orders first developed in the thirteenth century as a means to combat the increasingly worldly and wealthy direction that the Church was taking.

The intention of the orders was for friars to be free of all private property, including monasteries, in order to follow Jesus' example of meeting spiritual needs of a broader community wherever their travels took them. With no connection to a monastery that separated them from the rest of society, friars roamed the land, begging for their sustenance and in return providing spiritual guidance in the form of confessions, sermons, and the like.

Their involvement in the community made it nearly impossible for friars to uphold anything approaching the Rule of St. Benedict, and it is easy to see how they might also be swayed from the mendicant ideal as well. The mendicant orders at the institutional level had trouble maintaining

A woodcut of the Friar from a fifteenth-century edition of *The Canterbury Tales.* Courtesy of the Glasgow University Library.

their poverty as grateful nobles bequeathed land and property to their favorite orders. For the individual, resisting the allure of gifts of all sorts would require a strong faith and constitution indeed. Chaucer's characterization demonstrates just such a fall from grace past the mere temptation of gifts to the outright acceptance of bribes and the indulgence in several of the Seven Deadly Sins.

Mendicant orders were originally intended to counteract the problems with direction and dedication that were plaguing the Church in general and monastic orders specifically. As the Church grew ever wealthier and consequently worldlier, theologians sought a means to return to the strictest teachings of Jesus.

The Franciscans and Dominicans were the first of these orders, taking as their founding principles a vow of absolute poverty. Their goal was to live as Jesus did, preaching and begging for their living. As opposed to monks, who sought spirituality in an avoidance of society, mendicants brought the word into the urban areas and involved themselves deeply in the community.

This goal, as demonstrated by Chaucer's Friar, would be the downfall of many and brought heavy criticism to the orders who found themselves forced to rededicate themselves to their initial principles in much the same way as the monastic orders rededicated several times over the course of the Middle Ages.

See also St. Benedict

FURTHER READING

Benson, C. David, and Elizabeth Robertson, eds. *Chaucer's Religious Tales.* Rochester, NY: D. S. Brewer, 1990.

Duby, Georges. *The Three Orders: Feudal Society Imagined.* Translated by Arthur Goldhammer. Chicago: University of Chicago Press, 1980; reprinted 1982.

Farmer, Sharon, and Barbara H. Rosenwein, eds. *Monks and Nuns, Saints and Outcasts: Religion in Medieval Society: Essays in Honor of Lester K. Little.* Ithaca, NY: Cornell University Press, 2000.

Foster, Edward E., and David H. Carey, eds. *Chaucer's Church: A Dictionary of Religious Terms in Chaucer.* Brookfield, VT: Ashgate, 2002.

Hirsh, John C. *The Boundaries of Faith: The Development and Transmission of Medieval Spirituality.* New York: E. J. Brill, 1996.

Froissart

Born in Valenciennes, Hainault, to a middle-class family, Jean (or Jehan) Froissart (ca. 1333–1410) was a French poet, priest, historian, and courtier who would become the most famous chronicler of the Hundred Years War. Very little is known of his early life, although it is possible that his father was a painter of armor. Froissart was ordained as a priest, serving as

The Battle of Crécy as depicted in *The Chronicles of Froissart,* 1369–1373. © Bibliothèque nationale de France.

rector of Les Estinnes near Thun from 1373 to 1382, and as canon of Chimay in 1383.

Despite these posts, he essentially abandoned this career to live a more worldly life in the employ of Queen Philippa of England, for whom he acted as official historian. It was in this capacity that he was able to travel throughout England, Scotland, Wales, Flanders, Spain, and France, moving through the highest echelons of court society and gathering information for his *Chronicles.*

It is believed that Froissart knew Chaucer personally. They certainly traveled in the same circles, and both men, along with Petrarch, attended the wedding of the Duke of Clarence's daughter to Galeazzo Visconti, Petrarch's patron. The strengths of Froissart's *Chronicles,* covering the years 1322 to 1400, are also its weaknesses. Froissart has a flair for descriptive language and storytelling. As such, he brings a lively voice to the events he describes and illustrates the chivalric world better than anyone else of his time. His sympathy for the participants, however, which enables him to bring his society to life in the pages of the *Chronicles* also biases his historical account in favor of whomever was his patron of the moment. He also makes many factual errors in dates and frequently pads the numbers of participants in battle, most likely for dramatic effect.

See also Edward III; Hundred Years War; John of Gaunt; Richard II

FURTHER READING

Ainsworth, Peter F. *Jean Froissart and the Fabric of History: Truth, Myth, and Fiction in the* "Chroniques." New York: Oxford University Press, 1990.

Palmer, J.J.N. *Froissart: Historian.* Totowa, NJ: Rowman & Littlefield, 1981.

Patterson, Lee. *Chaucer and the Subject of History.* Madison: University of Wisconsin Press, 1991.

Furniture

Although we do not spend a great deal of time in any medieval homes in Chaucer's works, furniture and furnishings were, of course, an important facet of daily life. However, medieval homes, even those belonging to wealthy burghers and nobles, were scantly furnished by today's standards.

Furniture was time-consuming and expensive to make, and space was limited. Even the wealthiest homes faced heating challenges in colder months, and people tended to congregate in the heated areas of a home or palace, necessitating that furniture perform double or triple duty. Small chests were used for storage as well as for seating or as ad hoc tables, for instance. In very small or poor homes, beds performed double duty as seating as well.

For the nobles who moved frequently from home to home in order to keep tabs on the management of their multiple manors, furniture often had to be portable as well. Despite these practical requirements, furniture for those who could afford it was expected to be beautiful as well as functional. Medieval furniture was often embellished with painted or carved designs or beautiful fabric coverings.

As might be expected, peasant homes were the most spartanly furnished. Peasants would typically own a bed or two, with the mattress generally stuffed with straw. In addition, a couple of chests that functioned as storage, seating, and tables rounded out the home's furniture. Since the average peasant homes were never of more than two or three rooms, the lack of furniture often seemed more of a blessing than a detriment. There simply was not enough room to store and use a plethora of pieces.

The wealthy would have not only nicer furniture, but also more of it. Many chests of varying sizes were used again as tables and seats, as well as for storage. In addition to chests, wealthy merchants and nobles would have chairs and tables and benches. Tables were generally long, rather than square or round, and were constructed of heavy wood. Off to the side of the dinner table, food was served on long credenzas that were moved out of the way between mealtimes. In later centuries, these credenzas and chests would evolve into larger pieces such as cupboards, sideboards, and storage closets (armoires).

A bed was one of the more important pieces of furniture in a medieval home. As with everything else, beds provided a dual function and were used much like couches during the day. Beds of the wealthy were often very elaborate, with thick feather mattresses, piles of linens, curtained hangings, and heavy wooden frames. They were often also quite large. The linens and hangings were important for insulation and warmth and, in busy households, privacy. One could close the curtains around the bed and shut out the outside world if there was no door to close. These giant beds—sometimes as long as 11 feet—were often the most favored item in a king's palace and would be dismantled and moved when he went on progress.

See also Castles; Daily Life; Food; Private Houses; Tapestry

FURTHER READING

Britnell, Richard, ed. *Daily Life in the Late Middle Ages.* Stroud, England: Sutton, 1998.

Burns, E. Jane, ed. *Medieval Fabrications: Dress, Textiles, Clothwork, and Other Cultural Imaginings.* New York: Palgrave Macmillan, 2004.

Quiney, Anthony. *Town Houses of Medieval Britain.* New Haven, CT: Yale University Press, 2003.

Schofield, John. *Medieval London Houses.* New Haven, CT: Yale University Press, 1994.

Singman, Jeffrey L., and Will McLean. *Daily Life in Chaucer's England.* Westport, CT: Greenwood Press, 1995.

Wood, Margaret. *The English Mediaeval House.* London: Bracken Books, 1983; reprinted 1985.

G

Games

In Flaundres whilom was a compaignye
Of yonge folk that haunteden folye,
As riot, hasard, stywes, and tavernes,
Where as with harpes, lutes, and gyternes,
They daunce and pleyen at dees bothe day and nyght,
And eten also and drynken over hir myght
Thurgh which they doon the devel sacrifise
Withinne that develes temple in cursed wise
By superfluytee abhomynable.

In Flanders there was a group
Of young folk who courted folly,
In the form of gambling, dicing, brothels, and taverns,
And they danced and played all day and night
To the sounds of harps, lutes, and citerns,
While they ate and drank with all their might.
They offered the devil their sacrifices
In the devil's cursed temples
With these abominable excesses.

(*Canterbury Tales*,
"The Pardoner's Tale," VI (C), 463–71)

The game of chess is depicted in a thirteenth-century publication. © Bibliothèque nationale de France.

Although spare time was fleeting and often restricted to the hours past daylight for many, games and other pastimes were popular activities in the Middle Ages. Today, many people associate sports and games during the Middle Ages solely with jousting. However, there were a number of physical and mental activities that not only demonstrate a rich and varied leisure world but also reveal the roots of many of our own games today. Pastimes in the Middle Ages were perhaps more purposeful than they are in the modern world. Physical activities helped to develop skills and muscles for fighting and farming, while board games were designed to develop the mind.

Entertainment served the purpose of passing otherwise empty hours and created diversion, but in a harsher world where survival depended on one's abilities to deal with any kind of adversity that life dished out, even a pastime needed to be designed to instruct as well as amuse.

Despite the purpose-driven nature of medieval games, many within the Church especially looked upon them with suspicion as encouraging idleness and rough behavior, even sinful gambling and wagering. Two exceptions were archery and fencing, which specifically and obviously developed useful fighting skills. Many major cities throughout Europe had schools devoted to these two sports, even awarding diplomas to their best students. Fencing and sword-fighting exhibitions also were featured events at tournaments, another activity frowned upon by the Church, but which provided the most direct and realistic opportunities for developing warrior skills.

Tournaments are the activity that is perhaps most commonly associated with the Middle Ages. During their time, they were also the most popular of spectator sports, participation in a tournament being limited to knights.

One of the central activities of the tournament was the formal joust, where two knights attempted to knock one another from horseback with lances. In addition, there was the similar, but theoretically safer, baton, an activity requiring knights to knock the crests off of one another's helmets. The idea behind the baton was to test similar skills without the same danger of personal injury that the joust often posed.

Finally, the main event of any tournament was the melee, which involved a full-out simulated battle and sometimes resulted in serious injury to participants, even though the idea was merely to capture and ransom, not harm physically, one's opponents. Many a young, poor knight was able to accumulate some wealth through superior fighting skills that allowed him to best his elders and gather ransom in the form of coin and equipment.

The Queen from a thirteenth-century chess set. © Bibliothèque nationale de France.

"The Knight's Tale" features an extended description of the pomp and excitement that accompanied a medieval tournament, dwelling with intricate detail on the heraldic devices and weaponry of the participants:

Ther maystow seen devisynge of harneys
So unkouth and so riche, and wroght so weel
Of goldsmythrye, of browdynge, and of steel;
The sheeldes brighte, testeres, and trappures,
Gold-hewen helmes, hauberkes, cote-armures;
Lordes in paramentz on hir courseres,
Knyghtes of retenue, and eek squieres
Nailynge the speres, and helmes bokelynge;
Giggynge of sheeldes, with layneres, lacynge—
There as nede is they weren no thyng ydel;
  ...
Ther shyveren shaftes upon sheeldes thikke;
He feeleth thurgh the herte-spoon the prikke.

Up spryngen speres twenty foot on highte;
Out goon the swerdes as the silver brighte;
The helmes they tohewen and toshrede;
Out brest the blood with stierne stremes rede;
With myghty maces the bones they tobreste.
   ...

The jelous strokes on hir helmes byte;
Out renneth blood on bothe hir sydes rede.

There you might see such an array of harnesses
So exotic and expensive and made so carefully and well;
So much fancy embroidery, steelwork, and goldsmithery
Of shields brightly polished, and hauberks, trappings,
Helmets of gold, mail, and coats of arms;
Lords in costly robes on fine horses,
Knights of the retinue and their squires.
Nailing on the spear-heads and fastening the helmets;
Gigging the shields with lanyards and lacings,
There was need for activity everywhere and no one was idle.
   ...

There shafts shivered upon shields and split
Some of the men felt the shaft through the breast-bone prick
The spears reached up twenty feet in the air
Out come the swords, silver bright,
To hew and shred the helmets of the other side
Out of breasts flowed the blood, steady and thick
And under mighty maces the bones break.
   ...

The powerful strokes on their helmets bite
Out runs the red blood from both sides.

(*Canterbury Tales,*
"The Knight's Tale," I (A), 2496–2636)

Ball Games

Other games, while popular, were considered to be at the root of an assumed "decay" in English archery. In 1363, an edict was passed attempting to forbid sports such as handball, stickball, cambok, and football. However, these games all managed to survive, since the rule was so difficult to enforce.

Cambok was a game that resembled modern field hockey. It was thusly named for the curved sticks, which resembled a shepherd's crook, that were used to move the ball down the field. Stickball and handball, as their names imply, required striking a ball with a stick or hand, respectively. Balls were made of wood and did not bounce, making for what must have been an interesting challenge to consistently strike the ball hard enough to keep the game moving.

Medieval football—roughly akin to modern soccer—and a sport known as camp ball—which resembled rugby—were particularly popular among players and especially derided by moralists. Not only were they believed to encourage rowdy behavior among their fans, but they could be quite dangerous to the players themselves. Camp ball especially posed great danger to the participants because the purpose of the game was to convey the ball to the goal by any means possible. Because the goals could be placed miles apart, participants could use horses to speed travel. The potential for trampling conjures images of a battlefield melee in which foot soldiers grapple with mounted knights.

Lighter fare included shuttlecock, which was played with paddles like modern badminton, and a curious game called stoolball, in which a player threw a wooden ball at a stool while his opponent tried to deflect it with his hands. The roots of bowling appear in bowls, quits, and kailes, all of which required players to throw a ball or a stick at a specified target or, in the case of kailes, at a set of wooden pins with the intention to knock them down.

Child's Play and Other Pastimes

Children's games were very similar to those played today, although they were perhaps slightly more physical and rough. Tug-of-war was a favorite in the poorest villages where rope was readily and cheaply available. Leapfrog and blind-man's bluff both had no requirements beyond the physical presence of the players, making them available to any child, rich or poor.

Many games that were popular with children and adults centered around outdoor celebrations, such as May Day, and included more romantic and fanciful activities. Apple-bobbing and dancing around the May Pole allowed for incidental touching and flirting. There were some games that involved "fortune telling" in the most generic sense. Ragman's Roll, for instance, involved choosing sealed parchment rolls out of a hat. Each parchment, like the inside of a fortune cookie, contained a prediction of the future. These games, of course, were frowned upon by churchmen.

The development of the mind was stressed in board and card games, although the latter quickly led to unsavory pursuits such as gambling that made them seem illicit and potentially dangerous. Chess and backgammon were considered to be especially prestigious games. Chess had long been popular throughout the Islamic world after its invention in sixth-century India. Crusading knights brought the game back from the Middle East and thus introduced it to Europe. Chess was thought to develop a warrior's strategic planning because it is essentially a game of war. Chess pieces did not differ greatly from modern sets, in that there were the same pieces and two styles: the conventional stylized set and the figurative set in which a queen looked like a queen and so forth. However, there were many variations of piece movement.

A joust is depicted in this fourteenth-century illustration. © Bibliothèque nationale de France.

Although no examples of actual playing cards survive from earlier than the fifteenth century, there is ample evidence that card games were a popular pastime in earlier centuries of the Middle Ages. References from 1377 describe a deck containing four suits, 10 number cards and 3 face cards in each suit. Early Italian cards indicate that suits were rather like modern tarot cards and included batons, swords, cups, and coins. Games lent themselves easily to gambling, like today, and in medieval card games we find the predecessors of modern-day poker and blackjack.

Other wagering games included hazard, which was played with dice and resembles modern craps. Any number of players would gather around a table or in a circle and the dice would be rolled. One player would make a bet and the others would follow by wagering against part or all of the bet.

That dice was generally considered a low pursuit is indicated by "The Pardoner's Tale," which begins:

―――――――――

Now wol I yow deffenden hasardrye.
Hasard is verray mooder of lesynges,
And of deceite, and cursed forswerynges,
Blespheme of Crist, manslaughtre, and wast also
Of catel and of tyme; and forthermo,
It is repreeve and contrarie of honour
For to ben holde a commune hasardour.
And ever the hyer he is of estaat,
The more is he yholden desolaat.
If that a prynce useth hasardrye,
In alle governaunce and policye
He is, as by commune opinioun,
Yholde the lasse in reputacioun.

Now will I describe to you gambling.
Hazard is the veritable mother of lies,
And of deceit, and of cursed perjuries,
The blaspheming of Christ, manslaughter, and the complete waste
Of time and money; furthermore,
It is the opposite of honor, a reproach,
To be known as a common gambler.
And the higher a rank a man might hold,
The further he falls through gambling
Such that if a prince gambles,
Then those he governs and polices
Come to think of him in public opinion
Of having a sadly reduced reputation.

(*Canterbury Tales,*
"The Pardoner's Tale," VI (C), 590–629)

In the game of hazard, or raffle, several players bet an equal stake into the ante. The player who is chosen to cast throws two of three dice until he gets "doublets," or two of the same number. He then throws the third die and adds the total pips on all three dice. Each remaining player follows suit, the one with the highest score winning the pot.

See also Entertainment; Knight

FURTHER READING

Barker, Juliet R. V. *The Tournament in England, 1100–1400.* Wolfeboro, NH: Boydell Press, 1986.

Carter, John Marshall. *Medieval Games: Sports and Recreations in Feudal Society.* New York: Greenwood Press, 1992.

Wilkins, Sally E. D. *Sports and Games of Medieval Cultures.* Westport, CT: Greenwood Press, 2002.

Gentilesse

Vyce may wel be heir to old richesse,
But ther may no man, as men may wel see,
Bequethe his heir his vertuous noblesse
(That is appropred unto no degree
But to the firste fader in magestee,
That maketh hem his heyres that him queme),
Al were he mytre, croune, or diademe.

Vice might well be the heir to old money
But there is no man, as anyone can well see,
Who can give to his heir his noble virtue
(Which can be appropriated by anyone of any degree

Gentilesse

Except as it is given by the first father in heaven
Who make those his heirs who follow him)
As he would his crown or diadem.

("Gentilesse," 15–21)

————————

Gentilesse at its root simply means inborn superiority. Originally tied to gentle lineage, eventually it implied a range of qualities including refinement, morality, intelligence, nobility of character, and courtesy. During Chaucer's time it was undergoing this shift from a class-based notion to something that can be innate in even a peasant and that is not automatically passed through birth.

Love, in particular seems to bring out the *gentilesse* in a person, and many of Chaucer's female characters seem to embody it through their steadfast devotion to their mates, particularly Griselda of "The Clerk's Tale," who endures her husband's increasingly difficult tests of her love and devotion with steadfast dignity despite her peasant birth. In "The Knight's Tale," there is a twist to this notion, perhaps indicative of the Knight's personality. Arcite is disguised as lowborn, but his inborn nobility cannot help but shine through:

————————

But half so wel biloved a man as he
Ne was ther nevere in court of his degree;
He was so gentil of condicioun
That thurghout al the court was his renoun.
They seyden that it were a charitee
That Theseus wolde enhancen his degree,
And putten hym in worshipful servyse,
There as he myghte his vertu exercise.
And thus withinne a while his name is spronge,
Bothe of his dedes and his goode tonge,
That Theseus hath taken hym so neer
That of his chambre he made hym a squier,
And gaf hym gold to mayntene his degree.
And eek men broghte hym out of his contree,
From yeer to yeer, ful pryvely his rente;
But honestly and slyly he it spente,
That no man wondred how that he it hadde.

But half so well-beloved a man as he
Was never known at the court in his position;
He was so gently spoken and in his behavior
That he was renowned throughout the court.
Everyone said that it would be a fitting charity
If Theseus would raise him above his station
And allow him to come into the Duke's service

Where he might use his excellent virtue.
And so within a short time his name was carried about
Both because of his deeds and his noble speech
So that Theseus took him near to himself
So near as to make him a squire of his chamber
And gave him gold to maintain himself in his elevated position
And men from his own country also discretely
Came year after year, and gave him his income.
But he was so prudent in his spending
That no one wondered that he had so much.

(*Canterbury Tales,*
"The Knight's Tale," I (A), 1429–45)

This passage, of course, reveals the Knight's social bias and perhaps his insecurities. He believes that one of gentle birth cannot act as anything but noble, no matter how he or she dresses or appears.

However, the fact that Arcite is elevated to squire status despite his apparently low birth, reveals in a backhanded way Chaucer's belief in the inborn, classless nature of *gentilesse*. The knight in the tale of the Wife of Bath says boldly that *gentilesse* comes from an ancient name and wealth, but perhaps he is incorrect (*Canterbury Tales,* "The Wife of Bath's Tale," 1117–1212). Chaucer's own belief is aptly summed up in his short poem "Gentilesse" ("Gentilesse," 15–21).

See also Estates; Knight

FURTHER READING

Brown, Peter, ed. *A Companion to Chaucer.* Malden, MA: Blackwell, 2002.
Rossignol, Rosalyn. *Chaucer A to Z.* New York: Facts On File, 1999.

Gernade. *See* Grenada

Goose

"My wit is sharp; I love no taryinge;
I seye I rede hym, though he were my brother,
But she wol love hym, lat hym love another."

"My wit is sharp; I do not like to beat around the bush;
I say I will advise him, even as I would my own brother,
If she will not love him, then let him love another."

(*Parliament of Fowls,* 565–67)

Geese have a strangely mixed range of symbolic uses in literature and society. Domestic geese were said to represent home, hearth, and family life. Although often considered silly and stupid because of their habit of wandering and cackling, geese were actually prized in a capacity of guards in ancient times, and sacred geese were kept in the temples of Mars, Cupid, Priapus, and Venus. In Christian literature, the soberly colored grey goose was said to be like the modest and humble Christian, while the white goose represented the flashy dresser and gossip.

In Chaucer's *The Parliament of Fowls,* the goose is elected to represent the water fowls, and advises that the formel should choose the tercel she loves the best. The advice seems wise on the surface, but it is backwardly directed, apparently at the male eagles instead of the female (*Parliament of Fowls,* 565–67). The sparhawk mocks her, finding it ridiculous that the female should choose her own mate and the less noble one at that.

See also Animals; Birds

FURTHER READING

Rowland, Beryl. *Blind Beasts: Chaucer's Animal World.* Kent, OH: Kent State University Press, 1971.

Salisbury, Joyce E., ed. *The Medieval World of Nature: A Book of Essays.* New York: Garland, 1993.

Strickland, Debra Higgs. *Medieval Bestiaries: Text, Image, Ideology.* New York: Cambridge University Press, 1995.

Telesko, Werner. *The Wisdom of Nature: The Healing Powers and Symbolism of Plants and Animals in the Middle Ages.* New York: Prestel, 2001.

Great Schism

The Great Schism refers to the period of the Catholic Church that lasted from 1378 to 1415, when competing popes were elected by various means to the papacy. The result was widening cracks in the Church's foundation that eventually opened the door to the emergence of Protestantism from being considered just another troublesome group of heresies to a recognized alternative form of Christian worship.

The Great Schism is prefaced by the Avignon Papacy (1305–78), during which the papacy was removed from Rome to Avignon in France. During this time, the pope was increasingly viewed as little more than a French puppet, and anger and rebellion fomented throughout Christendom. To make matters worse, the Church provided little in the way of services to the sick and dying during the Black Death and did little to condemn or curtail the excesses of the Hundred Years War. In a time of increasing peasant unrest, the concurrent image of the Church as worldly and wealthy further undermined its position as the dominant authority in Europe.

Upon the death of Gregory XI in 1378, the College of Cardinals (made up of combined nationalities), threatened by an angry Roman mob, was forced to elect an Italian as his successor. This pope, Urban VI, decided the papacy should return permanently to Rome, a pronouncement that angered the French cardinals, who withdrew. In protest, the French cardinals elected a French pope who styled himself Clement VII, declaring Urban's election invalid because the College of Cardinals were acting under duress.

Understandably this resulted in great confusion among the faithful. There had been rival antipopes in the past, but never had the College of Cardinals elected one. When both Urban VI and Clement VII died in 1389 and 1394, respectively, successors to both were elected and the schism continued. Pope Boniface IX ruled in Rome until 1404 and Benedict XIII until 1418.

The Church, however, realized that this split could not continue without resulting in great damage. The cardinals asked the popes to resign but were met with stubborn refusal. The rival popes even went so far as to excommunicate one another. In 1409, a third pope, Alexander V, was elected in an effort to set the problem to rights, the idea being he would be recognized as the sole legitimate pope, the other two deposed as antipopes.

However, the unfortunate situation of three rival popes continued until 1417's Council of Constance, which finally succeeded in deposing John XXIII in Rome and Benedict XIII in Avignon, and received the resignation of the third pope Gregory XII. In their place, Martin V was elected and the schism ended. From this point on, the Church decreed that the only one who could undo the election of the pope was the pope himself.

The damage to the Church's image was enduring, and it is apparent how far individual church offices had fallen from grace before the Great Schism's resolution in Chaucer's depictions of church men and women. Madame Eglantyne, the Prioress, is more concerned with her manners and feeding dainties to her little dogs than in managing her nuns:

In curteisie was set ful muchel hir lest.
…
And sikerly she was of greet desport,
And ful plesaunt, and amyable of port
And peyned hire to countrefete cheere
Of court, and to been estatlich of manere,
And to ben holden digne of reverence.
But for to speken of hire conscience,
She was so charitable and so pitous
She wolde wepe, if that she saugh a mous
Kaught in a trappe, if it were deed or bledde.

Her demeanor was very pleasant
She was kind and courtly to all,
Very pleasant and amiable
And acted in such a way as to mimic the manners

Of court, so much so that she was thought to
Be a person of much renown.
But to speak of her conscience,
She was so charitable and so full of pity
That she would weep if she saw a mouse
Caught in a trap, if it was dead or had bled.

(*Canterbury Tales*,
General Prologue, I (A), 132–45)

The Monk and the Friar are both of questionable moral character, a fact revealed immediately in the General Prologue:

A MONK ther was, a fair for the maistreie,
An outridere, that lovede venerie.

...

The reule of Seint Maure or of Seint Beneit—
By cause that it was old and somdel streit
This ilke Monk leet olde thynges pace,
And heeld after the newe world the space.

...

Grehoundes he hadde as swift as fowel in flight;
Of prikyng and of huntyng for the hare
Was al his lust, for no cost wolde he spare.

...

A FRERE there was, a wantowne and a merye,
A lymytour, a ful solempne man.

...

Ful swetely herde he confessioun,
And plesaunt was his absolucioun:
He was an esy man to yeve penaunce,
Ther as he wiste to have a good pitaunce.
For unto a povre ordre for to yive
Is signe that a man is wel yshryve;

...

He knew the tavernes wel in every toun
And everich hostiler and tappestere
Bet than a lazar or a beggestere.

There was a Monk, who was a handsome man for the ministry
He was an outrider who loved good sport.

...

The rule of Saint Maurus or of Saint Benedict,
Because they were so old and straightlaced,
This monk let old things fall by the wayside
And instead let modern ideas guide him.

...

Greyhounds he owned, as swift as fowl in flight

Riding and hunting rabbits were all he cared for
And he spared no cost in his passion.
…
There was a Friar, a wanton and merry man
A Limiter, and an important personage.
…
He heard every confession with great sympathy
And his absolution was always given lightly
He was an easy man in assigning penance,
Especially when he was assured of getting a gift in return.
Because, of course, giving to a poor order
Is a sure sign that a man is shriven
…
He knew the taverns well in every town
And every hosteler and tapster,
Better than he did any lazar or beggar.

(*Canterbury Tales*,
General Prologue, I (A), 165–242)

See also Black Death; Estates; Friar; Monk; Nun; Prioress; Religion

FURTHER READING

Biller, Peter, and Barrie Dobson, eds. *The Medieval Church: Universities, Heresy, and the Religious Life: Essays in Honour of Gordon Leff.* Rochester, NY: Boydell Press, 1999.

Blumenfeld-Kosinski, Renate. *Poets, Saints, and Visionaries of the Great Schism, 1378–1417.* University Park: Pennsylvania State University Press, 2006.

Foster, Edward E., and David H. Carey, eds. *Chaucer's Church: A Dictionary of Religious Terms in Chaucer.* Brookfield, VT: Ashgate, 2002.

Grenada

In Gernade at the seege eek hadde he be
Of Algezir, and riden in Belmarye.

In Grenada he had been at the siege
Of Algeciras, and he had ridden in Morocco.

(*Canterbury Tales*,
General Prologue, I (A), 56–7).

Located in Andalusia on the southern coast of Spain, Grenada was one of the gateway cities to the Islamic world and, as a result, was the focus of much contention in the wars between the Spanish and the Moors to the south. Granada fell to the Banu Marin early in the fourteenth century and remained under their control until 1344.

The Knight's presence in Grenada places him in the middle of the wars between the Spanish and Muslim invaders (*Canterbury Tales,* General Prologue, I (A), 56–7). The implication is that the Knight was involved in minor skirmishes or battles that would benefit a mercenary more than a noble knight of the king's army.

See also John of Gaunt; Knight

FURTHER READING

Cantor, Norman. *The Civilization of the Middle Ages.* Rev. ed. New York: Harper Collins, 1993.

Jones, Terry. *Chaucer's Knight: The Portrait of a Medieval Mercenary.* Baton Rouge: Louisiana State University Press, 1980.

Kaeuper, Richard W. *Chivalry and Violence in Medieval Europe.* New York: Oxford University Press, 1999.

Labarge, Margaret Wade. *Medieval Travellers.* New York: Norton, 1983.

Le Beau, Bryan F., and Menachem Mor, eds. *Pilgrims and Travelers to the Holy Land.* Omaha, NE: Creighton University Press, 1996.

Tyerman, Christopher. *England and the Crusades, 1095–1588.* Chicago: University of Chicago Press, 1988.

Verdon, Jean. *Travel in the Middle Ages.* Notre Dame, IN: University of Notre Dame Press, 2003.

H

Hare

During the Middle Ages, the hare symbolized timorousness and hesitancy, making it an odd choice for heraldic devices, where it appeared on the arms of Edward I. However, it was also known for speed, gregariousness, and wisdom. The hare was thought to know its weaknesses and, through understanding its own limitations, was able to outwit and avoid its enemies. Its final symbolic connection was with sexual performance, as the hare is legendary for its ability to reproduce with abundance.

In Chaucer's works, the hare appears in a number of places and a variety of guises to represent a variety of character types. In the prologue to "Sir Thopas," Harry Bailly speaks directly to Chaucer, attempting to draw out the quiet poet. Bailly implies that there is something shady or shy about Chaucer's habit of staring at the ground "as thou woldst fynde an hare" (*as you would find a hare*) and follows by exhorting him to tell a tale (*Canterbury Tales,* "The Tale of Sir Thopas," VIII, 691–711). What follows is the jangly "The Tale of Sir Thopas," which manages to irritate Chaucer's pilgrims to the degree that he is begged to stop. Chaucer's description of the Pardoner's eyes in the General Prologue is that they are "glarynge" (*staring*) like a hare's, making him look shifty and easily spooked, while the Summoner in "The Friar's Tale" evokes the hearty but furtive sexual appetite of the rabbit (*Canterbury Tales,* General Prologue, I (A), 684; *Canterbury Tales,* "The Friar's Tale," III (D), 1325–29).

FURTHER READING

Rowland, Beryl. *Blind Beasts: Chaucer's Animal World.* Kent, OH: Kent State University Press, 1971.

Salisbury, Joyce E., ed. *The Medieval World of Nature: A Book of Essays.* New York: Garland, 1993.

Strickland, Debra Higgs. *Medieval Bestiaries: Text, Image, Ideology.* New York: Cambridge University Press, 1995.

Telesko, Werner. *The Wisdom of Nature: The Healing Powers and Symbolism of Plants and Animals in the Middle Ages.* New York: Prestel, 2001.

Hats. See Fashion

Helen of Troy

The most beautiful woman in the world, Helen was the daughter of Zeus and Leda. She was married to King Menelaus of Sparta. Prince Paris of Troy, however, had been promised the right to have the most beautiful woman in the world by Venus. Various versions of the legend survive. According to one, Paris came to her and persuaded her to leave with him. In another, he kidnapped her. Either way, her departure with him sparked the Trojan War.

Chaucer mentions Helen in *The Parliament of Fowls* as one of love's martyrs (*Parliament of Fowls*, 288–94). In "The Merchant's Tale," the delusional January humorously claims that he will ravish his new wife more vehemently than Paris did Helen: "But in his herte he gan hire to manace / That he that nyght in armes wolde hire streyne / Harder than evere Parys dide Eleyne" (*But in his secret heart he began to imagine / that he would that very night strain her in love / Harder even than Paris ever did Helen*") (*Canterbury Tales,* "The Merchant's Tale," IV (E), 1752–54).

Helen of Troy also makes an appearance in *Troilus and*

A depiction of the capture of Helen from a fifteenth-century French manuscript. © Bibliothèque nationale de France.

Criseyde, when she attends a dinner for one of Troilus's brothers and supports Criseyde's request for protection against Poliphete's legal actions against her.

FURTHER READING

Brown, Peter, ed. *A Companion to Chaucer.* Malden, MA: Blackwell, 2002.

Frye, Northrop. *Biblical and Classical Myths: The Mythological Framework of Western Culture.* Buffalo, NY: University of Toronto Press, 2004.

Hansen, William F. *Classical Mythology: A Guide to the Mythical World of the Greeks and Romans.* New York: Oxford University Press, 2005.

Manser, Martin H. *The Facts On File Dictionary of Classical and Biblical Allusions.* New York: Facts On File, 2003.

Morford, Mark P. O. *Classical Mythology.* 7th ed. New York: Oxford University Press, 2003.

Nolan, Barbara. *Chaucer and the Tradition of the Roman Antique.* New York: Cambridge University Press, 1992.

Powell, Barry B. *Classical Myth.* Translated by Herbert M. Howe. 4th ed. Upper Saddle River, NJ: Pearson/Prentice Hall, 2004.

Price, Simon, and Emily Kearns, eds. *The Oxford Dictionary of Classical Myth and Religion.* New York: Oxford University Press, 2003.

Heraldry

In stede of cote-armure over his harnays,
With nayles yelewe and brighte as any gold,
He hadde a beres skyn, col-blak for old.

Instead of a coat of arms over his harness,
With yellow nails, bright as any gold,
He had fastened a bear's skin, coal black and old.

(*Canterbury Tales,*
"The Knight's Tale," I (A), 2140–42)

Heraldry and the development of a distinctive familial coat of arms is another invention of the Middle Ages that had its origin in a very practical purpose. It would eventually, however, evolve into a symbolic and ceremonial practice. Heraldry emerged in the twelfth century from the need to be able to distinguish the knights on one's own side from those on the opponent's. In the heat and dust of battle, and with entire bodies and faces covered in protective armor, recognizing one's friends was impossible without some type of bright symbols that could quickly and clearly be seen at a glance. These symbols were first placed at obvious eye level on shields, and simple symbols, such as lines or crosses, were arranged to indicate family or allegiance.

Later, with the development of the surcoat and increasingly large protective helmets, these symbols were placed on clothing and armor. The term "coat of arms" in fact, came from this practice of wearing the symbols upon one's surcoat.

Heraldic devices were also placed on standards that flew high above the battlefield, enabling those both near and far to find one another. The use of standards, however, far predated heraldry, as the Vikings, Scots, Anglo-Saxons, and others had long utilized banners as a means of locating themselves as well as to symbolize their tribal or cultural affiliation.

As time wore on, these symbols became symbols of lineage, and they fit naturally into the conception of war as the glorious work of pure and aristocratic knights. The notion of chivalry, inborn nobility, and the special nature of knightly warfare all combined to make heraldry the perfect symbolic expression of a social hierarchy that increasingly elevated the knight above the rest of society.

For this reason, heraldic devices evolved from simple stylized symbols to increasingly intricate and colorful shields. Coats of arms were used on seals to authenticate documents, and they were worked into architecture and home decor. They were even used by institutions such as towns and universities, a practice that continues today.

The first recorded incidence of an individual heraldic device was in 1127, when Henry I gave his son Geoffrey a shield decorated with three golden lions. The shield was passed to Geoffrey's grandson, thereby investing heraldry with hereditary significance. Later Geoffrey's brother, Richard I, adopted a shield with two lions facing one another, perhaps an allusion to his long-standing feud with his father. He would eventually change his symbol to the three gold lions on a red background that remains the royal arms of England to this day.

As heraldry grew in complexity, a new array of patterns and colors emerged. There were two categories, which continued to reflect the practical roots of heraldic devices. The first was dark—purple, red, blue, black, or green—and light—typically yellow or white—which were used in conjunction so that the symbols could be seen from the distance of an arrow shot. The background color was known as the field, and the main design was called the charge—two names that evoke the battlefield and war. The color pattern was generally simpler than the actual design, although this would also evolve into more complex combinations as the art of heraldry evolved.

Symbols and color arrangement ultimately became governed by strict codes of meaning and order. Anyone who disobeyed could be banned from tournaments. Additional markings on individual knights—who typically would be marked with their own coat of arms as well as an indication of their loyalty to a king—would be placed on the helmet to indicate rank.

Finally, family crests, or coats of arms, were adapted to include a motto as well as some indication of the families that supported them. In order to police the proper use and display of heraldic crests, special classes of officers were created called heralds and pursuivants. They investigated for fraud or duplication of symbols and officiated at tournaments.

Unlike many other aspects of knighthood, heraldry survives to this day, perhaps because of the continuing fascination with that most elusively seductive of cultural notions, the special nature of noble blood and birth. However, the changes in the nature of warfare changed the needs on the battlefield, and heraldry further evolved into a purely ceremonial indicator of family lineage and rank.

Chaucer references the importance of heraldry in "The Knight's Tale" and alludes perhaps to his belief that such distinctions are ultimately obsolete when he says of Palamon that he had fastened a bear's skin over his armor, rather than a coat of arms (*Canterbury Tales*, "The Knight's Tale," I (A), 2140–42).

See also Animals; Knight; Scrope-Grosvenor Trial

FURTHER READING

Coss, Peter, and Maurice Keen, ed. *Heraldry, Pageantry, and Social Display in Medieval England*. Rochester, NY: Boydell Press, 2002.

De Pisan, Christine. *The Book of Deeds of Arms and of Chivalry*. Translated by Sumner Willard. Edited by Charity Cannon Willard. University Park: Pennsylvania State University Press, 1999.

Heresy

The issue of heresy—beliefs running counter to official Roman Catholic doctrine—became a sticky one for the Church in the closing decades of the Middle Ages. As the Church's political and social dominance weakened after the Black Death, increasingly bold religious and spiritual movements sprung up to provide alternative answers for the faithful but disenchanted.

Certainly, heresy was not a new phenomenon. Heretical movements had appeared and been repressed since the very earliest years of the Catholic Church. Donatism, Pelagianism, and Arianism all plagued the young Church, with their emphases on priestly good conduct, faith over good works, and the humanity of Christ. And while they were all suppressed by statute and/or force, the ideas they represented would return during the Middle Ages.

In 1227, the Church instituted the Inquisition to root out heresies throughout all of Christendom. The Franciscans and Dominicans proved to be useful orders for this task, and friars were sent to rural villages and urban centers alike to question priests and parishioners about their beliefs. Minor infractions were often gently corrected; however, the unrepentant and the relapsed were burned for their unorthodox beliefs.

The execution of Jan Hus following the Council of Constance. Courtesy of Dover Pictorial Archive.

The first group of victims was the Cathars or Albigensians, who posed a political threat in the attraction they held for many wealthy and powerful French aristocrats. From there, the papal Inquisition turned its attention to other groups, such as the Lollards in England, the Hussites in Bohemia, the Waldensians in Lyon, and the Knights Templar. Of these movements, the Hussites and the Lollards seem to have posed the biggest threat to the Church because their leaders proposed ideas that directly fed into Lutheranism and the Protestant Reformation.

The Lollards and Hussites both held firm to a system of beliefs that might loosely be termed proto-socialist in some ways, as there were serious political overtones to their message along with their religious beliefs. Both groups, the Lollards in particular, advocated the reading of scripture in the vernacular. Latin mass, they believed, did not allow the average person to comprehend the word of God. They criticized the worldliness and wealth of the Church as an institution, citing the example of the apostles as the guide to true Christian spirituality. They were also generally egalitarian, and the Lollards in particular advocated the equality of the sexes, even allowing for female preachers. The first Lollard martyr was burned at the stake in 1401.

See also Lollardy

FURTHER READING

Aston, Margaret, and Colin Richmond, eds. *Lollardy and the Gentry in the Later Middle Ages.* New York: St. Martin's Press, 1997.

Biller, Peter, and Barrie Dobson, eds. *The Medieval Church: Universities, Heresy, and the Religious Life: Essays in Honour of Gordon Leff.* Rochester, NY: Boydell Press, 1999.

Copeland, Rita. *Pedagogy, Intellectuals, and Dissent in the Later Middle Ages: Lollardy and Ideas of Learning.* New York: Cambridge University Press, 2001.

Broadside newsletter about the burning of three witches at Derneburg. Courtesy of the Dover Pictorial Archive.

Holidays and Holy Days

Holidays, or holy days, were days associated with religious events or personages, and as our modern definition indicates, were days off to celebrate and contemplate their significance. They shaped the course of daily life, along with the flow of the seasons, as everyone looked forward to a day devoted to pleasant pastimes, feasting, and music.

There were many saints days that were celebrated, although only the most important were chosen, or else nearly every day could have been counted as a holiday. Often the particular saint's day that was celebrated had some sort of local significance or occurred at a convenient point in the calendar. In East Anglia, St. Felix's day was celebrated on May 13, while in Wales, St. Dwynwen's day was celebrated on January 25.

In addition to the saints' days, the three most important holidays in the medieval calendar were Easter, Christmas, and Pentecost. All of these days were intended to be celebrated and observed as Sundays were—although, in practice, they were more festive. Typically there would be music and as much feasting as a budget allowed. The nobility would employ minstrels and often provided food for their peasants as well as a banquet for honored guests.

While each day in the calendar was named as today—Monday, Tuesday, etc.—days were also reckoned by which saints' or feast day fell near them. The day before would be the eve, as in All Hallow's Eve, while morrow indicated the day after. Some feast days also indicated important days in the agricultural calendar, such as Michelmas or Ascension Day.

See also Astrology and Astronomy; Calendar; Daily Life

FURTHER READING

Bentley, James. *A Calendar of Saints: The Lives of the Principal Saints of the Christian Year.* New York: Facts On File, 1986.

French, Katherine L. *The People of the Parish: Community Life in a Late Medieval English Diocese.* Philadelphia: University of Pennsylvania Press, 2001.

Horse

Horses in the Middle Ages served three main purposes: transportation, status, and agriculture. Unless someone wished to travel slowly on foot, the horse was the primary means of locomotion throughout the Middle Ages and well into the nineteenth century. Horses were instrumental to rapid travel and, in the interest of managing goods, in carting items to market towns for sale. They were necessary for moving armies across long distances and for enabling kings to go on progress to administer courts of law and keep local nobles in line.

Although oxen had generally been used to pull plows, the development of a new type of collar that allowed a horse to pull without strangling and of a stouter breed of horse, revolutionized agriculture in medieval Europe. By the fourteenth century, the *stot,* a breed of heavy plow horse ridden by the Reeve (*Canterbury Tales,* General Prologue, I (A), 615–16), was beginning to supplant oxen.

Of perhaps equal importance, from a socioeconomic standpoint, a man or a woman's worth could be judged by the quality of horse he or she owned. The variety of breeds developed by Chaucer's day provides an indication of the importance of both specialization of use and the subtle distinctions in classes of horseflesh. Cart horses, usually geldings, were used not only to carry goods to market but also as rides for peasants. Stockily built, they were a sturdy mount with little finesse of gait or appearance. Often a jade was used for this purpose. Jades were retired cart horses, too weak for pulling a loaded cart, but calm and placid mounts for inexperienced riders.

A hackney was the least expensive of riding horses, dependable but not flashy. A hackney was middling in size and could be used for carrying a knight on campaign, since he would need to save his war-horse (a much more expensive item of equipment) for battle. The Knight's horse, described as "goode, but ... nat gay" (*Good but ... not flashy*) is most likely a hackney (*Canterbury Tales*, General Prologue, I (A), 74–75). Slightly larger was the rouncey, a trotter typically used for hunting. It was a dependable mount with an excellent gait for travel, costing a bit more than the hackney.

Next on the scale of riding horses was the ambler, a pacer with an even better gait for long travel. The Wife of Bath rides an ambler, demonstrating her relatively high position within the middle class (*Canterbury Tales*, General Prologue, I (A), 469–70). Most expensive of all riding mounts was the palfrey. Palfreys cost nearly three times as much as hackneys, and were smooth gaited, elegantly built mounts, as beautiful to look at as they were to ride. The luxurious Monk rides a brown palfrey, and Chaucer notes the number of "deyntee" (*dainty*) horses in his stable (*Canterbury Tales*, General Prologue, I (A), 168, 207).

A final note of interest: the derivation of the term "canter" to describe the traveling gait between a trot and a gallop is from "Canterbury gallop," the pace set by the pilgrims on their way to Becket's shrine. The term was first recorded in 1631.

FURTHER READING

Rowland, Beryl. *Blind Beasts: Chaucer's Animal World*. Kent, OH: Kent State University Press, 1971.

Salisbury, Joyce E., ed. *The Medieval World of Nature: A Book of Essays*. New York: Garland, 1993.

Strickland, Debra Higgs. *Medieval Bestiaries: Text, Image, Ideology*. New York: Cambridge University Press, 1995.

Telesko, Werner. *The Wisdom of Nature: The Healing Powers and Symbolism of Plants and Animals in the Middle Ages*. New York: Prestel, 2001.

Humanism

Medieval humanism had its roots in a reaction against scholasticism, the dominant philosophical and intellectual movement of the twelfth and thirteenth centuries. Philosophers of the scholastic school sought to answer minute questions along the lines of how many angels could dance on the head of a pin, endlessly debating among themselves such purely theoretical notions with no recourse to practical implementation or experimentation. Humanists, on the other hand, returned to original classical texts from Greece and Rome in an effort to confront what were the first ideas and arguments regarding more practical issues. Their emphasis was more on the reality of human existence, and scientific humanists were at the forefront of experimental hypothesizing as opposed to theoretical. Although they still pondered intangible issues, such as the nature of God's love, the difference between humanists and scholastics was that the former analyzed such questions through tangible evidence in the surrounding world. We can see, for instance, the mirror of divine love in human relationships. Although we can never quite pin down what human love is precisely, we can experience it and make generalizations based on observation.

Undated portrait of Geoffrey Chaucer. Courtesy of the Glasgow University Library.

Throughout much of the Middle Ages, the classical texts referred to by humanists, written as they were by pagan authors, were off limits to scholars because of the influence and education of the Catholic Church. However, the increasing secularization of society that began in the late thirteenth and early fourteenth centuries—and eventually culminated in the Renaissance—allowed for the rediscovery, translation, and interpretation of these texts, albeit through a Christian lens.

The first true humanist is generally agreed to be Petrarch, the Italian poet most famous today for his Laura sonnets. Petrarch's greatest influences were Augustine and Cicero. Augustine provided him with the basis of his ideas of reconciling man's relationship with God—the human with the divine. Cicero, on the other hand, provided Petrarch with a model for the proper and eloquent use of language. As a disciple of Cicero's work, Petrarch translated the Roman's correspondence, discovering the man behind the politician. Cicero's devotion to philosophical thought and scholarship, combined with his sense of public duty, made him an ideal model of what a man should be, accomplished in many areas and deeply devoted to human endeavors and progress.

Humanism displaced the medieval focus on serving God as man's sole reason for existence with a newer enjoyment of the world and all it has to offer. A celebration of what it means to be human and experience the here and now characterized the philosophy, lending to the movement a practical aim. The medieval humanists gave human effort a distinctly Christian spin, emphasizing that man's accomplishments were ultimately meant to glorify God because we are his creation. However, the difference from earlier medieval thought was in striving to achieve greatness rather than embracing humility as the best way to please God. Based on the teachings of Augustine, the belief was that we are given unlimited potential because we are made in God's image, and we should always strive to achieve as much as we possibly can in order to honor that legacy. To be anything less and to shirk our duty to know the world around us is to disappoint God's plan in our creation.

One of the most important elements of humanist thought was its emphasis on education and this, too, finds its roots in Cicero's writings. Although the classical liberal arts program of the quadrivium (arithmetic, geometry, music, and astronomy) and the trivium (grammar, rhetoric, and logic) dates back to classical Roman times, it was the humanists who began to focus more on the trivium. The ability to think, speak, and write convincingly and persuasively—known as eloquence—became the mark of the truly educated man.

Chaucer's Clerk, despite his bookishness and interest in Aristotle, might best represent this trend, as his tale and envoy are both eloquent and calculated to convince the audience of the truth in his rather unorthodox viewpoints. Scholastics, on the other hand, focused on using language to achieve or derive some sort of certainty of knowledge. Chaucer's Doctour of Physik represents the scholastics, as he still relies on astrology and other theoretical ideas to diagnose patients. In short, the philosophical and intellectual focus shifted from seeking facts and proof (through theoretical approaches) to analyzing and exploring for the growth and joy that come from the process of learning and discovery.

The philosophical rooster, Chauntecleer, and his wife Pertelote of "The Nun's Priest's Tale," seem to reflect this trend in thought when they learnedly argue against each other citing classical sources. Chauntecleer argues that dreams signify future events, which indicates the existence of predestination and, thus, an omniscient God. However, they also reveal human curiosity and the desire to know and understand the world. Pertelote argues that dreams are mere physiological manifestations of humoral imbalance, thus revealing an interest in exploring science, perhaps in a way that is provable through experimentation:

"Lo Catoun, which that was so wys a man,
Seyde he nat thus, 'Ne do no fors of dremes?'"
"Now sire," quod she, "whan we flee fro the bemes,
For Goddes love, as taak som laxatyf.
Up peril of my soule and of my lyf,
I conseille yow the beste—I wol nat lye—
That bothe of colere and of malencolye
Ye purge yow; and for ye shal nat tarie
Though in this toun is noon apothecarie."

Look at Cato, who was the wisest of men
And who asked, 'Why would you fear dreams?'"
"Now sir," she said, "when we fly from these beams,
for God's love, please take some laxative.
Upon the peril of my soul and my life
I give you the best advice—I would not lie—
To purge yourself of the choler and melancholy
For there is no apothecary in this town."

"As touchyng daun Catoun,
That hath of wysdom swich a greet renoun,
Though that he bad no dremes for to drede,
By God, men may in olde bookes rede
Of many a man moore of auctoritie
Than evere Caton was, so moot I thee,
That al the revers seyn of this sentence,
And han wel founden by experience
That dremes been significaciouns
As wel of joye as of tribulaciouns
That folk endurn in this lif present.
Ther nedeth make of this noon argument;
The verray preeve sheweth it in dede."

"As touching upon Cato,
Who has such great renown as a wise man
Although he may have said that bad dreams are nothing to dread,
Nevertheless, men may read in old books
Of many men of more authority
Than ever Cato was on this subject, so your point is moot,
As they all say the opposite
That dreams are significant signs
Of happiness to come as well as trouble
That people endure in their daily lives.
You don't need to make any argument about this;
Experience proves it in fact."

(*Canterbury Tales,*
"The Nun's Priest's Tale," VII, 2940–83)

Chaucer himself, with his mastery of so many facets of learning—his skill in writing poetry, his knowledge of several languages, his various jobs in the king's service, his appreciation of music, and his knowledge of alchemy as well as of astronomy as is evidenced in his *Treatise on the Astrolabe*—embodies the ideal behind medieval humanism. In this last, he acknowledges his debt to and knowledge of the old classical masters: "But considre wel that I ne usurpe not to have founden this werk of my labour or of myn engyn. I n'am but a lewd compilator of the labour of olde astrologiens, and have it translated in myn Englissh oonly for thy doctrine. And with this swerd shal I sleen envie" (*Consider well that I do not pretend to have discovered this knowledge purely by my own labors and mental energies. I am simply a compiler of the works of classical astrologers and have translated their words into English solely to write this for you. And with this sword, I will slay any envy*) (*Treatise on the Astrolabe*, 59–64).

See also Astrology and Astronomy; Clerk; Medicine; Physician

FURTHER READING

Astell, Ann W. *Chaucer and the Universe of Learning.* Ithaca, NY: Cornell University Press, 1996.

Curry, Patrick, ed. *Astrology, Science, and Society: Historical Essays.* Wolfeboro, NH: Boydell Press, 1987.

French, Roger. *Canonical Medicine: Gentile da Foligno and Scholasticism.* Boston: Brill, 2001.

Gersh, Stephen, and Bert Roest, eds. *Medieval and Renaissance Humanism: Rhetoric, Representation and Reform.* Boston: Brill, 2003.

Kircher, Timothy. *The Poet's Wisdom: The Humanists, the Church, and the Formation of Philosophy in the Early Renaissance.* Boston: Brill, 2006.

Ullmann, Walter. *Medieval Foundations of Renaissance Humanism.* Ithaca, NY: Cornell University Press, 1977.

Hundred Years War

The Hundred Years War, rather than being a conflict that raged steadily over a century, was actually a series of wars fought between England and France between 1337 and 1453. It consisted of tense periods of truce punctuated by small raids and sieges, with a few monumental and famous land battles and some lesser known battles at sea to elevate it to the status of a war.

Throughout most of the war, England was the dominating force, and most of fighting and, hence, the destruction to property, took place on the continent in France. However, during the final years, the tables turned, and the French, aided by the psychological boost provided by Joan of Arc, managed to drive the English from every part of France, except for the city of Calais, which would remain in English hands until Mary I lost control of it in 1557.

In the macrocosm, the Hundred Years War was simply the culmination of the long-standing rivalry between France and England that had begun with the Norman Conquest, was exacerbated by the rise of the feudal system, and did not really end until the nineteenth century. At the root of the conflict was the issue of control of lands within France that lay in English hands; however, it was worsened and complicated by economic issues, such as England's desire to control Flanders.

The war began in 1337 when Edward III proclaimed himself King of France, tracing his claim to the crown through his mother's line. Edward was resentful of a number of things, including the requirement that he, the king of England, had to pay fealty (and thus be considered subordinate) to Philip, the King of France.

With Edward laying claim to the crown, the war entered its first phase, which would last until 1360. During this phase, the combined martial skills of Edward III and his eldest son, Edward the Black Prince, enabled the English to gain the advantage. They defeated the French fleet in the Battle

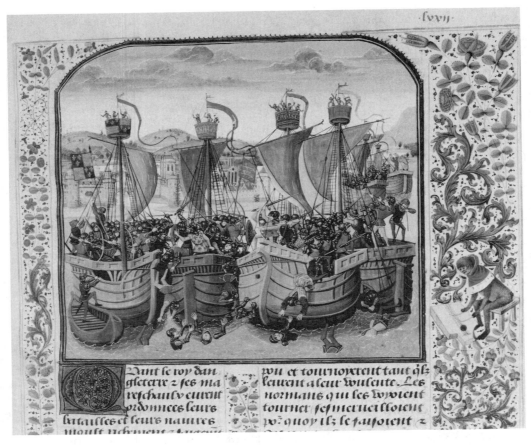

A fifteenth-century depiction of the Bataille de l'Ecluse. © Bibliothèque nationale de France.

of Sluis and invaded France, winning a crushing victory at Crécy in 1346.

After another victory for the English at Calais, the war was interrupted by the Black Death. When hostilities were renewed, the first major battle occurred in 1356 with the French defeat at Poitiers. The new French king, John II, was captured and held for ransom. The fact that the Treaty of Brétigny resulted in the king's ransom, the award of Calais to the English, and the recognition of Edward III as ruler of Aquitaine, but not of France, is testimony to the fact that his claim to the French crown was not serious.

Fierce fighting between soldiers and knights in armor during the Battle of Crecy, from *Les Chroniques de France*, ca. 1370. © HIP / Art Resource, NY.

Peace held until 1369, when the war entered its second phase, one that would last for the next 26 years. It began with the complaints of the nobles of Gascony, who, annoyed by the heavy tax imposed on them by Edward the Black Prince, revolted and asked for the help of the latest French king, Charles V. This phase went more in the favor of the French, who managed to win a few important battles, mainly because the English were experiencing political troubles at home.

The third phase was nearly disastrous for the French. It was sparked by Henry V's invasion of France in 1415, which resulted in the capture of Harfleur. Later that year, Henry defeated the flower of French knighthood in the war's most famous battle at Agincourt, which was won by common English foot soldiers. Over the next several years, Henry would conquer enough territory in France, including Normandy, to force Charles VI to sue for peace. In the treaty negotiations that followed, he awarded Henry his daughter's hand in marriage and recognized Henry's right to the lands he had conquered. As further proof of the French king's precarious position, he also formally recognized Henry as his heir, a move that disinherited his own son, Charles.

Henry might well have succeeded in uniting the two thrones; however, in one of history's interesting turns, he died in 1422, as did Charles VI. The heir to both thrones was nine-month-old Henry VI. Although Charles was fairly unpopular and known to be weak and uninspiring, his bid for the throne encompasses one of France's most exciting historical moments and introduces France's future patron saint, Joan of Arc. When Charles initially claimed the throne for himself, he was unable to rally the majority of the French to his cause. While the English and now the Burgundians swallowed greater pieces of France, Charles languished with only a small number of supporters in the south of France ready to acknowledge him as their king.

However, just when his defeat seemed inevitable, the war entered its fourth and final phase in 1429 with the appearance of young Joan. She approached the dauphin, requested an army and, while his support was reluctant, she raised the siege of Orléans and finally turned the tide to the side of the French. Upon the reclaiming of Rheims, the dauphin arranged for his coronation as Charles VII, which Joan attended.

However, while the French star was on the ascent, Joan's was waning and she was captured in 1430 by the Burgundians. For her trial, she was turned over to the English, who had much reason for vengeance upon this strange French anomaly who had motivated a fighting force of men in a way that their own commanders and monarch could not. She was tried for heresy (for wearing men's clothes, among other things) in Rouen, and burned at the stake May 30, 1431. By 1451, the French succeeded in driving the English out of France (but leaving them in possession of Calais).

As with the Black Death, the Hundred Years War was an important event in Chaucer's lifetime, yet it has little impact upon his writing. We are fairly certain that, as part of his job, he was sent to the Continent to deliver papers and negotiate in regard to the war. However, his professional lives did not cross, and there are no references to the war in any of his writings. A clue, perhaps, to his feelings regarding the war can be found in two places. First, the shabby condition of the Knight, who has not even fought in this monumental conflict, might indicate a certain apathy about the war and its value. However, it might also indicate that Chaucer finds it to be an important event and, were the Knight really worthy, he would have fought on the side of his king. Further evidence of Chaucer's familiarity with war, if not his support of it, can be found in the battle scenes of "The Knight's Tale" and *Troilus and Criseyde*.

See also Armor; Knight; Weapons

FURTHER READING

Ainsworth, Peter F. *Jean Froissart and the Fabric of History: Truth, Myth, and Fiction in the* "Chroniques." New York: Oxford University Press, 1990.

Barnie, John. *War in Medieval English Society: Social Values in the Hundred Years War 1337–99*. Ithaca, NY: Cornell University Press, 1974.

Bevan, Bryan. *Edward III: Monarch of Chivalry*. London: Rubicon Press, 1992.

Corfis, Ivy A., and Michael Wolfe, eds. *The Medieval City under Siege*. Rochester, NY: Boydell Press, 1995.

Dunn, Diana, ed. *War and Society in Medieval and Early Modern Britain*. Liverpool, England: Liverpool University Press, 2000.

Hilliam, David. *Medieval Weapons and Warfare: Armies and Combat in Medieval Times.* New York: Rosen, 2004.

Saunders, Corinne, Françoise Le Saux, and Neil Thomas. *Writing War: Medieval Literary Responses to Warfare.* Rochester, NY: D. S. Brewer, 2004.

Vernier, Richard. *The Flower of Chivalry: Bertrand Du Guesclin and the Hundred Years War.* Rochester, NY: D. S. Brewer, 2003.

Wright, Nicholas. *Knights and Peasants: The Hundred Years War in the French Countryside.* Rochester, NY: Boydell Press, 1998.

Hunting

Goddesse of maydens, that myn herte hast knowe
Ful many a yeer, and woost what I desire,
As keepe me fro thy vengeaunce and thyn ire,
That Attheon aboughte cruelly.
Chaste goddesse, wel wostow that I
Desire to ben a mayden al my lyf,
Ne nevere wol I be no love ne wyf.

Oh goddess of maidens, who my heart has known well
For many years, and who knows what I most desire,
Keep me from your vengeance and anger
That Actaeon bought so cruelly.
Chaste goddess, well you know my
Desire to remain a maiden my entire life,
And that I never wish to be a lover or a wife.

(*Canterbury Tales,*
"The Knight's Tale," I (A), 2300–06)

Perhaps the most popular sporting activity of the aristocracy and an important means of obtaining meat for the peasantry was the sport of hunting. Hunting was undertaken not only for pure sport, but also for honing warrior skills, providing food, and obtaining furs and skins. Hunters used falcons and hawks to catch and retrieve small prey such as rabbits, hares, and other fowl. They also tracked larger game such as bear, deer, wolf, or boar on horseback, often with the aid of dogs, and finished off the kill with arrows, knives, swords, or spears. There was no social class that did not hunt to some degree, but increasingly over the course of the medieval period, the nobility began to draw strict lines between what was their province and what was acceptable for the lower classes.

For the nobility, hunting served many functions. It was certainly an important source of additional food. It also gave knights an opportunity to hone their military skills, not only the obvious ones of killing and aiming, but of moving quietly through forests to practice ambush techniques.

Hunting was also a social occasion and, with the increasing popularity of falconry by Chaucer's day, many women also participated.

The importance socially of hunting is apparent from the literature and art of the time. It figures prominently in tapestries, where it is used as a metaphor for love. The woman is the deer who is pursued by her amorous hunter. Sometimes the goddess Diana is included, evoking notions of chastity along with the emotional dangers of courtship. The most famous of medieval hunt-themed tapestries is the Unicorn tapestry, which uses many panels to demonstrate the hunting and trapping of the rarest of creatures, the unicorn. In one panel, the unicorn is embraced by a virgin, the only human who can touch the rare beast.

Peasants were usually forbidden to hunt larger game or to use restricted forests. If they were caught hunting where and what they should not, they faced severe penalties up to and including execution. It was considered treasonous to trespass on the royal forests. However, hunting was a crucial element in the peasant diet, as wild game often provided the only meat a family saw for many months. What livestock they kept was limited, and chickens and cattle were only butchered when their egg- and milk-producing capacity had ceased. Sometimes a pig was kept and fattened for butcher-

An illustration of nobles hunting a stag, from an early fourteenth-century manuscript. © Bibliothèque nationale de France.

ing and salting over the long winter months, but for those who could not afford a pig, hunting filled the gap in an inexpensive way. It also enabled a family to obtain warm fur and skins for clothing that might otherwise be too costly to purchase.

Chaucer alludes to hunting and employs hunting metaphors in several of his works. In "The Knight's Tale," a scene of Actaeon's death is painted on the walls of Venus's temple while Emily prays to Diana to allow her to remain an unwed virgin (*Canterbury Tales,* "The Knight's Tale," I (A), 2300–06).

See also Allusions, Classical; Games

FURTHER READING

Barker, Juliet R. V. *The Tournament in England, 1100–1400.* Wolfeboro, NH: Boydell Press, 1986.

Carter, John Marshall. *Medieval Games: Sports and Recreations in Feudal Society.* New York: Greenwood Press, 1992.

Wilkins, Sally E. D. *Sports and Games of Medieval Cultures.* Westport, CT: Greenwood Press, 2002.

Hygiene

A SOMONOUR was ther with us in that place,
That hadde a fyr-reed cherubynnes face,
For saucefleem he was, with eyen narwe.
As hoot he was and lecherous as a sparwe.
With scalled browes blake and piled berd.
Of his visage children were aferd.
Ther nas quyk-silver, lytarge, ne brymstoon,
Boras, ceruce, ne oille of tartre noon,
Ne oynement that wolde clense and byte,
That hym myghte helpen of his whelks white,
Nor of the knobbes sittynge on his chekes.

A Summoner was there with us all at the Tabard,
Who had a fiery-red cherubic face,
His face was covered in eruptions and he had narrow, beady eyes,
And he was as hot and lusty as a sparrow,
With scaly black eyebrows and a mangy beard.
Children were afraid when they saw him.
There was no mercury, sulphur, or white lead,
Borax, ceruse, or cream of tarter,
No ointment that would clean and cure
To help him clear up neither his white head pimples,
Nor the bumps that covered his cheeks.

(*Canterbury Tales,*
General Prologue, I (A), 623–33)

Most people are convinced that the average person in the Middle Ages was far dirtier and, worse yet, completely unaware of that dirt, than we are today. Certainly, because of the lack of indoor plumbing and the expense of heating water for all but the wealthiest, medieval people did not bathe as frequently as we do today. And lack of proper dental information meant that their teeth were often in poor condition at an early age.

This does not mean, however, that they did not appreciate the benefits of cleanliness or did not notice foul odors. The Bible stresses that cleanliness is next to godliness, and with this in mind, the nobility in particular was taught to keep themselves clean. Manuals were written and published on the subject of good personal hygiene, offering suggestions for proper cleansing and maintaining a fresh smell. It was considered proper form for a nobleman to have clean clothes and a clean face and hands. If he was dirty, he was compared unfavorably to a peasant and mocked for his lack of manners and breeding.

For all social classes, cleaning the hands and face before a meal was imperative. The lowliest peasants would use precious water to cleanse the dirt of the fields from their heads and hands before approaching the dinner table. Because society was religious, peasants, as much as their economic betters, had standards that were influenced by the Bible, although the limitations placed on them by living conditions and poverty made high standards of cleanliness difficult to achieve.

Real baths during the Middle Ages were not common but were not completely out of the ordinary either. They were considered to be cleansing to both the soul and the body, although too many of them could be a form of luxurious indulgence that was considered sinful. However, the emphasis on the importance of such cleansing is evident in the use of a bath as part of the pre-dubbing ceremony for a new knight.

An elaborate bath is described in great detail in the *Secreta Secretorum,* a manual from the Middle Ages. This bath was accomplished in four stages that exposed the body to different temperatures and conditions—cold, then lukewarm, then hot, then dry—which served to balance the humors. Each stage was accompanied by appropriate perfumes, such as rosewater, and unguents.

That apparent lack of hygiene was considered a clue into a man's character is indicated by Chaucer's descriptions of some of his less savory pilgrims. The Miller, while his facial curiosities are not the result of poor hygiene, still imply a lack of care in his personal appearance:

Upon the cop right of his nose he hade
A werte, and theron stood a toft of herys,
Reed as the brustles of a sowes erys;
His nosethirles blake were and wyde.

On the end of his nose on the right he had
A wart which was topped by a tuft of hair,
Which was as red as the bristles in a sow's ears
His nose hairs were black and thick.

(*Canterbury Tales,*
General Prologue, I (A), 554–57)

The Summoner, on the other hand, has serious skin eruptions that make him frightening to little children (*Canterbury Tales,* General Prologue, I (A), 623–33).

See also Daily Life; Medicine

FURTHER READING

Britnell, Richard, ed. *Daily Life in the Late Middle Ages.* Stroud, England: Sutton, 1998.

French, Roger, Jon Arrizabalaga, Andrew Cunningham, and Luis García-Ballester, eds. *Medicine from the Black Death to the French Disease.* Aldershot, England: Ashgate, 1998.

Gottfried, Robert S. *Doctors and Medicine in Medieval England, 1340–1530.* Princeton, NJ: Princeton University Press, 1986.

Kibre, Pearl. *Studies in Medieval Science: Alchemy, Astrology, Mathematics, and Medicine.* London: Hambledon Press, 1984.

Hypsipyle

The daughter of King Toas, Hypsipyle became queen of Lemnos. During her reign, the women on her island were punished by Venus, because they had grievously offended the goddess by neglecting their rites to her. Venus responded by having all of their husbands take mistresses. The women, equally offended, responded by killing all of the men.

Later, when Jason and the Argonauts landed on Lemnos, Hypsipyle fell in love with him, and, as he did with so many other women in his travels, Jason promised to marry her. After they had produced two children, he decided to continue his search for the Golden Fleece and departed for Colchis to find it. Hypsipyle is mentioned in Chaucer's *The Legend of Good Women* and *The House of Fame* as one of the many women who has suffered betrayal by men (*Legend of Good Women,* 1467–1579; *House of Fame,* 400).

FURTHER READING

Brown, Peter, ed. *A Companion to Chaucer.* Malden, MA: Blackwell, 2002.

Frye, Northrop. *Biblical and Classical Myths: The Mythological Framework of Western Culture.* Buffalo, NY: University of Toronto Press, 2004.

Hansen, William F. *Classical Mythology: A Guide to the Mythical World of the Greeks and Romans.* New York: Oxford University Press, 2005.

Manser, Martin H. *The Facts On File Dictionary of Classical and Biblical Allusions.* New York: Facts On File, 2003.

Morford, Mark P. O. *Classical Mythology.* 7th ed. New York: Oxford University Press, 2003.

Nolan, Barbara. *Chaucer and the Tradition of the Roman Antique.* New York: Cambridge University Press, 1992.

Powell, Barry B. *Classical Myth.* Translated by Herbert M. Howe. 4th ed. Upper Saddle River, NJ: Pearson/Prentice Hall, 2004.

Price, Simon, and Emily Kearns, eds. *The Oxford Dictionary of Classical Myth and Religion.* New York: Oxford University Press, 2003.

Indulgences

His walet, biforn hym in his lappe,
Bretful of pardoun comen from Rome al hoot.
...
But of his craft, fro Berwyk into Ware
Ne was ther swich another pardoner.
For in his male he hadde a pilwe-beer,
Which that he seyde was Oure Lady veyl;
He seyde he hadde a gobet of the seyl
That Seint Peter hadde, whan that he wente
Upon the see, til Jhesu Crist hym hente.
He hadde a croys of latoun ful of stones,
And in a glas he hadde pigges bones.
But with thise relikes, whan that he fond
A povre person dwellynge upon lond,
Upon a day he gat hym moore moneye
Than that the person gat in monthes tweye;
And thus, with feyned flaterye and japes,
He made the person and the peple his apes.

He had his knap-sack in front of him on his lap
Full of pardons that had come from Rome.

Indulgences

...

But for his trade, from Berwick to Ware
There was not another such pardoner
For in his bag he had a pillow-case
That he said was actually Our Lady's veil;
He said he also had a portion of the sail
That Saint Peter had when he went
Upon the sea, until Jesus Christ found him.
He had a cross of brass, set with stones,
And in a glass he had pig's bones.
With these "relics" when he found a
Poor person dwelling in the country
In that day he'd make more money
Than the parson was likely to make in two months;
Thus with feigned flattery and trickery,
He made the parson and people his apes.

(*Canterbury Tales,*
General Prologue, I (A), 686–706)

Indulgences have their origin in two concepts: one, the Catholic doctrine that the sinner must repent and pay retribution; and, two, the need to raise money. The medieval doctrine of repentance required an external action—the proof of repentance—to demonstrate the internal state of the sinner. In order to accomplish this, temporal punishment was administered. In other words, the sinner had to perform some uncomfortable task or an act of charity or some other good works to prove contrition. For each act of penance, time was shaved off of one's sentence in Purgatory after death.

However, even if one were to perform enough penance to be considered utterly repentant, one could never quite do enough to progress straight from death to heaven. The effects of the sin would remain on the sinner's soul and would have to be cleansed by time in purgatory before entering heaven. Priests and religious thinkers of the Middle Ages, therefore, tried to create a system by which all the effects of sin could be erased, thereby allowing a soul direct entry into heaven.

Indulgences were the answer. Indulgences were created with the plan to prove repentance while raising funds for the Church. By the thirteenth century, Europe was increasingly developing a cash economy. Since the very concept of money is based on the notion of accepting it as a substitute for real things, the Church developed the idea of substituting money for someone's good works and, thus, outward demonstration of repentance. Priests, it was argued, were performing more good works than was necessary. Why should their flocks not benefit from them?

Indulgences allowed a parishioner to substitute the priest's or bishop's good works for his or her own. In return, the parishioner was given a piece of paper—the indulgence itself—that stated that he or she had done penance. Eventually, the potential for abuse caught up with the Church, and it was Pope Leo X's sale of indulgences to renovate St. Peter's Basilica in Rome that inspired Martin Luther to write his 95 Theses, sparking the Protestant Reformation.

It is the job of Chaucer's Pardoner to sell indulgences to help his church and its parishioners. In short, he is in the business of selling salvation. And, as the audience knows from Chaucer's description in the General Prologue, the Pardoner is not entirely scrupulous in the sort of salvation he sells. It is a business transaction, pure and simple, and he seeks to gain profit by whatever means he can.

See also Pardoner

FURTHER READING

DeWindt, Edwin Brezette, ed. *The Salt of Common Life: Individuality and Choice in the Medieval Town, Countryside, and Church: Essays Presented to J. Ambrose Raftis*. Kalamazoo: Medieval Institute Publications, Western Michigan University, 1995.

Foster, Edward E., and David H. Carey, eds. *Chaucer's Church: A Dictionary of Religious Terms in Chaucer*. Brookfield, VT: Ashgate, 2002.

Needham, Paul. The Printer & the Pardoner: *An Unrecorded Indulgence Printed by William Caxton for the Hospital of St. Mary Rounceval, Charing Cross*. Washington, DC: Library of Congress, 1986.

Slater, T. R., and Gervase Rosser, eds. *The Church in the Medieval Town*. Brookfield, VT: Ashgate, 1998.

Thomson, John A. F. *Popes and Princes, 1417–1517: Politics and Polity in the Late Medieval Church*. Boston: Allen & Unwin, 1980.

Jerusalem

The most important city of the Holy Land for three major religions, Jerusalem was first settled in 3500 B.C. The city figures prominently in the history of the area, first as the capital of Israel, when the Jewish King David established it in 1003. Jerusalem would be captured by Alexander the Great in 332 B.C., and then fall successively under the control of the Egyptian Ptolemies from 320 to 198 B.C. and the Syrian Seleucids from 198 to 167 B.C. Although Antiochus IV Epiphanes outlawed Judaism in 169 B.C., Judah Maccabee recaptured Jerusalem and restore its Temple for the Jews in 164 B.C. In 326, the Roman government officially recognized the city when Helena, mother of Emperor Constantine, visited Jerusalem and commissioned churches to be built on the location of events associated with Jesus' last days. The most important of these would be the Church of the Holy Sepulcher.

The fact that Palestine and Jerusalem eventually fell into the hands of the Muslims prompted the series of Crusades that defines the militant aims of the Catholic Church during much of the Middle Ages, the first of which resulted in its recapture by Christians in 1099 and its establishment of the Crusader State of Jerusalem. In 1187, Saladin, who permitted Jews and Christians to settle the city alongside Muslims, recaptured it. Although it would remain a battleground throughout the twelfth and most of the thirteenth centuries, Marmeluk Turks, who ruled there until 1517, eventually captured Jerusalem.

Absalom's Pillar and the city wall of Jerusalem. Courtesy of the Library of Congress.

A council is held in Jerusalem to discuss an attack on Damascus. Courtesy of Corbis.

Despite the dangers in the Holy Land, Jerusalem remained a popular destination for pilgrimage throughout the fourteenth and fifteenth centuries. The Wife of Bath, for instance, visited there three times: "And thrice hadde she been at Jerusalem; / She hadde passed many a straunge strem" (*and she had been three times to Jerusalem; / she had passed many a foreign stream*) (*Canterbury Tales*, General Prologue, I (A), 463–64). Pilgrims would visit the sites associated with the life of Christ, following the Via Dolorosa (Walk of Sorrow), developed by Franciscan friars in the fourteenth century. In "The Parson's Tale,"

Chaucer also mentions that life itself is a metaphorical pilgrimage to Jerusalem (*Canterbury Tales,* "The Parson's Tale," X (I), 51).

See also Pilgrimage

FURTHER READING

Blick, Sarah, and Rita Tekippe, eds. *Art and Architecture of Late Medieval Pilgrimage in Northern Europe and the British Isles.* Boston: Brill, 2005.

Dyas, Dee. *Pilgrimage in Medieval English Literature, 700–1500.* Rochester, NY: D. S. Brewer, 2001.

Lasansky, D. Medina, and Brian McLaren, eds. *Architecture and Tourism: Perception, Performance and Place.* New York: Berg, 2004.

Le Beau, Bryan F., and Menachem Mor, eds. *Pilgrims and Travelers to the Holy Land.* Omaha, NE: Creighton University Press, 1996.

Swatos, Jr., William H., and Luigi Tomasi, eds. *From Medieval Pilgrimage to Religious Tourism: The Social and Cultural Economics of Piety.* Westport, CT: Praeger, 2002.

Jews

Children an heep, ycomen of Cristen blood,
That lerned in that scole yeer by yere.
. . .

Fro thennes forth the Jues han conspired
This innocent out of this world to chace.
An homycide therto han they hyred,
That in an aleye hadde a privee place;
And as the child gan forby for to pace,
This cursed Jew hym hente, and heeld hym faste,
And kitte his throte, and in a pit hym caste.
. . .

"My throte is kut unto my nekke boon,"
Seyde this child, "and as by wey of kynde
I sholde have dyed, ye, longe tyme agon."
. . .

O yonge Hugh of Lyncoln, slayn also
With cursed Jewes, as it is notable,
For it is but a litel while ago,
Preye eek for us, we sinful folk unstable,
That of his mercy God so merciable
On us his grete mercy multiplie,
For reverence of his mooder Marie. Amen.

There was a group of children, all of Christian blood
Who learned in that school, year after year.
. . .

From that moment forward the Jews had conspired
To chase this innocent soul out of the world

And with his homicide in mind they planned
To take him to an ally where there was privacy.
And as this child walked past the place
This cursed Jew snatched him up and held him fast
And slit his throat and threw him into a pit.
    . . .

"My throat is cut down to my neck bone,"
Said the child, "and by the means of nature
I should have died a long time ago."
    . . .

O young Hugh of Lincoln, slain as well
By cursed Jews, as is well noted,
Because it is only a little while ago this happened,
Pray for us, as we are such unstable and sinful folk,
That God in his mercy is so kind and just
And let him multiply that mercy upon us
In the name of his mother Mary. Amen.

(*Canterbury Tales*, "The Prioress's Tale," VIII,
497–98, 565–71, 649–51, 684–90)

The history of the Jewish people in medieval Europe is generally a sad tale of intolerance and persecution from the Christian majority who accused them of everything from poisoning wells to engineering the Black Death. However, the reality, as with so many other historical issues, is far more complex than this summary would indicate. In the early years of the growth of western and central Europe, the Jews enjoyed the patronage of the Carolingian rulers who controlled France, parts of northern Italy, and most of western Germany. They were also protected by the Norman rulers of England and in France from the eleventh century forward.

This protection, quite simply, stemmed from an economic need. The Jewish merchants and bankers were crucial in establishing international commerce in Europe, and, through them, the European states were able to finance the economic growth that characterizes the high to late Middle Ages. Not only were the Jewish bankers important for lending money and financing partnerships, but Jewish merchants were leading importers of luxury items such as silk, perfume, gems, and spices into Germany.

Jewish merchants were also an important link with the Middle East and exported furs, lumber, and white slaves to the Arabic world. The slave trade from northern and central Europe to the Middle East was an important and lucrative one in the early Middle Ages and one that is typically elided by historians.

Because of their dietary restrictions and other social and cultural differences (including the fact that they were required to wear distinguishing markers on their clothing), Jews in Europe—and in England especially—tended to live in small, concentrated and exclusive communities that were dominated by a few wealthy and powerful merchant families who married their sons and daughters into the rabbinical elite to create a sort of aristocracy. This created the main method of social mobility among Jewish communities. Otherwise, the majority of the Jewish population was comprised of artisans, craftsmen, and other lower middle-class occupations (very few Jews in England were farmers).

Their exclusivity made it difficult for Jews to move out of their communities and take up other occupations or join the Christian community through conversion. They simply lacked a support system if they ventured out of their enclaves. For the devoutly Christian convert, even monasteries proved to be a difficult transition because most by the twelfth and thirteenth centuries had become quite selective and did not welcome impoverished novices.

In the period between 1050 and 1200, the Jewish communities of Europe experienced a prolonged decline in economic prosperity due to the growth of Christian banking and mercantile families. No longer did the Jews enjoy exclusive control of the economic motor of Europe. Jews may have started the engine, but, as the Church imposed restrictions on Christians lending one another money with interest loosened, they would be left behind at the station. By the year 1200, the old school of Jewish banking was obsolete. From this point forward, persecutions increased because kings no longer kept the Jews under special protection. In England, the monarchy managed to maintain this protection the longest, simply because enough wealth remained among the Jewish elite families for the monarchy to draw 20 percent of its income from taxing them.

With royal protection a thing of the past, the growth of the Inquisition, and militant Christianity on the rise, the Jews of Europe faced the sort of persecution with which we are familiar. Popular support backed Church attacks on Jews, and demonstrations against them were often violent. Forced conversions were the most common result, although records exist of more troublesome, even murderous, persecutions. By Chaucer's day, nearly all Jews had left England for Germany.

With this in mind, it is curious that the Prioress tells a tale so virulently anti-Semitic. After all, there really were not that many Jews left in England at this time, and chances were good that those who remained worked hard to not draw undue and negative attention to themselves. Yet she deliberately chooses a story that paints Jews as wicked and cold-blooded murderers of an innocent Christian child, a tale of martyrdom that rings hollow from a woman who is obviously light on devout spirituality.

It is this tale that has earned Chaucer a rather unfair reputation as an anti-Semite. Because his character—a rather questionable character at that—espouses a certain philosophy, he has been painted with the same brush. However, there are distinct clues that he disagrees with the Prioress's prejudice, not least of which is his slyly negative characterization of her in the General Prologue. The audience knows from the outset that she is a fraud. Therefore, her attempts with her story to appear pious are undermined. Whatever negative statement the Prioress makes about Jews will thus fall under scrutiny and be judged according to their source:

Ther was in Asye, in a greet citee,
Amonges Cristene folk a Jewerye,
Sustened by a lord of that contree
For foule usure and lucre of vileynye,
Hateful to Crist and to his compaignye;
And thurgh the strete men myghte ride or wende,
For it was free and open at eyther ende.

There was in Asia, in a great city,
Where a Jewery existed in the midst of Christian folk,
And it was sustained by a lord of that country
So that they could practice foul usury and the money of villany,
Which is hateful to Christ and his apostles;
And through the streets men could ride or stroll,
As it was free and open at either end.

(*Canterbury Tales,*
"The Prioress's Tale," VIII, 488–94)

The Prioress's reference to the usury of the Jews is curious, as there were no longer restrictions limiting money-lending to Jews by this time. This suggests that the Prioress, who obviously loves fine things, is in debt herself and is resentful of those to whom she owes money. Her repeated references to blood throughout the tale, and the gruesome details of the boy's cut throat are also very cold and curious coming from someone who weeps over the death of a mouse.

See also Jerusalem; Religion

FURTHER READING

Delany, Sheila, ed. *Chaucer and the Jews: Sources, Contexts, Meanings.* New York: Routledge, 2002.

Schildgen, Brenda Deen. *Pagans, Tartars, Moslems, and Jews in Chaucer's* Canterbury Tales. Gainesville: University Press of Florida, 2001.

Skinner, Patricia, ed. *The Jews in Medieval Britain: Historical, Literary, and Archaeological Perspectives.* Rochester, NY: Boydell & Brewer, 2003.

Job

Job (Old Testament) is one of the most striking figures of the Bible, inspiring awe, pity, and exasperation in many. His story begins with a wager between God and Satan. In response to some cynical taunting regarding the fickle nature of man's devotion, God tells Satan that the faithful, yet prosperous, Job will remain faithful to him no matter what adversity comes.

When Satan maintains that Job will only remain faithful as long as it profits him, God proceeds to systematically snatch away everything that Job holds dear and allows Satan to inflict him with a painful skin ailment.

Reduced to his lowest point, Job continues to be devoted to God, who rewards him with even greater prosperity and happiness. He becomes the archetype of patience rewarded.

Chaucer uses Job in a number of *The Canterbury Tales.* The Wife of Bath tells her husbands that they could learn a thing or two from Job about patience: "Ye sholde been al pacient and meke, / And han a sweete spiced conscience, / Sith ye so preche of Jobes pacience. / Suffreth alwey, syn ye so wel kan preche" (*You should be patient and meek, / and have a sweet conscience, / Since you preach so much about Job's patience. / Suffer on, since you preach so well, you should practice what you preach*) (*Canterbury Tales,* "The Wife of Bath's Tale," III (D), 434–37).

Job folio, from a twelfth-century Latin text. © Bibliothèque nationale de France.

An obvious parallel is drawn between Grisilde and Job in "The Clerk's Tale" as well as in "The Man of Law's Tale." Finally, in "The Friar's Tale," the devil tells the Summoner that those who are faithful, like Job, sometimes are tormented by him and God allows it: "And somtyme, at oure prayere, han we leve / Oonly the body and nat the soule greve; / Witnesse on Job, whom that we diden wo" (*And sometimes when we get the chance, / we can torment a man in his body, but not in his soul; / Such as the case of Job, whom we caused great harm*) (*Canterbury Tales,* "The Friar's Tale," III (D), 1489–91).

FURTHER READING

Brown, Peter, ed. *A Companion to Chaucer.* Malden, MA: Blackwell, 2002.

Frye, Northrop. *Biblical and Classical Myths: The Mythological Framework of Western Culture.* Buffalo, NY: University of Toronto Press, 2004.

Manser, Martin H. *The Facts On File Dictionary of Classical and Biblical Allusions.* New York: Facts On File, 2003.

John of Gaunt

John of Gaunt was born in Ghent in 1340, the third son of Edward III and Philippa of Hainault. Brother to the legendary Black Prince, Gaunt was

John of Gaunt hosts John I, king of Portugal at a banquet, from Froissart's *Chronicles*. © Snark / Art Resource, NY.

destined to become not only the most powerful man in England, but also the founder of the House of Lancaster, a lineage that sparked the fierce struggle for the crown known as the War of the Roses. He would also be Chaucer's patron at court and relative by marriage, taking Chaucer's sister-in-law as his third wife.

Gaunt's early career was tied to that of his older brother, Edward the Black Prince, and the latter's role in the Hundred Years War. He provided limited support in the Gascony campaign of 1370 and was present at the siege of Limoges and the city's subsequent destruction. Gaunt's attack on the king's ministers for the apparent failure of the war made his loyalties suspect to many, and it was his marriages rather than any early military prowess that brought him his great power.

In 1359, he married Blanche (1341–68), the heiress to the duchy of Lancaster. She bore him three children, including the future Henry IV. Gaunt became duke upon Blanche's father Henry's death in 1362. As duke, Gaunt was the first to take the red rose as his device, providing the counterpart to York's white rose in a later generation's bid for the throne. He also became perhaps the greatest lord in England through this marriage, with more than thirty castles and manors and a measure of independence from the crown. He retained the title after his wife's death and attempted to extend his power through his second marriage in 1371 to Constanza of Castile (13??–1394), daughter of Pedro the Cruel. It was through Constanza that he laid claim to the throne of Castile. His bid was unsuccessful, although he styled himself King of Castile in formal documents. His great power heightened suspicion and resentment about Gaunt's influence over the English crown, and his cause was not helped by his support of John Wyclif, the accused heretical founder of the Lollards. When the deaths of first the Black Prince (heir to the throne) in 1376 and Edward III the following year placed the 10-year-old Richard II on the throne, worries ran high that Gaunt planned to depose the boy king and seize the crown for himself.

Instead, he proved himself to be Richard's loyal supporter. He arranged the young king's coronation himself. In addition, as Steward of England, he acted in a supervisory capacity over the regency council that in essence ran England during the first dozen years of Richard's reign. Despite Gaunt's own apparent loyalty, his son Henry Bolingbroke deposed Richard and took the throne himself as Henry IV.

In 1396, Gaunt married his long-time mistress Katherine Swynford (1372–1418), Chaucer's sister-in-law, and had his children by her legitimized under the name of Beaufort. Gaunt's great-great-grandson took the throne as Henry VII, staking his claim over the house of York based on John of Gaunt's place in the succession, born one year earlier than Edmund, Duke of York.

The Book of the Duchess is supposedly written for Gaunt in response to his grief at his wife Blanche's untimely passing. The many references to the lost lady as "white" and a reference in *The Legend of Good Women* to another poem called "The Deeth of Blaunche the Duchesse" are strong evidence for this conclusion (*Legend of Good Women*, F, 418). Gaunt was laid to rest beside Blanche upon his death in 1399.

See also Edward III; Lollardy; Richard II

FURTHER READING

Bennett, Michael. *Richard II and the Revolution of 1399*. Gloucestershire, England: Sutton, 1999.

Bevan, Bryan. *Edward III: Monarch of Chivalry*. London: Rubicon Press, 1992.

Cantor, Norman. *The Encyclopedia of the Middle Ages*. New York: Viking Press, 1999.

Collins, Hugh E. L. *The Order of the Garter, 1348–1461: Chivalry and Politics in Late Medieval England*. New York: Oxford University Press, 2000.

Fraser, Antonia, ed. *The Lives of the Kings and Queens of England*. Rev. ed. Berkeley: University of California Press, 1998.

Staley, Lynn. *Languages of Power in the Age of Richard II*. University Park: Pennsylvania State University Press, 2005.

Joseph

Joseph (Old Testament) was the eleventh son of Jacob, and the first born to Jacob's second wife Rachel. Because Joseph was his father's obvious favorite, his outraged and jealous brothers sold him into slavery in Egypt, an event that brought him into the household of Potiphar, an officer of the Pharaoh. Although he was able to rise to a position of trust within Potiphar's household, he became a victim of his own honor and good looks when Potiphar's wife attempted to seduce him. Joseph's refusal earned him her vengeful scorn, and she told her husband that Joseph tried to have his unwanted way with her—a lie that landed the hapless Joseph in jail.

While in jail, his reputation as an interpreter of dreams gained him the interest of the Pharaoh, who had been haunted by some disturbing ones. Joseph saw impending famine in the Pharaoh's dreams and, because of the early warning, a period of seven potentially disastrous years became simply lean years. Joseph's happy ending was complete when his brothers came to Egypt and he, unbeknownst to them, was able to test them successfully to see if they were repentant for their past bad behaviors.

Because dreams are very important in Chaucer's work, it is not surprising that the dream interpreter should be referenced in several tales in this capacity. In *The Book of the Duchess,* the Narrator compares his dream to that of the Pharaoh, complaining that even Joseph would probably be unable to interpret it (*Book of the Duchess,* 282), an idea that is echoed in *The House of Fame* (*House of Fame,* 516). In "The Nun's Priest's Tale," Chaunticleer cites the Pharaoh's dream as solid evidence that dreams like his own contain specific warnings for events that could happen in the future (*Canterbury Tales,* "The Nun's Priest's Tale," 3133–35).

FURTHER READING

Brown, Peter, ed. *A Companion to Chaucer.* Malden, MA: Blackwell, 2002.
Frye, Northrop. *Biblical and Classical Myths: The Mythological Framework of Western Culture.* Buffalo, NY: University of Toronto Press, 2004.
Manser, Martin H. *The Facts On File Dictionary of Classical and Biblical Allusions.* New York: Facts On File, 2003.

Judas

Judas Iscariot (New Testament) bears the dubious distinction of having been the apostle who betrayed Jesus to the Romans and took 30 pieces of silver—the so-called blood money—for his necessary part in the drama that would provide the foundation to one of the world's dominant religions. He is the archetypal figure of the betrayer of a friend and almost never appears in a positive light.

Chaucer mentions Judas in a number of tales. In "The Nun's Priest's Tale," he refers to the fox as the "newe Scariot" (*new Iscariot*) (*Canterbury Tales,* "The Nun's Priest's Tale," VII, 3227). In "The Canon Yeoman's Tale," the Yeoman points out that the company should not judge all canons by his employer's bad behavior. After all, Judas's sin did not corrupt the other apostles:

Ye woot wel how
That among Cristes apostelles twelve
Ther nas no traytour but Judas hymselve.
Thanne why sholde al the remenant have a blame
That giltlees were? By yow I seye the same,
Save oonly this, if ye wold herkne me;
If any Judas in youre covent be,
Remoeveth hym bitymes, I yow rede,
If shame or los may causen any drede.

You know well that
Among Christ's twelve apostles
There was no other traitor than Judas.
So why should all of the other apostles be blamed
That are guiltless? I say the same about priests,
Except only this, if you will listen to me;
If there is any Judas in your company,
Get rid of him quickly, I warn you,
Or you will suffer great shame and loss.

(*Canterbury Tales,*
"The Canon's Yeoman's Tale," VIII (G), 1001–09)

FURTHER READING

Brown, Peter, ed. *A Companion to Chaucer.* Malden, MA: Blackwell, 2002.
Frye, Northrop. *Biblical and Classical Myths: The Mythological Framework of Western Culture.* Buffalo, NY: University of Toronto Press, 2004.
Manser, Martin H. *The Facts On File Dictionary of Classical and Biblical Allusions.* New York: Facts On File, 2003.

For Reference

Not to be taken from this room